2

Second Edition

INTRODUCING
MICROSOFT®
.NET

Microsoft·
.net™

David S. Platt

PUBLISHED BY
Microsoft Press
A Division of Microsoft Corporation
One Microsoft Way
Redmond, Washington 98052-6399

Library of Congress Cataloging-in-Publication Data pending.

Printed and bound in the United States of America.

2 3 4 5 6 7 8 9   QWE   7 6 5 4 3 2

Distributed in Canada by Penguin Books Canada Limited.

A CIP catalogue record for this book is available from the British Library.

Microsoft Press books are available through booksellers and distributors worldwide. For further information about international editions, contact your local Microsoft Corporation office or contact Microsoft Press International directly at fax (425) 936-7329. Visit our Web site at www.microsoft.com/mspress. Send comments to *mspinput@microsoft.com*.

ActiveX, Authenticode, BizTalk, FrontPage, Hotmail, IntelliSense, JScript, Microsoft, Microsoft Press, MS-DOS, MSDN, MSN, Outlook, Visual Basic, Visual C++, Visual C#, Visual J++, Visual Studio, Windows, and Windows NT are either registered trademarks or trademarks of Microsoft Corporation in the United States and/or other countries. Other product and company names mentioned herein may be the trademarks of their respective owners.

The example companies, organizations, products, domain names, e-mail addresses, logos, people, places, and events depicted herein are fictitious. No association with any real company, organization, product, domain name, e-mail address, logo, person, place, or event is intended or should be inferred.

Acquisitions Editor: Danielle Bird
Project Editor: John Pierce
Technical Editor: Jean Ross

Body Part No. X08-77657

To my daughter,
Annabelle Rose Platt

Table of Contents

Preface   ix

1   Introduction   1

    The Big Internet   1
    Raising the Bar: Common Infrastructure Problems   2
    The Best Laid Plans   4
    What the Heck Is .NET, Anyway?   6
    About This Book   9
    Sing a Song of Silicon   10

2   .NET Objects   13

    Problem Background   13
    Solution Architecture   17
        Oh Yeah? What Does It Cost?   19
    Simplest Example   20
    More on .NET Namespaces   26
    Assemblies   29
        Concept of an Assembly   29
        Assemblies and Deployment   31
        Assemblies and Versioning   34
    Object-Oriented Programming Features   40
        Inheritance   41
        Object Constructors   46
    .NET Memory Management   48
    Interoperation with COM   54
        Using COM Objects from .NET   55
        Using .NET Objects from COM   59
    Transactions in .NET   61
    Structured Exception Handling   65
    Code Access Security   70

3   ASP.NET   **79**

    Problem Background   79

    Solution Architecture   82

    Simplest Example: Writing a Simple ASP.NET Page   85

    More on Web Controls   89

    Managing and Configuring Web Application Projects: The Web.config File   96

    ASP.NET State Management   100

    Security in ASP.NET   105

        Authentication   106

        Authorization   116

        Identity   122

    Process Management   125

4   .NET Web Services   **129**

    Problem Background   129

    Solution Architecture   132

    Simplest Example: Writing an XML Web Service   135

    Self-Description of XML Web Services: The WSDL File   140

    Writing XML Web Service Clients   142

    XML Web Service Support in Visual Studio .NET   149

    XML Web Service Design Considerations   150

        Make Them Chunky   151

        Think Carefully About Their State   152

        Handling Exceptions   155

        Replacing the Namespace URI   156

        XML Web Service Security   157

5   Windows Forms   **159**

    Problem Background   159

    Solution Architecture   161

    Simplest Example   162

    More Complex Example: Controls and Events   165

    Hosting ActiveX Controls in Windows Forms   168

    Form Enhancements   172

	Drawing	173
	Mouse Handling	175
	Menu Handling	176
	Keyboard Handling	179
	Dialog Boxes	179

6 Data Access in .NET   **181**

	Problem Background	181
	Solution Architecture	183
	Simplest Example	187
	More Complex Example: Disconnected Operation	191
	Visual Studio Support and Typed *DataSet* Objects	199

7 Handling XML   **207**

	Problem Background	207
	Solution Architecture	209
	Simplest Example: Basic Serialization	210
	More Complex Example: Controlling Serialization	214
	XML Schemas and Serialization	218
	Generic Parsing	222

8 Events and Delegates   **225**

	Problem Background	225
	Solution Architecture	227
	Simplest Example	228
	More Complex Example	235
	Delegates	239

9 Threads   **245**

	Problem Background	246
	Solution Architecture	248
	Simplest Threading Example: Using The Process Thread Pool	250
	More Complex Example: Thread Safety	256
	Still More Complex Example: Managing Your Own Threads	264

10   Windows Forms Controls   **269**

    Problem Background   269

    Solution Architecture   271

    Simplest Control Example   273

    More Complex Example: Extending an Existing Control   280

    User Control Example: Containing Other Controls   282

11   Web Forms Controls   **287**

    Problem Background   287

    Solution Architecture   288

    Simplest Web Forms Control Example   292

    More Complex Web Forms Example   296

    View State Management   303

    Client-Side Scripting   304

Epilogue and Benediction   311

Index   313

Preface

I always thought that the product now named Microsoft .NET sounded very cool. I remember reading Mary Kirtland's articles in the November and December 1997 issues of *Microsoft Systems Journal* describing what was then called COM+, a run-time environment that would provide all kinds of useful services, such as cross-language inheritance and run-time access control, to object programmers. As a COM geek, I liked the way this environment promised to solve many of the problems that kept hanging me up in COM.

Microsoft then decided that the next version of Microsoft Transaction Server would be called COM+ 1.0 and would be integrated into Windows 2000; what Mary had described would be COM+ 2.0. Later, Microsoft renamed COM+ Microsoft .NET, and I coined the term MINFU, Microsoft Nomenclature Foul-Up, for all this jumping around. But the product still sounded cool, and I was thrilled when Microsoft Press asked me to write a book about it with the same high-level treatment as I had given COM+ 1.0 in *Understanding COM+* (Microsoft Press, 1999). You are holding, and, I hope, buying, the result.

I was afraid that Microsoft wouldn't let me tell the story my own way, that they would insist that I hold to the party line. That didn't happen in this book, not even once. Everything that I say in this book, whether you agree or disagree with it, is my own call. Obviously, I like .NET and think it will make its users a heck of a lot of money, and Microsoft doesn't disagree. When a prospective employer asks you for a reference, do you provide someone who thinks you're a demigod, or someone who thinks you're a turkey? Most programmers I know could provide some of both. In some internal correspondence about an early draft, a project manager took exception to one of my rants about administrative tools and wrote to me, "it makes the purpose of the book more editorial than instruction, IMO. Is that your intention?" I wrote back to this person, "I am proud that my book points out the bad parts of

.NET as well as the good, the costs as well as the advantages. I'd be a weasel if I did anything else. IMHO, I consider this to be instruction. If you're accusing me of calling 'em as I see 'em, I plead guilty, as charged."

I can't stand dry reading, any more than I can stand eating dried-out fish or meat. I remember my freshman year in college, when I tried to spice up a chemistry lab report with a couple of jokes and got flunked for my pains. "Levity has no place in science," my professor said. "Do it over again. Passive voice should be used throughout." He's the only guy I've ever met with a mustache carefully shaved into a permanent frown. You didn't get tenure, did you, Phillip? Lighten up, you'll live longer, or at least enjoy it more. Maybe he was trying to keep himself bored to make his life *seem* longer, but he shouldn't inflict it on the rest of us.

To me, the best authors are also the best storytellers, even in, or especially in, the often dry fields of science and history. For example, I greatly admire Laurie Garrett's *The Coming Plague* (Penguin, 1995), Evan S. Connell's *Son of the Morning Star* (North Point Press, 1997), and William Manchester's biography of Winston Churchill entitled *The Last Lion* (Little Brown, 1983). Think about your college textbooks, written by people like my former professor. What could be a bigger turnoff? Then read this excerpt about Emile Roux's development of diphtheria antitoxin and the first human trials, during a vicious outbreak among children in Paris in 1894:

Roux looked at the helpless doctors, then at the little lead-colored faces and the hands that picked and clutched at the edges of the covers, the bodies twisting to get a little breath....
Roux looked at his syringes—did this serum really save life?
"Yes!" shouted Emile Roux, the human being.
"I don't know—let us make an experiment," whispered Emile Roux, the searcher for truth.
"But, to make an experiment, you will have to withhold the serum from at least half of these children—you may not do that." So said Emile Roux, the man with a heart, and all voices of all despairing parents were joined to the pleading voice of this Emile Roux.

You can read about Roux's choice and its results in *Microbe Hunters* by Paul de Kruif, originally published in 1926 and periodically reissued, most recently in 1996 by Harcourt Brace. Not much academic objectivity there, but which would you rather read? I know which I'd rather write. I do not come close to de Kruif's eloquence, and I seriously doubt that anyone will be reissuing this book when I'm 112 years old. But I've done my best to make it slide down easily, and how many technical authors even try?

De Kruif closes his book by saying, "This plain history would not be complete if I were not to make a confession, and that is this: that I love these microbe hunters, from old Antony Leeuwenhoek to Paul Ehrlich. Not especially for the discoveries they have made nor for the boons they have brought mankind. No. I love them for the men they are. I say they are, for in my memory every man jack of them lives and will survive until this brain must stop remembering." As I say in my epilogue (no fair jumping there now; you have to read the whole book first), the Internet is doing nothing more nor less than evolving the human species. Microsoft .NET is the product that's going to crack it wide open. And I find it extremely cool to be chosen to tell the story and to tell it my own way. To talk with the project team, to discuss what the future of computing will be and why, is the reason I switched to Microsoft Press from my former publisher. Early readers have told me that comes through in my text. I certainly tried for that, and I hope they are right.

Every book is a team effort, like a moon launch but on a smaller scale. The authors, like the astronauts, get such glory as there is (you're all coming to my ticker tape parade, aren't you?), but without all the other people who worked so hard on this project, you'd never get to read it. Like the thousands of Project Apollo team members, most of them get very little acknowledgment (although I think the chain-smoking, vest-wearing flight controller Gene Kranz, played by Ed Harris, nearly stole the show from Tom Hanks's Jim Lovell in the movie *Apollo 13*.) Until someone makes *Introducing Microsoft .NET* into a movie (a fine idea, any producers out there?), I'm afraid they're stuck with only this acknowledgment to tell the world of their deeds.

First honors must go to John Pierce, the lead editor on this book. He played a secondary role on my last Microsoft Press book, *Understanding COM+*, a couple of years ago. I was very happy to find out that he was available for the lead role on this book. His sense of humor is as warped as mine. I knew he wouldn't cramp my style or change my voice, which, love it or hate it, you'll have to agree is distinctive. He shaped my prose in a better way than I could have.

Next come Jean Ross and Marc Young, the technical editors. They tracked down the answers to all of my technical questions, usually under great time pressure and in the face of daily changes to the code builds. In addition to Jean and Marc, many of the .NET project development team took time from their brutal schedules to set me straight on things. I'd like to especially thank Keith Ballinger, Susan Warren, Mark Boulter, Loren Kohnfelder, Erik Olson, John Rivard, Paul Vick, Jeffrey Richter, and Sara Williams.

On the acquisition side, Ben Ryan started the process two years ago, and Danielle Bird took over when he moved on. Anne Hamilton backstopped the process. Teresa Fagan, a Microsoft Press group product manager, upon hearing the working title *Introducing Microsoft .NET* had the idea, "Hey, you ought to get that as a web address," and I ran through the rain back to my lonely writer's garret (OK, it was the Bellevue Club Hotel's concierge floor) and snagged it before anyone else could act on the thought. That was the cherry on top of the sundae.

Finally, I need to thank my wife Linda, now a mother to our daughter, Annabelle, and Annabelle herself, who now not only names individual objects ("Simba") and calls methods on those objects ("Feed Simba") but recognizes that objects are instances of classes ("Simba is a kitty cat").

David S. Platt
www.rollthunder.com
Ipswich, Massachusetts, USA
April 2001 and March 2002

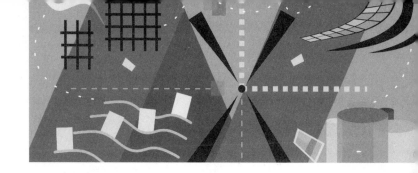

1

Introduction

I cannot get my sleep to-night; old bones are hard to please;
I'll stand the middle watch up here—alone wi' God an' these
My engines, after ninety days o' race an' rack an' strain
Through all the seas of all Thy world, slam-bangin' home again.
　　　　　—Rudyard Kipling, writing on the importance of 24/7
　　　　　　　availability under load, "McAndrew's Hymn," 1894

The Big Internet

The Internet is Big. (Annoyed Reader: "I paid you HOW MUCH to tell me that?" Royalty-Counting Author: "What, you mean, it's NOT?")

On its own, a desktop PC is boring, much as a single-cell amoeba is boring. Sure, you can use it (the PC, not the amoeba) to play a mean game of Solitaire and it won't let you cheat (this is an advantage?), and Notepad comes in handy on occasion. But unlike the evolutionary value of the amoeba, the economic benefits to society of the stand-alone desktop PC have yet to be satisfactorily proven. It just can't do that much interesting or useful stuff as long as its horizons remain limited to its own box. However, when you use the Internet to link your PC to every other PC in the world, and to every intelligent non-PC device (palmtops, refrigerators, and so on) as well, for essentially no extra hardware cost, fun things start to happen—just as when enough single cells connect and evolve to form the human brain, which can

Stand-alone PCs are much less useful than networked PCs.

1

compose, play, and appreciate a symphony; fly to the moon; or obliterate its own species. Beats the heck out of Solitaire, doesn't it?

The Internet continues to change society ever more rapidly.

The Web started out as a means for browsing boring physics reports and took off (understatement of the century) from there. It dramatically lowered the friction of distributing all types of data. Expanded content attracted more users to the Internet, and the increasing numbers in the audience drew in more content providers in a virtuous cycle that not only shows no signs of ending but is accelerating even as I write these words. Yesterday I used the Web to watch video highlights of a hockey game that I missed. After that, I used Morpheus to find some good music among 500,000 different songs (I only look at the legal ones, naturally) on 10,000 different users' hard drives. Then I talked to my mother about setting up a video camera link so that she could look into her first grandchild's crib from her home 500 miles away. The Internet has made ours a completely different world from that of even 5 years ago.

Internet hardware and bandwidth are cheap and getting cheaper.

Hardware for connecting to the Internet and bandwidth for transmitting data are cheap and getting cheaper. The Web camera that lets my mother watch my daughter cost only a couple of hundred bucks to install in my PC and essentially nothing extra to operate over my existing cable modem. Think what it would have cost 10 years ago, or even 5, to buy video hardware and lease a dedicated line from Ipswich, Massachusetts, to Orwigsburg, Pennsylvania. The prices of Internet hardware and bandwidth will soon fall to Cracker Jack prize level, if they haven't already.

Raising the Bar: Common Infrastructure Problems

Internet software poses new classes of problems that are difficult and expensive to solve.

The hardware and bandwidth are cheap, but there's a snag. Platt's Second Law states that the amount of crap in the universe is conserved.[1] If someone has less crap to deal with, it's because he's managed to dump his ration on someone else's head, but there's no such thing as making it disappear. If hardware and bandwidth are so much easier and cheaper to get, that means writing the software to run that environment must, by the laws of the universe, be harder and more expensive by a corresponding amount. And so indeed it has proved, as anyone who's tried lately will confirm. The problem in your Internet application isn't the business logic, which is much the same as a desktop case (a certain number is less than zero, indicating that your checking account is overdrawn). However, the fact that you're implementing an application on different boxes connected by the Internet introduces new

---

1. Platt's First Law is called "Exponential Estimation Explosion." It states that every software project takes three times as long as your best estimate, even if you apply this law to it.

classes of problems, because of the Internet's public, uncontrolled, and heterogeneous nature. Think how (relatively) easy it is to handle a toddler in your own living room. Then think how much harder it is to handle that same toddler in Grand Central Station. Same kid, same goals (safety, fun), entirely different requirements.

Consider the question of security, for example. Many users keep their personal financial records on stand-alone PCs, using Quicken or similar products. Developers of early versions of Quicken didn't write any security code. They were comfortable, or more properly, their customers were comfortable, that if they kept their PCs physically locked up, no one would steal their money. Paranoid users could buy a product that would password-protect their entire PC, but hardly anyone did this.

<aside>Desktop applications generally didn't have any security at all.</aside>

But Quicken on the desktop wasn't that useful, as many users discovered once the novelty wore off. It did very little more than what your paper check register already did—often more quickly and more easily than the silly program. Quicken didn't become a net benefit to users until it could connect to the Internet and interact with other financial parties, with features such as electronic bill receipt and payment and automatic downloading of bank and credit card statements. (That is, it would become a net benefit to users if its user interface wasn't so lame. It doesn't handle the complexity of these new features well at all, overwhelming the user with far too many indistinguishable choices at any given time. But that's not an Internet problem.)

However, once Quicken's operations leave the secure cocoon of the single box on which they're running, they run smack into a massive new need for security. For example, when the user tells the electronic bill paying center to write a check to the phone company, the bill paying center needs to ensure that the request comes from the genuine owner of the account and not from the phone company desperately trying to stave off bankruptcy by advancing itself a couple of months' worth of payments. We also need to encrypt all the data that flows between the parties. You don't want your neighbor's geeky teenage son using a packet sniffer on your cable modem line to see your account numbers and what you bought—"$295 to Hunky Escort Service, eh? Wonder if her husband knows about that?"

<aside>Internet applications need security for all phases of their operations.</aside>

This security code is extremely difficult to write—and to test, and debug, and deploy, and support, and maintain, while employees come and go. You have to hire people who know everything about security—how to authenticate users, how to decide whether a user is allowed to do this or that, how to

<aside>Security code is extremely difficult to develop.</aside>

encrypt data so that authorized users can easily read it but snoopers can't, how to design tools that administrators can use to set or remove users' security permissions, and so on.

Security and similar problems in distributed computing belong to the generic category of infrastructure.

Internet computing raises other similar classes of problems, which I'll discuss later in this chapter. All of them share the characteristic that, as I first explained in my book *Understanding COM+* (Microsoft Press, 1999), they have nothing whatsoever to do with your business process, the stuff that your clients are paying you to get done. Instead, these problems represent infrastructure, like the highway system or the electric power grid, the framework on which you and other people weave your day-to-day lives.

Infrastructure, not business logic, is what kills projects.

Developing infrastructure kills projects. I have never seen a project fail over business logic. You know your business process better than anyone else in the world; that's why you're writing software to assist it. But you don't know the infrastructure (unless that's your product, as it is for Microsoft). Almost no one is an expert on security authentication algorithms or encryption. If you try to write that code yourself, one of two things will happen. You'll either write a lame implementation because you don't know what you're doing (and you had better hope no bad guys notice it), or you'll try to write an implementation and fail to complete it before the money runs out. When I worked on a pre-Internet distributed foreign exchange application twelve years ago (also described in *Understanding COM+*), we did both.

The Best Laid Plans

Software developers delude themselves.

Software developers always begin a project with the best of intentions and the loftiest of promises. Like an alcoholic heading to a party, we swear that we'll avoid bugs through careful design and that we'll document our code thoroughly. We'll test it all the way through, and we won't add features after the code freeze. Above all, we'll make realistic schedule estimates and then stick to them. ("That operating system feature doesn't do exactly what we want, but I can write a better one in a week, so there's no need to modify our program requirements. Two weeks at the outside. Unless I hit a snag. Oh, will we need testing time, too?") A robust, useful application (sobriety) is within our grasp, all we have to do is stay disciplined. No Solitaire at all. At least not until after five. OK, one game at lunch. "Dang, I lost; just one more to get even, OK? Hey, how'd it get to be 4:00?" Every single project I've ever seen has begun with this rosy glow.

Has any developer ever kept these promises? No. Never has, never will. We know in our hearts that we're lying when we promise. It's a disease. Like addicts, there's only one way out (not counting dying, which everyone does at exactly the same rate: 1.000 per person.) To write successful Internet applications, we of the software development community need to do what recovering addicts do and embrace at least two steps on our path to righteousness:

1. Admit that we are powerless—that our lives have become unmanageable.

2. Come to believe that a power greater than ourselves can restore us to sanity.

Application programmers must admit that we are powerless over Internet infrastructure. It makes our projects unmanageable. We cannot build it; it takes too long, it costs too much, and we don't know how. We must not even try, for that way lies sure and certain doom. In the extremely unlikely event that we do accidentally write some decent infrastructure code, our competitors who don't will have long since eaten our lunches, and breakfasts and dinners besides. You don't build your own highway to drive your car on, nor do you install your own power generating equipment (unless you lived in California in early 2001).

You can't afford to build infrastructure yourself.

Fortunately, your Internet application's infrastructure requirements are the same as everyone else's, just as your requirements for highways and electricity are similar to those of many other people. Because of this large common need, governments build highways and power companies build power plants, which you use in return for a fee, either directly through tolls and bills, or indirectly through taxes. Governments and utilities reap large economies of scale because they can hire or develop the best talent for accomplishing these goals and because they can spread the development cost over many more units than you ever could.

What we really need is for someone to do for distributed computing what the government does for highways (maybe not exactly what the government does for highways, but you get the basic idea). As recovering addicts believe that only the power who created the universe in which we compute can restore their lives, so developers need a higher power in computing to provide our Internet infrastructure, restoring our development efforts to sanity.

You want someone else to build it and for you just to use it.

What the Heck Is .NET, Anyway?

Microsoft .NET provides prefabricated infrastructure for solving the common problems of writing Internet software.

That's what Microsoft .NET is—prefabricated infrastructure for solving common problems in Internet applications. Microsoft .NET has been getting an enormous amount of publicity lately, even for this industry. That's why 5000 rabid geeks, crazed on Jolt Cola, converged on Orlando, Florida, in July 2000. Not because they can't pass up a bargain off-season airfare, even if it's not somewhere they want to go, or because they enjoy punishing heat and sunstroke. It was to hear about Microsoft .NET for the first time.

The server-side features of Microsoft .NET run on Windows NT, Windows 2000, and Windows XP Professional. The client-side features run on these plus Windows 98, Windows Me, and Windows XP Home. While it's currently an add-on service pack, later versions of .NET will probably be made part of the operating system. Later versions may or may not be announced to allow at least portions of it to run on other versions of Windows or, as we shall see, perhaps for other operating platforms as well. Microsoft .NET provides the following services, all discussed later in this book.

- **A new run-time environment, the .NET Framework.**   The .NET Framework is a run-time environment that makes it much easier for programmers to write good, robust code quickly, and to manage, deploy, and revise the code. The programs and components that you write execute inside this environment. It provides programmers with cool run-time features such as automatic memory management (garbage collection) and easier access to all system services. It adds many utility features such as easy Internet and database access. It also provides a new mechanism for code reuse—easier to use and at the same time more powerful and flexible than COM. The .NET Framework is easier to deploy because it doesn't require registry settings. It also provides standardized, system-level support for versioning. All of these features are available to programmers in any .NET-compliant language. I discuss the .NET Framework in Chapter 2.

- **A new programming model for constructing HTML pages, named ASP.NET.**   Even though intelligent single-use programs are on the rise, most Internet traffic for the near- to middle-term future will use a generic browser as a front end. This requires a server to construct a page using the HTML language that browsers understand and can display to a user. ASP.NET (the next version of Active Server Pages) is a new environment that runs on Internet

Information Services (IIS) and makes it much easier for programmers to write code that constructs HTML-based Web pages for browser viewing. ASP.NET features a new language-independent way of writing code and tying it to Web page requests. It features .NET Web Forms, which is an event-driven programming model of interacting with controls that makes programming a Web page feel very much like programming a Visual Basic form. ASP.NET contains good session state management and security features. It is more robust and contains many performance enhancements over original ASP. I discuss ASP.NET in Chapter 3.

■   **A new way for Internet servers to expose functions to any client, named XML Web services.**   While generic browsers will remain important, I think that the future really belongs to dedicated applications and appliances. The Web will become more of a place where, instead of data being rendered in a generic browser, a dedicated client (say, Napster, for music searching) will make cross-Internet function calls to a server and receive data to be displayed in a dedicated user interface or perhaps without a user interface at all for machine-to-machine communications. Microsoft .NET provides a new set of services that allows a server to expose its functions to any client on any machine running any operating system. The client makes calls to the server using the Internet's lowest common denominator of XML and HTTP. A set of functions exposed in this manner is called an XML Web service. Instead of sitting around waiting for customers to see the light and embrace the One True Operating System (Hallelujah!), the new design seems to say, "Buy our operating system because we provide lots of prefabricated support that makes it much easier to write applications that talk to anyone else in the entire world, no matter what or where they're running." I discuss XML Web services in Chapter 4.

■   **Windows Forms, a new way of writing rich client applications using the .NET Framework.**   A dedicated client application that uses XML Web services needs to provide a good user interface. A high-quality interface can provide a much better user experience, as the dedicated interface of Microsoft Outlook is better than the generic Web user interface of Hotmail. Microsoft .NET provides a new package, called .NET Windows Forms, that makes it easy to write dedicated Windows client applications using the

.NET Framework. Think of Visual Basic on steroids, available in any language, and you'll have imagined the right model. I describe .NET Windows Forms in Chapter 5.

■ **ADO.NET, which provides good support for database access within the .NET Framework.**   No Internet programming environment would be complete without some mention of database access. Most Internet programs, at least today, spend most of their time gathering information from a client, making a database query, and presenting the results to the client. .NET provides good support for database operations using ADO.NET. I cover ADO.NET in Chapter 6.

■ **Outstanding support for handling XML documents and streams.**   Operating in the modern distributed computing environments requires applications to handle XML. The .NET Framework contains outstanding support for writing applications that handle XML documents and streams. I discuss XML in Chapter 7.

■ **A standardized mechanism for signaling asynchronous events.**   Providing a standardized mechanism for callbacks from a server to its client was a large stumbling block in pre-.NET COM-based programming. The .NET Framework provides a standardized mechanism for one party to make an asynchronous call to another. I discuss this eventing mechanism in Chapter 8.

■ **Support for writing multithreaded code.**   The Windows operating system acquired preemptive multithreading in 1993 with the release of 32-bit Windows NT. Unfortunately, multithreaded programs have been difficult to write due to the low level of support from the operating system. The .NET Framework contains much more support for allowing everyday programmers to make use of the operating system's multithreading capabilities. I discuss threading in Chapter 9.

■ **Support for writing your own Windows Forms and Web Forms controls.**   The concept of a control, a prepackaged unit of functionality dealing with a user interface, has been fantastically successful. Both Windows Forms (Chapter 5) and ASP.NET Web Forms (Chapter 3) get most of their functionality from their ability to host controls. .NET also provides excellent support for users to develop their own controls, either for internal use or for sale to third parties. Chapter 10 and Chapter 11, respectively, discuss writing Windows Forms controls and Web Forms controls.

About This Book

Until I wrote *Understanding COM+*, all of my books had been low-level how-to manuals and tutorials, with the samples written in C++. This worked beautifully for hard-core programmers who write in C++, but unfortunately this is a small percentage of the people who buy computer books, which made my creditors very unhappy. I wanted to make this book accessible to developers who didn't know or didn't like C++. Furthermore, I found that managers got essentially nothing out of my C++-based approach because they never worked with the sample programs (with only one exception I know of, and I'm sending him a free copy of this book for working so hard to understand my last one). I really wanted to reach that audience, even more than programmers. An ignorant (or worse, half-educated) manager is an extremely dangerous beast. Eliminating that species would be my grand contribution to civilization.

This book uses the basic style I experimented with in my last book, in which I adapted the format that David Chappell used so successfully in his book *Understanding ActiveX and OLE* (Microsoft Press, 1996): lots of explanations, lots of diagrams, and very little code in the text descriptions. As much as I liked David Chappell's book, I still felt hungry for code (as I often need a piece of chocolate cake to top off a meal of delicate sushi). I found myself writing code to help me understand his ideas, much as I wrote equations to understand the textual descriptions in Stephen Hawking's *A Brief History of Time*. (OK, I'm a geek.) So my book comes with sample programs for all the chapters, some of which I wrote myself and some of which I adapted from Microsoft's samples. These sample programs are available on this book's Web site, which is *http://www.introducingmicrosoft.net*, naturally. Managers and architects will be able to read the book without drowning in code, while code-hungry programmers will still be able to slake their appetites. Most of the sample code I present in the text of this book is written in Visual Basic .NET because that's the language that most of my readers are familiar with. However, I got so many requests for C# code after the first edition of this book that I've also provided C# versions of all the samples on the book's Web site. If you want to run the sample programs, you'll need a computer running

Sample programs and installation instructions are available on this book's Web site.

Windows 2000 Server or Windows XP Professional, the Microsoft .NET Framework SDK, and Visual Studio .NET. Detailed system and installation requirements for the sample programs are available on the book's Web site.

Each chapter presents a single topic from the top down. I start by describing the architectural problem that needs to be solved. I then explain the high-level architecture of the infrastructure that .NET provides to help you solve that problem with a minimum amount of code. I next walk you through the simplest example I can imagine that employs the solution. Managers may want to stop reading after this section. I then continue with a discussion of finer points—other possibilities, boundary cases, and the like. Throughout, I've tried to follow Pournelle's Law, coined by Jerry Pournelle in his "Chaos Manor" computing column in the original *Byte* magazine, which states simply, "You can never have too many examples."

Each chapter of this book presents a single topic from the top down.

Sing a Song of Silicon

I can't stand modern poetry.

Modern poetry bores me silly. I find most of it indistinguishable from pompous politicized prose strewn with random carriage returns. It has no rhyme, no rhythm, just an author (usually with a private income or taxpayer's grant, else he'd starve to death) who suffers from the fatal delusion that he has Something Important To Say. Maybe my feeble mind just doesn't want to make the effort of parsing his intentional dislocations. Don't know about you, but I've got other things to do with my few remaining brain cycles.

Rudyard Kipling's poetry is great.

On the other hand, I love older poetry, especially Rudyard Kipling. He's not politically correct these days—read his poem "The White Man's Burden" if you want to know why. In his defense, I'll say that he was a product of his times, as we all are. And he won the Nobel Prize for Literature in 1907, so someone must have liked him then. My grandparents gave me a copy of his *Just So Stories*. My parents used that book to read me to sleep, and it was one of the first books I learned to read myself. I graduated to Kipling's poetry in high school English class, where I found reading his section of the literature book far more interesting than listening to the teacher. His poems still sing to me as no one else's ever have, before or since.

Kipling wrote a poem celebrating a marine engineer named McAndrew, almost all of which applies to programmers today.

What does this have to do with computer geekery, you ask? The incredible acceleration of technological innovation in the last few years brings to my mind Kipling's poem "McAndrew's Hymn," published in 1894. Most of us think of modern times as different from a hundred years ago and nowhere more so than in technology. Still, I'm astounded at how much of McAndrew's feelings resonate with me today. The title character is an old oceangoing Scottish engineer musing on the most brilliant technological accomplishment of his day: the marine steam engine. That was the beginning of the death of distance, a process that you and I, my fellow geeks, will complete ere we rest. I like this poem so much that I've started every chapter with an excerpt from it. You can read the whole thing on line at *http://home.pacifier.com/~rboggs/ KIPLING.HTML*. You may think of Scotty on Star Trek as the prototypical Scottish engineer, but I'm convinced that Gene Roddenberry based him on Kipling's McAndrew.

Every programmer, for example, knows Moore's law, right? It says that computing power at a given price point doubles every eighteen months. Many programmers also know its reciprocal, Grosch's law, which states that it doesn't matter how good the hardware boys are because the software boys will piss it away. A few even know Jablokow's corollary, which states simply, "And then some." But McAndrew figured this out a hundred years ago, way before some plagiarist stuck Moore's name on the idea and called it a law. I think of Kipling's words as I contemplate the original 4.77 MHz IBM PC (with two floppy drives and 256 KB of memory) that I use as a planter:

The poem includes an early formulation of Moore's Law.

[I] started as a boiler-whelp when steam and [I] were low.
I mind the time we used to serve a broken pipe wi' tow.
Ten pound was all the pressure then - Eh! Eh! - a man wad drive;
An' here, our workin' gauges give one hunder' fifty-five!
We're creepin' on wi' each new rig - less weight an' larger power:
There'll be the loco-boiler next an' thirty mile an' hour!

Like Rodney Dangerfield, we geeks yearn for respect and appreciation. Society has looked askance at us ever since the first cave-geek examined a sharp stone and said, "Cool fractal patterns. I wonder if it would scale to spearhead size?" Remember how girls in high school flocked around football players, most of whom (not all, Brian) were dumb as rocks? A straight-A average was uncool (mine would have been if I'd had one), and even my chess championship trophy couldn't compete with a varsity letter. Even though I knew that in the long run I'd make far more money than the high-school jocks (which my father pointed out is far more attractive to the opposite sex), it still burned. McAndrew cried aloud for the same thing, only far more eloquently (my emphasis added):

Romance! Those first-class passengers they like it very well,
Printed an' bound in little books; but why don't poets tell?
I'm sick of all their quirks an' turns-the loves an' doves they dream-
Lord, send a man like Robbie Burns to sing the Song o' Steam!

"Lord, send a man like Robbie Burns to sing the Song o' Steam!"

No Robbie Burns am I, and not even my mother likes hearing me sing. But I've done my best to tell the story as I see it today. I hope you enjoy reading it.

2

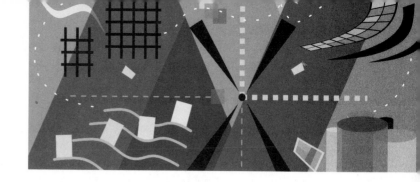

.NET Objects

To match wi' Scotia's noblest speech yon orchestra sublime
Whaurto-uplifted like the Just—the tail-rods mark the time.
The Crank-throws give the double-bass; the feed-pump sobs an' heaves:
An' now the main eccentrics start their quarrel on the sheaves.
Her time, her own appointed time, the rocking link-head bides,
Till-hear that note?—the rod's return whings glimmerin' through the guides.

> —Rudyard Kipling, writing about the vastly different types
> of components that any large application needs to work
> together harmoniously, "McAndrew's Hymn," 1894.

Problem Background

Good code is hard to write. It's never been easy, and the problems that developers need to solve to produce useful applications grow ever more complex in today's distributed, heterogeneous Internet world. I sometimes catch myself longing for the good old days, when software development meant writing an input processor that read characters directly from the keyboard and parsed them into recognizable tokens to be fed to a command processor. It doesn't work that way any more. Here are several of the difficult problems dogging the efforts of developers today.

Good code is hard to write.

First, we have the ongoing controversy over which programming language to use. While in theory any language can produce binary code that takes advantage of the entire operating system, it's all too common to hear something like, "Hey, you're using COBOL, so you can't have automatic memory management. Get yourself a real language, kid," or "Visual Basic

We need all system features to be available to programmers in any language.

doesn't do uncouth things like threads" [nose in air]. We'd like the choice of language to be dictated by how well it matches the problem domain, not by how well it matches the system features. We don't want any more second-class citizens. What's probably going to be the downfall of the Java language is that you can only use its cool features from Java. I have no patience for anyone who insists that I embrace the One True Programming Language; instead, I believe that salvation ought to be available to believers of any development creed.

COM helped us develop applications by assembling purchased components; we didn't have to write everything from scratch.

With the release of COM in 1993, Microsoft Windows developers found that they didn't have to write all of their application's code from scratch. COM allowed a client to call functions on a server at a binary level, without needing to know the server's source code implementation. Using COM meant that we could buy components—say, a calendar control—from third-party vendors and wire them into our apps by writing a relatively thin layer of "glue" code to express our business logic. We got faster application development and better functionality than we could have written ourselves, and the third-parties got a much higher unit volume over which to amortize their development efforts. Microsoft also used COM to provide access to operating system functionality, such as queuing and transactions, again making apps faster and easier to write. It was a good idea, and the software gods smiled. For a while.

COM only went so far. We need to abstract away the differences in implementations.

As with most software architectures, COM helped to a certain point, but its internal structure has now become an obstacle rather than a help. COM has two main problems: First, it requires a substantial infrastructure from each application; for example, class factories and interface marshalers. Every development environment has to supply its own implementation of these mechanisms, so they're all slightly different and not as compatible as we'd like. Second, COM operates by keeping client and server at arm's length. They deal with each other through external interfaces, not through sharing their internal implementations. You might say that a COM client and server only make love by telephone. Unfortunately, everyone's implementation of a COM interface differs in sneaky and hard-to-reconcile ways. For example, strings are implemented differently in C++ than they are in Microsoft Visual Basic, and both are implemented differently than strings in Java. Passing a string from a COM server written in Visual Basic to a COM client written in C++ requires work on someone's part to iron out the differences, usually the C++ application because Visual Basic's implementation isn't negotiable. Programmers spend an inordinate amount of time ironing out these differences. That wastes valuable programmer time (and annoys programmers, making them change jobs to do something more fun), and you never know when you have it right, when any COM client regardless of implementation can use your server. We need to iron out differences in implementation, allowing our apps to interoperate on a more intimate basis.

The Web is nothing if not heterogeneous. That's the dominant feature that any successful software architecture has to deal with. Much as Microsoft would like to see Windows PCs everywhere, they're starting to realize that it isn't going to happen. We'd like to be able to write software once and run it on a variety of platforms. That's what Java promised but hasn't quite delivered. (Spare me the righteous e-mails disagreeing with that statement; this is MY book.) Even if we can't make that approach work completely today, we'd like our software architecture to allow platform interoperability to evolve in the future.

We'd like our code to be able to run on a variety of platforms.

One of the major causes of program failure today, particularly in applications that run for a long time, is memory leaks. A programmer allocates a block of memory from the operating system, intending to free it later, but forgets and allocates another block. The first block of memory is said to be "leaked away," as it can't be recovered for later use. If your app runs long enough, these leaks accumulate and the app runs out of memory. That's not a big deal in programs like Notepad that a user runs for a few minutes and then shuts down, but it's fatal in apps like Web servers that are supposed to run continuously for days or weeks. You'd think we could remember to free all of our memory allocations, but they often get lost in complex program logic. Like an automatic seat belt that passengers couldn't forget to buckle, we'd like a mechanism that would prevent memory leaks in some way that we couldn't forget to use.

We need automatic memory management to prevent leaks.

When you ship a product, it's never perfect. (I know, yours are, but you'll have to agree that no one else's are, right? Besides, with no updates, how would you get more money from your existing customers?) So some time after you ship the first version, you ship an updated version of the product with new features and bug fixes for the old ones. Now the fun starts. No matter how hard you try to make your new release backward compatible with all of its old clients, this is very hard to do and essentially impossible to prove that you have done it. We'd really like some standardized mechanism whereby servers can publish the version level they contain. We'd like this mechanism to enable clients to read the version level of available servers and pick one with which they are compatible or identify exactly what they are missing if they can't.

We need help with managing different versions of the same software package.

Object-oriented programming, using such techniques as classes and inheritance, has permeated the software development world. That's about the only way you can manage programming efforts above a certain, not-very-high level of complexity. Unfortunately, every programming language provides a different combination of these features, naturally all incompatible, which

We'd like object-oriented programming features to be available in and between all programming languages.

means that different languages can interoperate with each other only at a very low level of abstraction. For example, COM does not allow a Visual Basic programmer to use the convenient mechanism of inheritance to extend an object written in C++. Instead, COM requires cumbersome workarounds. We'd like object-oriented programming techniques to be available in and between all programming languages.

For safety, we want to be able to restrict the operations of pieces of code we don't fully trust.

The Web is fast becoming the main avenue by which users acquire software, which leads to major security problems. While current versions of Windows use digital certificates to identify the author of a piece of downloaded code, there is currently no way to ensure that a piece of code can't harm our systems, say, by scrambling files. We can choose to install or not install a downloaded component on our system, but there is no good way to restrict its activities once it's there. It's an all-or-nothing decision, and we really don't like that. We'd like some way of setting allowed and forbidden operations for various pieces of code and of having the operating system enforce those restrictions. For example, we might like to say that a piece of code we've just downloaded can read files but can't write them.

We need a better way of organizing operating system functions for better access.

The Windows operating system has grown almost unimaginably complex. From its humble beginnings as a Solitaire host with just a couple of hundred functions, it's mushroomed into a behemoth FreeCell host with over 5000 separate functions. You can't find the one you want simply by looking at an alphabetical list; it takes too long. Programmers manage complex projects by organizing their software into logical objects. We need a similar method of organizing the functionality of the operating system into logically related groups so that we have at least some chance of finding the function we want.

Our new object model needs to seamlessly interoperate with COM, both as client and as server.

Finally, I don't want to dump on COM too badly. It was revolutionary in its day, and we're going to have a lot of it with us for the foreseeable future. Just as the first color TV sets needed to also receive the black and white broadcasts that predominated at the time, so does whatever object model we start using need to seamlessly interoperate with COM, both as client and as server.

It should be obvious that this long list of requirements is far more than any application vendor can afford to develop on its own. We have reached the limit of our potentialities. To move into the Internet world, we need a higher power that can provide us with a world we can live in.

Solution Architecture

The .NET Framework is Microsoft's operating system product that provides prefabricated solutions to these programming problems. The key to the framework is *managed code.* Managed code runs in an environment, called the *common language runtime*, that provides a richer set of services than the standard Win32 operating system, as shown in Figure 2-1. The common language runtime environment is the higher power that we have to turn our code over to in order to deal with the harsh, savage world that is modern Internet programming.

The solution is managed code, executing in the common language runtime.

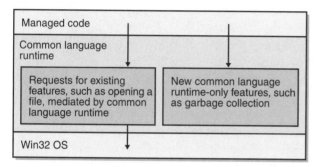

Figure 2-1   Managed execution in the common language runtime.

But with that architecture, how can the common language runtime work with any language? Not to sound Clintonesque, but that depends on what your definition of "language" is. Every common language runtime–compliant development tool compiles its own source code into a standard *Microsoft Intermediate Language* (MSIL, or IL for short), as shown in Figure 2-2. Because all development tools produce the same IL, regardless of the language in which their source code is written, differences in implementation are gone by the time they reach the common language runtime. No matter how it's presented in the source code programming language itself, every program's internal implementation of a string is the same as every other program's because they all use the *String* object within the common language runtime. The same holds true for arrays and classes and everything else.

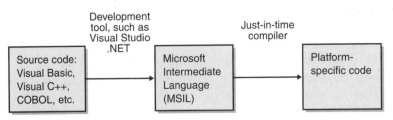

Figure 2-2   Different source code programming languages are compiled into MSIL.

All common language runtime–compliant source code languages compile to the same intermediate language.

Any company that wants to can write a common language runtime–compliant language. Microsoft Visual Studio .NET provides common language runtime–compliant versions of Visual Basic, C# (pronounced C sharp), JScript, and C++. Third parties are producing many others, including APL, COBOL, and Perl.

The IL is compiled just-in-time to run on the target machine.

The IL code produced by the development tool can't run directly on any computer. A second step is required, called *just-in-time* (JIT) compilation, as shown in Figure 2-2. A tool called a *just-in-time compiler*, or JITter[1], reads the IL and produces actual machine code that runs on that platform. This provides .NET with a certain amount of platform independence, as each platform can have its own JITter. Microsoft isn't making a huge deal about just-in-time compiling, as Sun did about Java 5 years or so ago, because this feature is still in its infancy. No common language runtime implementations for platforms other than Windows (98, NT4 SP6, Me, 2000, or XP for clients; 2000 or XP Professional for servers) have currently been announced, although I expect some will be over time. It's probably more a strategy for covering future versions of Windows, like the forthcoming 64-bit version and now Windows XP, than it is for covering different operating systems, like Linux.

The .NET Framework provides automatic memory management via garbage collection.

The .NET Framework provides automatic memory management, using a mechanism called *garbage collection*. A program does not have to explicitly free memory that it has allocated. The common language runtime detects when the program is no longer using the memory and automatically recycles it. Wish I had a maid that did that with my laundry!

The .NET Framework supports explicit standardized version management.

The .NET Framework finally supports versioning. Microsoft .NET provides a standardized way in which developers of servers can specify the version that resides in a particular EXE or DLL and a standardized mechanism that a client uses to specify which version it needs to run with. The operating system will enforce the version requests of clients, both providing a reasonable default set of versioning behavior and allowing a developer to override it and specify explicit versioning behavior.

---

1. Defects in this piece of software are known, of course, as jitterbugs.

Because each language compiles to the same IL, all languages that support the common language runtime have the potential to support the same set of features. While it is possible to write a common language runtime language that does not expose this or that underlying common language runtime feature to a programmer, I expect the brutal Darwinian jungle that is the modern software marketplace to kill off such an ill-conceived idea very quickly. The common language runtime provides a rich set of object-oriented programming features, such as inheritance and parameterized object construction. Don't worry if these sound like complicated concepts—they aren't hard to use; they save you a lot of time and potential errors; and you'll grow to like both of them.

The .NET Framework extends rich object-oriented programming features to all languages.

The .NET Framework organizes operating system functionality through the *System* namespace. All operating system objects, interfaces, and functions are now organized in a hierarchical manner, so it's much easier to find the things you want. It also keeps your object and function names from colliding with those of the operating system and those of other developers.

The .NET Framework organizes system functionality into a hierarchical namespace.

The .NET Framework supports code access security. You can specify that a piece of code is allowed to perform this operation but not that one. For example, you can allow a piece of code to read files but not write them, and the common language runtime will enforce your specifications and block any attempt to go outside them. This means that you can apply different levels of trust to code from different sources, just as you apply different levels of trust to different people that you deal with. This capability lets you run code from the Web without worrying that it's going to trash your system.

The .NET Framework supports code security

Finally, the .NET Framework provides seamless interoperability with COM, both as client and as server. The framework puts a wrapper object around a COM object that makes the object look like a native .NET object. This means .NET code doesn't know or greatly care which kind of object it's running with. On the flip side, .NET objects know how to register themselves with an abstraction layer so that they appear to COM clients to be COM servers.

The .NET Framework provides seamless interoperability with COM, both as client and as server.

Oh Yeah? What Does It Cost?

But what about Platt's Second Law? (The amount of crap in the universe is conserved; see Chapter 1.) If I have less crap to deal with—for example, if I no longer have to worry about freeing memory that I've allocated—whose head did that crap get dumped on because it didn't just disappear? In the case of .NET, it got dumped primarily on two sets of heads, namely Microsoft's and Intel's. (All of my readers who work for Sun just stood up and cheered. Both of them.) In Microsoft's case, the operating system itself got harder to write. An automatic garbage collection mechanism like the one in .NET is several orders of magnitude harder to write than a simple in-out heap manager of the

The operating system got harder to write, but you don't really care about that.

type that Windows 2000 contains. Since Microsoft hopes to sell millions of copies of .NET, they can afford to hire lots of smart programmers and engineer the heck out of it. This division of labor—letting Microsoft develop infrastructure while you worry less—makes economic sense.

The computational task also got harder, requiring more computing horsepower.

In the case of Intel, the new .NET Framework will keep them busy producing faster CPUs and more memory chips. Applications built on .NET will run slower in some operations than those that aren't, but they'll be easier to write and debug. Sophisticated garbage collection requires more computation than simple heap allocation, just as an automatic seatbelt requires more parts than a manual one. Plus, since garbage collection doesn't take place as often, your computer probably needs more memory so that your app still has enough while objects are hanging around waiting to be garbage collected. (Remember Grosch's Law? Go check the end of Chapter 1 if you don't.) But I don't think that the additional memory and CPU cycles a .NET program requires are being squandered, as they are on that stupid dancing paper clip in Microsoft Office. I think they're being wisely invested, saving you time and money by letting you write code faster and with fewer bugs because the operating system is doing more of the scut work for you. An application using a general disk operating system will never run as fast as one that programs absolute sector and track disk head movements. But you can't afford to do that; it takes too long, it costs too much, and you can't manage very much data. You'll spend all your time on the silly disk sectors and never get any paying work done. Once it becomes possible to abstract away these infrastructural problems, doing so becomes an economic necessity. If your own memory management was working well enough, you wouldn't be spending your debugging time tracking memory leaks.

Simplest Example

A .NET Framework object sample begins here.

As I'll do throughout this book, I've written the simplest example I could think of to demonstrate the operation of the .NET Framework. You can download this sample and all the other code examples in this book from *www.introducingmicrosoft.net*. For this sample I wrote a .NET object server, the .NET replacement for an ActiveX DLL in Visual Basic 6, and its accompanying client. The server provides a single object exposing a single method, called *GetTime*, that provides the current system time in the form of a string, either with or without the seconds digits. Even though I wrote the server in Visual Basic and the client in C#, I didn't have to use Visual Studio. In fact, I wrote both applications in Notepad and built them with the command line tools provided in the .NET Framework SDK. I do show examples of using

Visual Studio .NET in other sections of this chapter. Note: You can download a copy of the .NET Framework SDK at *www.msdn.microsoft.com/net*.

You'll notice when we begin looking at the code that it seems, at least superficially, quite similar to the classic Visual Basic code you are already familiar with. However, Microsoft made a number of important changes to the .NET version of Visual Basic to enable it to use the .NET common language runtime classes and interoperate correctly with the other common language runtime languages. A full discussion of these changes is far beyond the scope of this book, but here are two examples. The text string displayed in a button is now stored in a property called *Text* (as for a *TextBox*) rather than in the *Caption* property used in Visual Basic 6. This change will break your existing app's compilation but is trivial to fix once the compiler shows it to you. Other changes won't break your compilation, but they can change your program's behavior in subtle and far-reaching ways. For example, a Visual Basic 6 object is destroyed immediately when its reference count reaches zero, but a zero-reference Visual Basic .NET object won't actually be destroyed until a garbage collection occurs, some indeterminate amount of time later. (See the discussion later in this chapter.) Your app might be able to live with the new behavior, or it might require a redesign. These changes mean that you cannot simply compile your existing Visual Basic code in Visual Studio .NET and expect it to work correctly. It will take some effort to port; probably not an enormous amount, but more than the zero-level you were hoping for.

Visual Basic .NET contains a number of critical language differences from Visual Basic 6.

> **Note** Visual Studio .NET contains an upgrade tool that runs automatically when you open a Visual Basic 6 project. It flags the changes that it detects and suggests fixes. The language has definitely gotten more powerful. If you want the cool Internet features of .NET, you'll probably think it's worth the effort to switch. Even if you're just writing single-user desktop form applications, you may still find the versioning support and the easier deployment and cleanup to be worth it.

Figure 2-3 shows the code listing for my sample object server. Looking at this code, we first see the *Imports* directive. This new feature of Visual Basic .NET tells the compiler to "import the namespaces." The term *namespace* is a fancy way to refer to the description of a set of prefabricated functionality provided by some class somewhere. It is conceptually identical to a reference in your Visual Basic 6 project. The names following *Imports* tell the engine which sets of functionality to include the references for. In this case, *Microsoft.VisualBasic* is the one containing the definition of the *Now* function that I use to fetch the time. If you use Visual Basic from within Visual Studio .NET, the *Microsoft.VisualBasic* namespace is imported automatically without needing an explicit *Imports* statement.

We next see the directive *Namespace TimeComponentNS*. This is the declaration of the namespace for the component we are writing, the name that clients will use when they want to access this component's functionality. I discuss namespaces later in this chapter. Again, if you are using Visual Studio .NET, this declaration is made automatically.

```
' Import the external Visual Basic namespace, allowing me to
' access the Now function by its short name.

Imports Microsoft.VisualBasic

' Declare the namespace that clients will use to access
' the classes in this component.

Namespace TimeComponentNS

' Declare the class(es) that this DLL will provide to a client.
' This is the same as Visual Basic 6.

Public Class TimeComponent

    ' Declare the function(s) that this class will provide to a client.
    ' This, too, is the same as VB6.

    Public Function GetTime(ByVal ShowSeconds As Boolean) As String

        ' The formatting of dates, and the returning of values of
        ' functions, changed somewhat in Visual Basic .NET.

        If (ShowSeconds = True) Then
            Return Now.ToLongTimeString
        Else
            Return Now.ToShortTimeString
        End If

    End Function

End Class

End Namespace
```

Figure 2-3 Visual Basic code listing of simplest object server.

Next come the class and function declarations, identical to Visual Basic 6. Finally, I put in the internal logic of fetching the time, formatting it into a string and returning it to the client. These too have changed slightly. The property *Now* still fetches the date, but formatting it into a string is now done with a method of the new .NET class *DateTime* rather than a separate function. Also, a Visual Basic function specifies its return value using the new keyword *Return* instead of the syntax used in earlier versions.

This section describes the code of my .NET object server

I next compiled my code into a DLL, named timecomponent.dll, using the command line tools that come with the .NET Framework SDK. Anyone who cares to can find the command line syntax in the sample code you can download from the book's Web site. The result may look like a plain old DLL to you, but it's actually very different inside. The Visual Basic .NET compiler didn't convert the Visual Basic code to native code; that is, to specific instructions for the microprocessor chip inside your PC. Instead, the DLL contains my object server's logic expressed in MSIL (again, for Microsoft Intermediate Language; IL for short), the intermediate language that I introduced in the "Solution Architecture" section in this chapter. All common language runtime language compilers produce this IL rather than native processor instructions, which is how the runtime can run seamlessly with so many different languages. The DLL also contains *metadata* that describes the code to the common language runtime system. This metadata is in a runtime-required format that describes the contents of the DLL: what classes and methods it contains, what external objects it requires, what version of the code it represents, and so on. Think of it as a type library on steroids. The main difference is that a COM server could sometimes run without a type library, whereas a .NET object server can't even begin to think about running without its metadata. I discuss this metadata further in the section "Assemblies" later in the chapter.

Compiling the Visual Basic code produces a DLL containing intermediate language and metadata.

Having written my server, I next need a client to test it. To demonstrate the fact that .NET works between different languages, I wrote this client in C#. I know that not many of you are familiar with this language, but if you look at the code in Figure 2-4, you'll see that it's fairly easy to understand at this level of simplicity. In fact, given the enhancements to Visual Basic .NET to support the common language runtime's object-oriented features such as inheritance (described later in this chapter), I've heard programmers after a few beers describe C# as "VB with semicolons" or occasionally "Java without Sun." Either one of these can start a fistfight if you say it too loudly in the wrong bar in Redmond or Sunnyvale.

Visual Basic and C# resemble each other more than either community likes to admit.

```
// Import the namespaces that this program uses, thereby allowing
// us to use the short names of the functions inside them.

using System ;
using TimeComponentNS ;

class MainApp
{

    // The static method "Main" is an application's entry point.

    public static void Main()
    {

        // Declare and create a new component of the class
        // provided by the VB server we wrote.

        TimeComponent tc = new TimeComponent ( ) ;

        // Call the server's GetTime method. Write its
        // resulting string to a console window.

        Console.Write (tc.GetTime (true)) ;
    }
}
```

Figure 2-4   C# code listing of simplest object client.

Our client example starts with importing namespaces, which in C# requires the directive *using*. Our sample client imports the *System* namespace (described in detail later in this chapter), which contains the description of the *Console.Write* function, and also imports our time component's namespace. Additionally, we have to explicitly tell the compiler in which DLL it will find our component's namespace, which we do in the compiler batch file (not shown). Visual Studio .NET provides an easy user interface for this.

The C# client also compiles to intermediate language.

Execution of any C# program begins in a static (shared) method called *Main*. In that method, we can see that our client program uses the C# *new* operator to tell the runtime engine to find the DLL containing our *TimeComponent* class and create an instance of it. The next line calls the object's *GetTime* method and then uses the system's *Console.Write* method to output the time string in a command line window. The C# compiler in this case produces an EXE file. Like the server DLL, this EXE does not contain native instructions, but instead contains intermediate language and metadata.

When I run the C# client executable, the system loader notes that the executable is in the form of managed code and loads it into the runtime engine. The engine notes that the EXE contains IL, so it invokes the just-in-time compiler, or JITter. As I discussed earlier, the JITer is a system tool that converts IL into native code for whichever processor and operating system it runs on. Each different architecture will have its own JITter tailored to that particular system, thereby allowing one set of IL code to run on multiple types of systems. The JITter produces native code, which the common language runtime engine will begin to execute. When the client invokes the *new* operator to create an object of the *TimeComponent* class, the common language runtime engine will again invoke the JITter to compile the component DLL's IL just-in-time and then make the call and report the results. The output is shown in Figure 2-5.

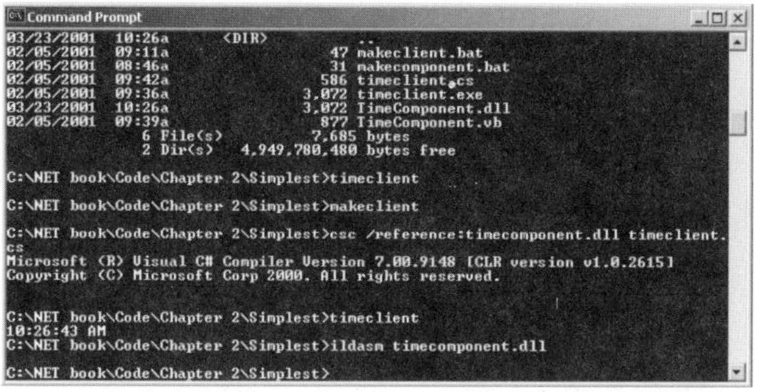

Figure 2-5   Console output of sample TimeClient program.

This run-time compilation model works well for some classes of applications, such as code downloaded from the Internet for a page you just surfed to, but not for others, say, Visual Studio, which you use all day, every day, and update once or twice a year. Therefore, an application can specify that JIT compilation is to be performed once, when the application is installed on a machine, and the native code stored on the system as it is for non-.NET applications. You do this via the command-line utility program Ngen.exe, the native image generator, not shown in this example.

The IL is compiled just-in-time when the client and its component are run.

When the client used the *new* operator to create the object, how did the loader know where to find the server DLL? In this case, the loader simply looked in the same directory as the client application. This is known as a *private assembly*, the simplest type of deployment model in .NET. A private assembly can't be referenced from outside its own directory. It supports no version checking or any security checking. It requires no registry entries, as a COM server would. To uninstall a private assembly, all you have to do is delete the files, without performing any other cleanup. Obviously, this simple

The loader finds the DLL requested by the client by looking in the client application's directory.

case, while effective in situations like this, isn't useful in every situation—for example, when you want to share the same server code among multiple clients. I discuss these more complex scenarios in the section on assemblies later in this chapter.

More on .NET Namespaces

Selecting items from a short alphabetical list is easy. It's much harder when the list gets longer.

I remember programming Windows version 2.0, scanning the alphabetical list of operating system functions (on paper, that's how long ago this was) until I found the one whose name seemed to promise that it would do what I wanted. I'd try it, and sometimes it would work and sometimes it wouldn't. If it didn't, I'd go back to scanning the list again. Listing the functions alphabetically worked reasonably well on Windows 2.0, which contained only a few hundred different functions. I could see at a glance (or two or three) everything that the operating system could do for me, which gave me a fighting chance at writing some decent, albeit limited, code.

Organizing operating system functions into one alphabetical list won't work with today's 32-bit Windows. It's enormous—over 5000 functions and growing. I can't scan through a list that long to find, for example, console output functions; they're scattered among far too many unrelated functions for me to pick them out. It's a problem for operating system designers, too. When they want to add a new function, they have to choose a name for it that is descriptive but that doesn't conflict with any of the other function names already implemented. Application programmers also need to make sure that their global function names don't conflict with operating system functions. The signal-to-noise ratio of this approach gets lower as the list of functions gets longer, and it's approaching absolute zero today. We say that the *namespace*, the set of names within which a particular name needs to be unique, has gotten too large.

The best way to handle large lists is to break them down into smaller logical groups.

The way to handle large lists is to break them down into smaller sublists that you can more easily digest. The classic example of this is the Start menu in Windows. If every application on your entire computer were listed on one gigantic menu, you'd never be able to find the one that you wanted. Instead, the Start menu provides a relatively short (10 or so) list of groups, easy to scan and pick from. Each group contains a list of logical subgroups, nested as deeply as you feel is cost-effective, eventually terminating in a short list of actual applications. By the time you pick the application you want, you've looked at maybe 50 different choices, rarely more than a dozen or so at a time. Think how much easier this is compared to selecting the one application you want out of the thousand or so installed on most computers.

The .NET Framework provides a better way of organizing operating system functions and objects. This same mechanism keeps the names of functions and objects that you write from interfering with the names of objects and functions written by other developers. It uses the concept of a namespace, which is a logical subdivision of software functionality within which all names must be unique. It's not a new concept; object-oriented languages have used it for decades. But its use in .NET is the first time I know of that an entire operating system's functionality has been organized in this way.

All .NET common language runtime objects and functions are part of a namespace called *System*. When you look them up in the documentation, you'll find that all names begin with the characters "System." We say that all the objects and functions whose names begin this way "belong to the *System* namespace." The *System* namespace is naturally quite large, as it contains the names of all functional elements of a rich operating system. It is therefore subdivided into a number of subordinate namespaces—for example, *System.Console*, which contains all the functions dealing with input and output on a console window. Some of these subnamespaces contain their own sub-subnamespaces, and so on down the line until the developers got tired of it. The *fully qualified name* of a function, sometimes called the *qualified name* or *q-name*, is the name of the function preceded by its full namespace location, also known as a *qualifier*. For example, *System.Console.Write* is the fully qualified name of the system function that writes output to a console window. You can call a function by means of its fully qualified name from anywhere in your code.

The *System* namespace is very large. Consequently, it is implemented in several separate DLLs. Just because a function or an object is part of the *System* namespace does not necessarily mean that your editor, compiler, and linker will automatically be able to find it. You generally have to tell your development tools which of the *System* namespace DLLs you want to include when building a project. For example, when I build .NET components in Visual Studio, I often like them to pop up message boxes during debugging. The *MessageBox* object is part of the *System.Windows.Forms* namespace, which is implemented in System.Windows.Forms.dll. Visual Studio does not automatically include this DLL in its reference list when I create a component library project, probably because its authors figured that components would work behind the scenes and not interact with the user. That's generally true in production. To gain access to the *MessageBox* object during debugging, I have to explicitly add that reference to my project.

.NET provides the concept of a namespace, a logical division within which a name needs to be unique.

All .NET common language runtime objects and functions live within the *System* namespace.

The *System* namespace is implemented in several separate DLLs. You have to be sure that your development tools know to include all the ones you need.

Importing a namespace allows you to use short names when calling a function within that namespace.

This organization of functions into logical groups is very handy for finding the one you want with a minimum of fuss. The only drawback is that fully qualified names can get very long. For example, the function *System.Runtime.InteropServices.Marshal.ReleaseComObject* is used for releasing a specified COM object immediately without performing a full garbage collection. (See the section ".NET Memory Management" for an explanation of the latter.) Most .NET applications won't use this function at all, but the ones that do will probably use it in many places. Typing this whole thing in every time you call it could get very tedious very quickly. You can see that it barely fits on one line of this book. My wife does not address me as "David Samuel Platt, son of Benjamin, son of Joseph" unless she is exceptionally angry, a state she is incapable of occupying for very long. Therefore, just as people address their most intimate relations by their first names, the common language runtime allows you to *import a namespace*, as shown earlier in the programming examples in Figures 2-3 and 2-4. When you import a namespace, you're telling your compiler that you use the functions in that namespace so often that you want to be on a first-name basis with them. Importing a namespace is done in Visual Basic by using the keyword *Imports*, and in C# via the keyword *using*. For example, in Figure 2-4, I imported the namespace *System*, which allowed me to write to the console by calling *Console.Write*. If I hadn't imported the *System* namespace, I would have had to use the fully qualified name *System.Console.Write*. Choosing which namespaces to import is entirely a matter of your own convenience and has no effect on the final product (IL always contains full names) other than allowing you to organize your own thought processes so as to produce your best output. Since the whole point of using separate namespaces is to separate functions with the same name to prevent conflicts, you can't import them all at the same time. To avoid confusion, I strongly urge you to pick a consistent set of rules for choosing which namespaces to import and follow it throughout your entire project.

Your own code will also live in a namespace, with a name you define.

When you write a .NET object server, you specify the name of the namespace in which your code lives. This is done via the *Namespace* directive, as shown in Figure 2-3. The namespace will often be the same as the name of the file in which the code lives, but it doesn't have to be. You can put more than one namespace in the same file, or you can spread one namespace among multiple files. Visual Studio .NET or other development environments will often automatically assign a namespace to your project. But how do you know that your namespace won't conflict with the namespace chosen by another vendor for a different component? That's what assemblies are for, which is our next topic of conversation.

Assemblies

The .NET Framework makes extensive use of *assemblies* for .NET code, resources, and metadata. All code that the .NET common language runtime executes must reside in an assembly. In addition, all security, namespace resolution, and versioning features work on a per-assembly basis. Since assemblies are used so often and for so many different things, I need to discuss assemblies in some detail.

.NET makes extensive use of a new packaging unit called an assembly.

Concept of an Assembly

An assembly is a logical collection of one or more EXE or DLL files containing an application's code and resources. An assembly also contains a *manifest*, which is a metadata description of the code and resources "inside" the assembly. (I'll explain those quotes in a second.) An assembly can be, and often is, a single file, either an EXE or a DLL, as shown in Figure 2-6.

When we built the simple example of a time server earlier in this chapter, the DLL that our compiler produced was actually a single-file assembly, and the EXE client application that we built in that example was another one. When you use tools such as Visual Studio .NET, each project will most likely correspond to a single assembly.

Our simple example produced two single-file assemblies.

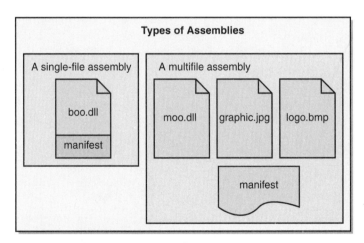

Figure 2-6   Single-file and multifile assemblies.

Although an assembly often resides in a single file, it also can be, and often is, a logical, not a physical, collection of more than one file residing in the same directory, also shown in Figure 2-6. The manifest specifying the files that make up the assembly can reside in one of the code-containing EXEs or DLLs of the assembly, or it can live in a separate EXE or DLL that contains

An assembly can also be a logical collection of more than one file.

nothing but the manifest. When dealing with a multifile assembly, you *must* remember that the files are not tied together by the file system in any way. It is entirely up to you to ensure that the files called out in the manifest are actually present when the loader comes looking for them. The only thing that makes them part of the assembly is that they are mentioned in the manifest. In this case, the term *assembly*, with its connotation of metal parts bolted together, is not the best term. Perhaps "roster" might be a better one. That's why I put quotes around the term "inside" the assembly a few paragraphs ago. You add and remove files from a multifile assembly using the command line SDK utility program AL.exe, the Microsoft Assembly Linker. Smart development environments such as Visual Studio do this automatically for you.

You can view an assembly's manifest with ILDASM.exe

You can view the manifest of an assembly using the IL Disassembler (ILDASM.exe). Figure 2-7 shows the manifest of our time component. You can see that it lists the external assemblies on which this assembly depends. In this case, we depend on mscorlib.dll, the main .NET common language runtime DLL, and on an assembly called Microsoft.VisualBasic, which contains Visual Basic's internal functions such as *Now*. It also lists the assembly names that we provide to the world, in this case, TimeComponent.

```
MANIFEST                                                    _|□|×|
.assembly extern mscorlib
{
  .publickeytoken = (B7 7A 5C 56 19 34 E0 89 )              // .z\V.4.
  .hash = (B0 73 F2 4C 14 39 0A 35 25 EA 45 0F 60 58 C3 84  // .s.L.9.5%.E.`X..
           E0 3B E0 95 )                                    // .;..
  .ver 1:0:2411:0
}
.assembly extern Microsoft.VisualBasic
{
  .publickeytoken = (B0 3F 5F 7F 11 D5 0A 3A )              // .?_....
  .hash = (A3 11 69 32 7F 24 F4 A4 0D EB '55 F9 31 63 78 BD // ..i2.$....U.lcx.
           A8 BE 91 FB )
  .ver 7:0:9135:0
}
.assembly TimeComponent
{
  .hash algorithm 0x00008004
  .ver 0:0:0:0
}
.module TimeComponent.dll
// MVID: {20A87166-3129-4FD2-9B47-FF675C9F66E0}
.subsystem 0x00000002
.file alignment 512
.corflags 0x00000001
// Image base: 0x03060000
```

Figure 2-7 Assembly manifest of our sample time component.

In addition to the code objects exposed by and required by the assembly, the manifest also contains information that describes the assembly itself. For example, it contains the assembly's version information, expressed in a standardized format described later in this section. It can also describe the culture (fancy name for human language and sublanguage, say, Australian English) for which the assembly is written. In the case of a shared assembly, of which more anon, the manifest contains a public cryptographic key, which is used to ensure that the assembly can be distinguished from all other assemblies regardless of its filename. You can even add your own custom attributes to the manifest, which the common language runtime will ignore, but which your own applications can read and use. You set manifest attributes with the Assembly Linker mentioned previously or with Visual Studio .NET.

Assemblies and Deployment

The central question in dividing your code among assemblies is whether the code inside the assembly is intended solely for your own application's use or will be shared with any other application that wants it. Microsoft .NET supports both options, but it requires more footwork in the latter case. In the case of code that you write for your own applications, say, the calculation engine for a complex financial instrument, you'd probably want to make the assembly private. On the other hand, a general utility object that could reasonably be used by many applications—a file compression engine, for example—might be more widely used if you make it shared.

You need to think carefully about whether your assemblies should be private or public.

Suppose you want your assemblies to be private. The .NET model couldn't be simpler. In fact, that's exactly what I did in the simplest example shown previously. You just build a simple DLL assembly, and copy it to the directory of the client assembly that uses it or to a subdirectory of that client. You don't have to make any entries in the system registry or Active Directory as you had to do when using COM components. None of the code will change unless you change it, so you will never encounter the all-too-familiar situation in which a shared DLL changes versions up or down and your app breaks for no apparent reason.

Assemblies can be private to an application, which simplifies your life in certain cases.

The obvious problem with this approach is the proliferation of assemblies, which was the problem DLLs were originally created to solve back in Windows 1.0. If every application that uses, say, a text box, needs its own copy of the DLL containing it, you'll have assemblies breeding like bacteria all over your computer. Jeffrey Richter argues (in *MSDN Magazine*, March 2001) that this isn't a problem. With 40 gigabyte hard drives selling for under $200 (then; today for $200 you can get 100 GB), everyone can afford all the disk space they need, so most assemblies should be private; that way your application will never break from someone else messing with shared code. That's like an emergency room doctor saying that the world would be a far better place if people didn't drink to excess or take illegal drugs. They're both absolutely right, but neither's vision is going to happen any time soon in the real world. Richter's idea is practical for developers, who usually get big, fast PCs, but a customer with a large installed base of two-year-old PCs that it can't junk or justify upgrading at that point in its budget cycle isn't going to buy that argument *or* bigger disks. Fairly soon in your development process, you

However, sometimes you want the code in assemblies to be shared.

will need to share an assembly among several applications, and you want the .NET Framework to help you do that.

Shared assemblies live in the global assembly cache, administered by a number of tools.

The .NET Framework allows you to share assemblies by placing them in the *global assembly cache* (GAC, pronounced like the cartoon exclamation). This is a directory on your machine, currently \winnt\assembly or \windows\assembly, in which all shared assemblies are required to live. You can place assemblies into the cache, view their properties, and remove them from the cache using a .NET Framework SDK command line utility called GACUTIL.exe, which works well when run from scripts and batch files. Most human users will prefer to use the Assembly Cache Viewer, which is a shell extension that installs with the .NET Framework SDK. It automatically snaps into Windows Explorer and provides you with the view of the GAC shown in Figure 2-8.

Shared assemblies use public key cryptography to ensure that their names are unique.

Whenever you share any type of computer file, you run up against the problem of name collisions. Because all .NET shared assemblies have to go in the GAC so that they can be managed, we need some way of definitively providing unique names for all the code files that live there, even if their original names were the same. This is done with a *strong name*, otherwise known as a *shared name*. A strong name uses public key cryptography to transparently produce a name that is guaranteed to be unique among all assemblies in the system. The manifest of a shared assembly contains the public key of a public/private key pair. The combination of the file's name, version, and an excerpt from this public key is the strong name.

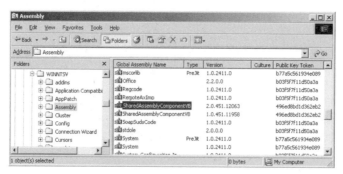

Figure 2-8 Global Assembly Cache Viewer.

This paragraph contains instructions for generating a shared assembly.

Suppose we want to write a shared assembly that lives in the GAC. I've switched to Visual Studio .NET for this example, both to demonstrate it and because I find it easier to operate than the command line tools. I've written a different Visual Basic .NET component that does the same thing as our simplest time example, except that it adds the version number to its returned time string. Once I build the component, I need to generate and assign a strong name for it, also known as *signing* the component. Visual Studio .NET can be configured to do this automatically if you provide a file containing the public/private key pair. You generate this file with the SDK command line utility program SN.exe. You tell Visual Studio about the key file by specifying the filename in the AssemblyInfo.vb file in the project, as shown in Figure 2-9. When I build the component, Visual Studio .NET signs it automatically. I then manually put it in the GAC by using Windows Explorer.

```
<Assembly: AssemblyKeyFileAttribute("mykeys.snk")>
```

Figure 2-9   AssemblyInfo.vb file entry specifying key pair for generating strong name.

I've also provided a client, this one written in Visual Basic using Visual Studio .NET, that uses the shared assembly. I tell Visual Studio .NET to generate a reference to the server DLL by right-clicking on the References folder in Solution Explorer, selecting Add Reference to open the Add Reference dialog box (shown in Figure 2-10), and then clicking Browse and surfing over to the shared assembly file that resides in a standard directory. Visual Studio .NET generates a reference accessing that namespace.

This paragraph contains instructions for writing a client that uses an object from the GAC.

Visual Studio cannot currently add a reference to an assembly in the GAC, although this feature has been proposed for a future release. This happened because the GAC's design hadn't yet stabilized by the time the Visual Studio developers needed to design their reference mechanism. Therefore, unless they're building client and server together as part of the same project, developers must install two copies of their components, one in a standard directory to compile against and another in the GAC for their clients to run against. Users will require only the latter.

Finally I need to set the *CopyLocal* property of the newly-added reference to False, thereby telling Visual Studio .NET that I don't want it to make a local copy. When the client runs, the loader looks for a local copy, doesn't find it, and therefore checks the GAC, where the shared component does indeed live.

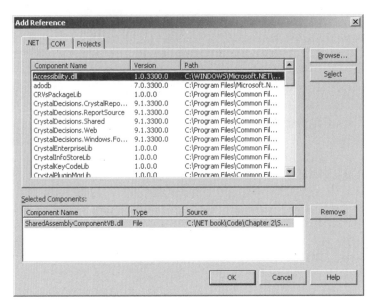

Figure 2-10   Adding a reference to a shared component.

The public/private key algorithm also provides a check on the integrity of the assembly's files.

As an added benefit of the public key cryptography scheme used for signing shared assemblies, we also gain a check on the integrity of the assembly file. The assembly generator performs a hashing operation on the contents of the files contained in the manifest. It then encrypts the result of this hash using our private key and stores the encrypted result in the manifest. When the loader fetches an assembly from the GAC, it performs the same hashing algorithm on the assembly's file or files, decrypts the manifest's stored hash using the public key, and compares the two. If they match, the loader knows that the assembly's files haven't been tampered with. This doesn't get you any real identity checking because you can't be sure whose public key it really is, but it does guarantee that the assembly hasn't been tampered with since it was signed.

Assemblies and Versioning

Versioning of code is an enormous, painful, unsexy problem.

Dealing with changes to published code has historically been an enormous problem, often known as DLL Hell. Replacing with a newer version a DLL used by an existing client bit you two ways, coming and going. First, the new code sometimes broke existing applications that depended on the original version. As hard as you try to make new code backward compatible with the old, you can never know or test everything that anyone was ever doing with it. It's especially annoying when you update a new DLL and don't run the now-broken old client until a month later, when it's very difficult to remember what you might have done that broke it. Second, updates come undone when installing an application copies an older DLL over a newer one that's already on your computer, thereby breaking an existing client that depended on the newer behavior. It happens all the time, when an installation script says, "Target file *xxx* exists and is newer than the source. Copy anyway?" and 90 percent of the time the user picks Yes. This one's especially maddening because someone else's application caused the problem, but your app's the one that won't work, your tech support line is the one that receives expensive calls and bomb threats, and you better hope you haven't sold any copies of the program to the Postal Service. Problems with versions cost an enormous amount of money in lost productivity and debugging time. Also, they keep people from buying upgrades or even trying them because they're afraid the upgrade will kill something else, and they're often right.

Windows has so far ignored this versioning problem, forcing developers to deal with it piecemeal. There has never been, until .NET, any standardized way for a developer to specify desired versioning behavior and have the operating system enforce it. In .NET, Microsoft seems to have realized that this is a universal problem that can be solved only at an operating system level and has provided a system for managing different versions of code.

.NET finally incorporates some functionality for versioning.

Every assembly contains version information in its manifest. This information consists of a *compatibility version*, which is a set of four numbers used by the common language runtime loader to enforce the versioning behavior requested by a client. The compatibility version number consists of a major and minor version number, a build number, and a revision number. The development tools that produce an assembly put the version information into the manifest. Visual Studio .NET produces version numbers for its assemblies from values that you set in your project's AssemblyInfo.vb (or .cs) file, as shown in Figure 2-11. Command line tools require complex switches to specify an assembly's version. You can see the version number in the IL Disassembler at the bottom of Figure 2-12. You can also see it when you install the assembly in the GAC, as shown previously in Figure 2-8.

Each assembly contains information telling the runtime what version number it represents.

```
' Version information for an assembly consists of the following
' four values:
'
'       Major Version
'       Minor Version
'       Revision
'       Build Number
'
' You can specify all the values or you can default the Build and
' Revision Numbers by using the '*' as shown below:

<Assembly: AssemblyVersion("2.0.*")>
```

Figure 2-11   AssemblyInfo.vb file showing version of component assembly.

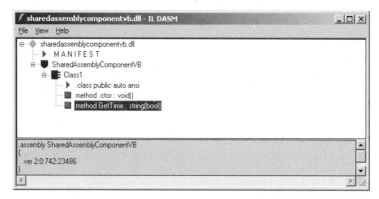

Figure 2-12   ILDASM showing version of a server component.

The manifest can also contain an *informational version*, which is a human readable string like "Microsoft .NET 1.0 January 2002." The informational version is intended for display to human viewers and is ignored by the common language runtime.

Every client assembly contains information about the versions it was built against.

When you build a client assembly, you've seen that it contains the name of the external assemblies on which it depends. It also contains the version number of these external assemblies, as you can see in Figure 2-13.

```
.assembly extern SharedAssemblyComponentVB
{
  .publickeytoken = (49 6E D8 BD 1D 36 2E B2 )
  .hash = (A0 82 D1 EB BB 29 8F 64 FE EA 1B 42 F2 1F E5 11
           C1 58 DC 64 )
  .ver 1:0:449:10749
}
```

Figure 2-13   ILDASM showing required version in a client.

When the client runs, the common language runtime looks to find the version that the client needs. The default versioning behavior requires the exact version against which the client was built; otherwise the load will fail. Since the GAC can contain different versions of the same assembly, as shown in Figure 2-8, you don't have the problem of a new version breaking old clients, or an older version mistakenly replacing a new one. You can keep all the versions that you need in the GAC, and each client assembly will request and receive the one that it has been written and tested against.

By default, a client requires the exact version of the server against which it was built.

Occasionally this exact-match versioning behavior isn't what you want. You might discover a fatal defect, perhaps a security hole, in the original version of the server DLL, and need to direct the older clients to a new one immediately. Or maybe you find such a bug in the new server and have to roll the new clients back to use the old one. Rather than have to recompile all of your clients against the replacement version, as would be the case with a classic DLL, you can override the system's default behavior through the use of configuration files.

You can override default versioning behavior by using configuration files.

The most common way to do this is with a *publisher policy*, which changes the versioning behavior for all clients of a GAC assembly. You set a publisher policy by making entries in the master configuration file machine.config, which holds the .NET administrative settings for your entire machine. Machine.config is an XML-based file, and you might be tempted to go at it with Notepad or your favorite XML editor. I strongly urge you to resist this temptation; wipe out one angle bracket by accident or get the capitalization wrong on just one name and your entire .NET installation may become unusable (shades of the registry, except no one used Notepad on that, at least not for long). Instead, use the .NET Framework Configuration utility mscorcfg.msc, shown in Figure 2-14, which comes with the .NET SDK. This utility allows you to view the GAC, similar to the Windows Explorer add-in I showed in Figure 2-8. In addition, it allows you to configure the behavior of assemblies in the GAC.

A publisher policy changes the versioning behavior of a GAC assembly for all its clients.

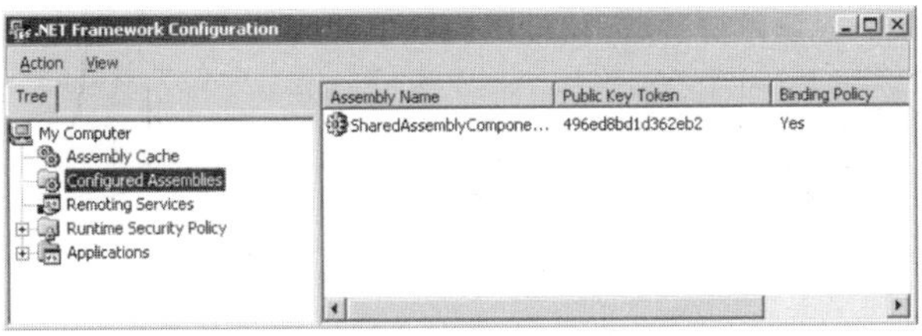

Figure 2-14   The .NET Framework Configuration utility.

You set a publisher policy using the .NET Framework Configuration utility mscorcfg.msc.

You set a publisher policy by making your server assembly into a *configured assembly*, which is a GAC assembly for which a configuration file holds entries that change the assembly's behavior from default GAC assembly behavior. You do this by right-clicking the Configured Assemblies tree item, selecting Add, and either entering a specific assembly or selecting the assembly you want from the list you're offered. Once you have made the assembly into a configured assembly, you can then change its behavioral properties by right-clicking on the assembly in the right-hand pane and choosing Properties from the context menu. Figure 2-15 shows the resulting dialog box. You enter one or more binding policies, each of which consists of a set of one or more old versions that the assembly loader will map to exactly one new version. The configuration utility will write these entries into the configuration file in the proper format. When a client creates an object requesting one of the specified older versions, the loader checks the configuration file, detects the publisher policy, and automatically makes the substitution. You can also enter a codebase for an assembly, which tells the loader from where to download a requested version if it isn't already present on the machine.

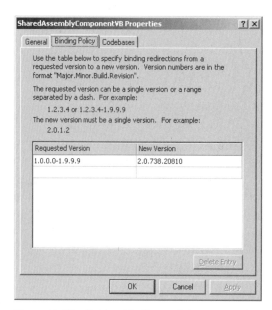

Figure 2-15 Setting binding policies.

An individual application can override a publisher policy's versioning behavior with its own configuration file.

If you need to redirect all the clients of one object version to a different version instead of leaving the original version on the machine for its original clients, then the machine-wide substitution that I just described is probably what you want. Occasionally, however, you might need to tell one old client to use a newer version of its server without changing the behavior of other old clients. You can do this with an application configuration file, which is an XML-based configuration file that modifies the behavior of a single application. The name of this file is the *full* name of the application that it configures, including the extension, with the additional extension ".config" tacked onto the end (e.g., SharedAssemblyClientVB.exe.config). This file lives in the client application's own directory. While masochists can produce it by hand, anyone who values her time will use the configuration utility on the client application itself. You add the client application to the Applications folder in the .NET Framework Configuration window. You must then add assemblies individually to the application's Configured Assemblies section. You aren't moving the assemblies anywhere, you are simply adding configuration information to the local application's configuration file. The settings modify the default behavior of the assembly loader when accessed by this client only, even if the assembly lives in the GAC. When you set the configured assembly's properties, you'll see an option to allow you to ignore publisher policies. Selecting this option writes this information into your app configuration file, which will cause the loader to give you the app's original versioning behavior regardless of publisher policies. You can also specify a different version redirection, pointing your client app to someplace completely different. Just so you have an idea of what it looks like internally, Figure 2-16 shows the relevant portions of an application configuration file that ignore publisher policies and provide its own version redirection:

```
<configuration>
  <runtime>
    <assemblyBinding xmlns="urn:schemas-microsoft-com:asm.v1">
      <publisherPolicy apply="no" />
      <dependentAssembly>
        <assemblyIdentity name="SharedAssemblyComponentVB"
          publicKeyToken="496ed8bd1d362eb2" />
        <publisherPolicy apply="no" />
        <bindingRedirect oldVersion="1.0.0.0-1.9.9.9"
          newVersion="2.0.0.0" />
      </dependentAssembly>
    </assemblyBinding>
  </runtime>
</configuration>
```

Figure 2-16 Sample configuration file.

Object-Oriented Programming Features

Organizing the internal functionality of software projects is difficult.

When a software project reaches a certain level of complexity, the sheer effort of organizing the source code, of remembering the internal workings of every function, overwhelms the effort of dealing with your problem domain. No single person can remember what all the functions do and how they fit together, and chaos results. This critical size isn't very large, perhaps a five-programmer project, arguably less. To develop larger and more functional pieces of software—Microsoft Word for example—we need a better way of organizing code than providing global functions all over the place. Otherwise, the effort of picking our way through our spaghetti code overwhelms the work of figuring out how to process words.

The only way to successfully develop software projects that require the work of more than a few developers is to partition the projects into classes of objects.

The techniques of object-oriented programming were developed to solve this problem and allow larger, more complex programs to be developed. Exactly what someone means when he uses the term "object-oriented" is hard to pin down. The meaning depends heavily on the term's usage context and the shared background of the listeners. It's sort of like the word "love." I once watched, amused, as two respected, relatively sober authors argued vehemently for half an hour over whether a particular programming technique truly deserved the description "object-oriented" or only the lesser "object-based." But like love, most developers agree that object-oriented software is a Good Thing, even if they're somewhat vague on why and not completely sure about what. As most people will agree that the word "love," at the minimum, indicates that you like something a lot, so most programmers will agree that object-oriented programming involves at least the partitioning of a program into *classes*, which combine logically related sets of data with the functions that act on that data. An *object* is an individual instance of a class. *Cat* is a class, my pet Simba is an instance of the class, an object. If you do a good job of segregating your program's functionality into classes that make sense, your developers don't have to understand the functionality of the entire program. They can concentrate on the particular class or classes involved in their subset of it, with (hopefully) minimal impact from other classes.

.NET provides all languages with the object-oriented features of inheritance and constructors.

Providing object-oriented functionality to a programmer has historically been the job of the programming language, and different languages have taken it to different levels. Standard COBOL, for example, doesn't do it at all. Visual Basic provides a minimal degree of object-oriented functionality, essentially classes and nothing else. C++ and Java provide a high level of object-oriented features. Languages that want to work together seamlessly need to share the same degree of support for object-orientation, so the question facing Microsoft and developers was whether to smarten up Visual Basic and other non-object-oriented languages or dumb down C++ and other languages that did support object-orientation. Because the architects of .NET belong (as do I) to the school of thought that says object-orientation is the only way to get anything useful done in the modern software industry, they decided that object-oriented features would be an integral part of the common language runtime environment, and thus available to all languages. The two most useful object-oriented techniques provided by the common language runtime are inheritance and constructors. I'll describe each of them in the following sections.

Inheritance

Essentially no manufacturer in modern industry, with the possible exception of glassmakers, builds their products entirely from nature, starting with earth, air, fire, and water. Instead, almost everyone reuses components that someone else has built, adding value in the process. For example, a company that sells camper trucks doesn't produce engine and chassis; instead they buy pickup trucks from an automaker and add specialized bodies to them. The automaker in turn bought the windshields from a glass manufacturer, who bought sand from a digger. We would like our software development process to follow this model, starting with generic functionality that someone else has already written and adding our own specialized attachments to it.

Essentially all modern economic processes involve adding value to existing components.

The object-oriented programming technique known as inheritance makes development of components much easier for programmers of software objects than it is for makers of physical objects. Someone somewhere uses a programming language that supports inheritance to write an object class, called the *base class,* which provides some useful generic functionality, say, reading and writing bytes from a stream. We'd like to use this basic functionality, with our own twists in it, in a class that reads and writes like the base class but that also provides statistics such as length. So we write a piece of software, known as the *derived class*, that incorporates the base class's functionality but modifies it in some manner, either adding more pieces to it, replacing some portion of it while leaving the rest intact, or a combination of both. We do this by simply telling the compiler that our derived class inherits from the base class, using the syntax of our programming language. The compiler will automatically include the base class's functionality in our derived class by reference. Think of it as cutting and pasting without actually moving anything. The derived class is said to *inherit from, derive from,* or *extend* the base class. The process is shown in Figure 2-17 with several intervening classes omitted for clarity.

Object-oriented programming provides this concept in software by means of inheritance.

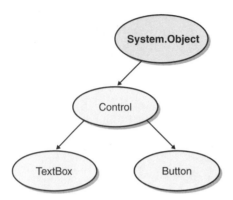

Figure 2-17 Object-oriented programming inheritance.

Every .NET object inherits from the system base class *System.Object*.

The .NET Framework uses inheritance to provide all kinds of system functionality, from the simplest string conversions to the most sophisticated Web services. To explore inheritance further, let's start as always with the simplest example we can find. The time component I wrote previously in this chapter offers a good illustration of .NET Framework inheritance. Even though I didn't explicitly write code to say so, our time component class derives from the Microsoft-provided base class *System.Object*. You can see that this is so by examining the component with ILDASM, as shown in Figure 2-18. All objects in the .NET system, without exception, derive from *System.Object* or another class that in turn derives from it. If you don't specify a different base class, *System.Object* is implied. If you prefer a different base class, you specify it by using the keyword *Inherits* in Visual Basic, as shown in Figure 2-19, or the colon operator in C#.

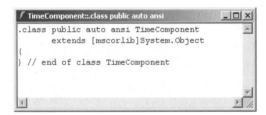

Figure 2-18 ILDASM showing inheritance from System.Object.

```
Public Class WebService1
    Inherits System.Web.Services.WebService
```

Figure 2-19 Explicit declaration of inheritance.

In more complex cases, the Visual Studio .NET Object Browser shows us the inheritance tree. This case is too simple for it to handle. Figure 2-20 shows the Object Browser.

Figure 2-20   The Visual Studio .NET Object Browser showing the inheritance tree.

OK, our time component inherits functionality from *System.Object*, but how do we know what was in the will? We find that out with a little old-fashioned RTFM (Read The Funny Manual, more or less). When we do that, we find that our base class has the public methods shown in Table 2-1. That means that our derived class, the time component, knows how to do these things even though we didn't write code for them.

Table 2-1 **Public methods of *System.Object***

Method name	Purpose
Equals	Determines whether this object is the same instance as a specified object.
GetHashCode	Quickly generates and returns an integer that can be used to identify this object in a hash table or other indexing scheme.
GetType	Returns the system metadata of the object
ToString	Returns a string that provides the object's view of itself.

The *Equals* method determines whether two object references do or do not refer to the same physical instance of an object. This determination was surprisingly difficult to make in COM and could easily be broken by an incorrectly implemented server, but in .NET our objects inherit this functionality from the base class. I've written a client application that creates several instances of our time component and demonstrates the *Equals* method, among others. It's shown in Figure 2-21.

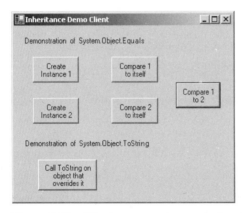

Figure 2-21 Client program demonstrating *System.Object* features inherited by time component.

You can override a base class's methods to replace part of its functionality.

Sometimes your component doesn't want everything it inherits from a base class, just like human heirs. You love the antique table your Aunt Sophie left you, but you aren't real crazy about her flatulent bulldog (or vice versa). Software inheritance generally allows a derived class to *override* a method that it inherits from the base class: that is, provide a replacement for it. A good example of this is the method *System.Object.ToString*, which tells an object to return a string for display to a programmer who is debugging the application.

The implementation that we inherit from *System.Object* simply returns the name of the derived class, which isn't that illuminating. To make our component easier to debug, we'd like this method to return more detailed information. For example, an object that represents an open file might return the name of that file. We do that by overriding the base class's method, as shown in Figure 2-22. We write a method in our derived class that has the same name and parameters as the method in the base class, specifying the keyword *Overrides* (*override* in C#) to tell the compiler to replace the base class's implementation with our derived class's new one.

```
' This method overrides the ToString method of the
' universal base class System.Object.

Public Overrides Function ToString() As String

    ' Call the base class's ToString method and get the result.
    ' You don't have to do this if you don't want to. I did,
    ' for demo purposes.

    Dim BaseResult As String
    BaseResult = MyBase.ToString

    ' Construct response string with base class's string plus
    ' my own added information. The net result here is that
    ' I'm piggybacking on the base class, not completely
    ' replacing it.

    Return "You have reached the overriding class. " + _
           "The base class says: " + BaseResult

End Function
```

Figure 2-22   Overriding base class method.

If your derived class wants to provide its own functionality in addition to that of the base class—rather than instead of the base class—it can call the overridden base class's method explicitly. In Visual Basic, the base class is accessible through the named object *MyBase*, and in C# it's called *base*. The sample component calls the base class to get its string and then appends its own string to that of the base class. The result is that the component is piggybacking on the base class's functionality rather than completely replacing it. Not all base class methods can be overridden. A base class method must be

An overriding method can access the base class's method that it overrides.

written with the keyword *Overridable* in Visual Basic or *virtual* in C# if you want to allow this.

.NET inheritance works between different languages.

Much is made of the ability of .NET to provide cross-language inheritance, that is, to allow a class written in one language, Visual Basic, for example, to derive from a base class written in another language, say C#. COM couldn't provide this feature because the differences between language implementations were too great. However, the standardized IL architecture of the common language runtime allows .NET applications to use it. In fact, the simple time component example does exactly that with no effort on my part. I guarantee you that the *System.Object* class is written in one language and not any other, yet every .NET object, without exception and regardless of language, inherits from it.

Object Constructors

Objects need a standard place for putting initialization code.

As the Good Rats sang a couple of decades ago, "birth comes to us all." As humans mark births with various rituals (religious observances, starting a college fund), so objects need a location where their birth-ritual code can be placed. Object-oriented programming has long recognized the concept of a *class constructor*, a function called when an object is created. (Object-oriented programming also uses the concept of a *class destructor*, a function called when the object is destroyed, but this concept has been replaced in .NET with the system garbage collector described in the next section.) Different languages have implemented constructors differently—C++ with the class name, Visual Basic with *Class_Initialize*. As with so many features that have varied widely among languages, the rituals for object creation had to be standardized for code written in different languages to work together properly.

.NET object classes provide for initialization through an object constructor.

In .NET, Visual Basic lost its *Class_Initialize* event, and the model looks much more like a C++ model, primarily because parameterized constructors are needed to support inheritance. Every .NET class can have one or more constructor methods. This method has the name *New* in Visual Basic .NET or the class name in C#. The constructor function is called when a client creates your object using the *new* operator. In the function, you place the code that does whatever initialization your object requires, perhaps acquiring resources and setting them to their initial state. An example of a constructor is shown in Figure 2-23.

```
Public Class Point

    Public x, y As Integer

    ' Default constructor accepts no parameters,
    ' initializes member variables to zero

    Public Sub New()
        x = 0
        y = 0
    End Sub

    ' This constructor accepts two parameters, initializing
    ' member variables to the supplied values.

    Public Sub New(ByVal newx As Integer, ByVal newy As Integer)
        x = newx
        y = newy
    End Sub

End Class
```

Figure 2-23   Constructor declaration example.

One of the more interesting things you can do with a constructor is allow the client to pass parameters to it, thereby allowing the client to place the object in a particular state immediately upon its creation. For example, the constructor of an object representing a point on a graph might accept two integer values, the X and Y location of that point. You can even have several different constructors for your class that accept different sets of parameters. For example, our *Point* object class might have one constructor that accepts two values, another that accepts a single existing point, and yet a third that accepts no parameters and simply initializes the new point's members as zero. An example is shown in Figure 2-24. This flexibility is especially useful if you want to make an object that requires initialization before you can use it. Suppose you have an object that represents a patient in a hospital, supporting methods such as *Patient.ChargeLotsOfMoney* and *Patient.Amputate (whichLimb)*. Obviously, it is vital to know which human being each individual instance of this class refers to or you might remove money or limbs from the wrong patient, both of which are bad ideas, the latter generally more so than the former. By providing a constructor that requires a patient ID—and not providing a default empty constructor—you ensure that no one can ever operate on an unidentified patient or inadvertently change a patient's ID once it's created.

Object constructors can accept different sets of parameters, allowing an object to be created in a particular state.

```
Dim foo As New Point ( )

Dim bar As New Point (4, 5)
```

Figure 2-24   Constructor call example.

.NET Memory Management

Manual memory management leads to costly, hard-to-find bugs.

One of the main sources of nasty, difficult-to-find bugs in modern applications is incorrect use of manual memory management. Older languages such as C++ required programmers to manually delete objects that they had created, which led to two main problems. First, programmers would create an object and forget to delete it when they finished using it. These leaks eventually consumed a process's entire memory space and caused it to crash. Second, programmers would manually delete an object but then mistakenly try to access its memory location later. Visual Basic would have detected the reference to invalid memory immediately, but C++ often doesn't. Sometimes the transistors that had made up the deleted object memory would still contain plausible values, and the program would continue to run with corrupted data. These mistakes seem painfully obvious in the trivial examples discussed here, and it's easy to say, "Well, just don't do that, you doofus." But in real programs, you often create an object in one part of the program and delete it in another, with complex logic intervening—logic deleting the object in some cases but not others. Both of these bugs are devilishly difficult to reproduce and harder still to track down. Programming discipline helps, of course, but we'd really like some way to keep our programmers thinking about our business logic, not about resource management. You can bet that Julia Child, the *grand dame* of TV chefs, hires someone to clean up her kitchen when she's done with it so that she can concentrate on the parts of cooking that require her unique problem-domain expertise.

Automatic memory management and resource recovery of the type built into Visual Basic and Java is a very useful feature.

Modern languages such as Visual Basic and Java don't have this type of problem. These languages feature "fire-and-forget" automatic memory management, which is one of the main reasons that programmers select them for development. A Visual Basic 6.0 programmer doesn't have to remember to delete the objects that she creates in almost all cases. (Remember that "almost"; it will figure into an important design decision later.) Visual Basic 6.0 counts the references to each object and automatically deletes the object and reclaims its memory when its count reaches zero. Her development environment provides her with an automatic scullery maid cleaning the used pots and pans out of her sink and placing them back on her shelves. Wish I could get the same thing for my real kitchen. Maybe if you tell all your friends to buy this book....

Microsoft has made automatic memory management part of the .NET common language runtime, which allows it to be used from any language. It's conceptually simple, as shown in Figure 2-25.

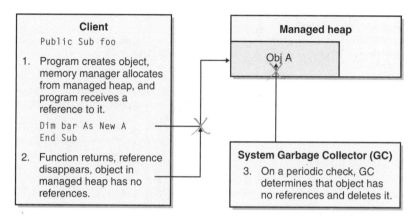

Figure 2-25 Automatic memory management with garbage collection.

A programmer creates an object using the *new* operator and receives a reference to it. The common language runtime allocates that object's memory from the *managed heap*, a portion of a process's memory reserved by the runtime for this purpose. Every so often, a system thread examines all the objects in the managed heap to see which of them the program still holds outstanding references to. An object to which all references have disappeared is called *garbage* and is removed from the managed heap. The objects remaining in the managed heap are then compacted together, and the existing references in the program fixed to point to their new location. The entire operation is called *garbage collection*. It solves the aforementioned problems of manual memory management without you having to write any code. You can't forget to delete an object because the system cleans up after you. And you can't access a deleted object through an invalid reference because the object won't be deleted as long as you hold any reference to it. Obviously, garbage collection is going to take more CPU cycles to run than just a standard in-out heap allocator, even though it is written to ensure that it doesn't check an object twice or get caught in circular object references. As I said previously, I think this is a good investment of CPU cycles because it gets you faster development time with fewer bugs.

The common language runtime garbage collector makes automatic memory management available to any application.

This magical collection of garbage takes place when the garbage collector darn well feels like it. Apart from detecting no more available memory in the managed heap in response to an allocation request, no one really knows

The garbage collector runs when it feels like it, but you can force a garbage collection manually.

what the exact algorithm is for launching a garbage collection, and I wouldn't be surprised to see it vary from one version to another of the released product. You can force a garbage collection manually by calling the function *System.GC.Collect*. You might want to make this call at logical points in your program; for example, to clear away the debris just after a user saves a file or perhaps to clear the decks just before starting a large operation. Most of the time you just let the garbage collector do its thing when it wants to.

Automatic garbage collection looks great so far, but it leaves us with one gaping hole. What about the cleanup that an object needs to do when it gets destroyed? C++ applications usually cleaned up in an object's destructor, and Visual Basic classes did the same thing in their *Class_Terminate* methods. This is a good location for cleanup code because a client can't forget to call it, but how can we handle this with automatic garbage collection? First, let's realize that the problem has gotten considerably smaller. The main cleanup task we performed in C++ destructors was to delete additional objects to which the destructing object held references, and now garbage collection takes care of that for us automatically. But occasionally we'll need to do some cleanup that doesn't involve local garbage-collected resources; for example, releasing a database connection or logging out from a remote system.

The common language runtime garbage collection supports the notion of a *finalizer*, an object method that is called when the object is garbage collected. It is somewhat analogous to a C++ class destructor and also to the Visual Basic *Class_Terminate* method, both of which it replaces. However, a finalizer is significantly different from both of these other mechanisms in ways you may find unsettling. The universal runtime base class *System.Object* contains a method called *Finalize*, which we override as shown in Figure 2-26. When the object is garbage collected, the garbage collection thread detects the fact that our object has a *Finalize* method and calls it, thereby executing our cleanup code. Although early versions didn't do it, the released version of .NET calls all outstanding finalizers automatically when an application shuts down.

In C#, you supply a finalizer by writing what looks like an ordinary destructor, but under the hood your compiler is overriding the *Finalize* method and it behaves as a garbage-collected finalizer and not a deterministic destructor as in C++. This is the only case I've ever seen in which Visual Basic code provides a clearer view of what's really going on behind the scenes than a C-family language does.

Before garbage collection, we often put cleanup code in an object's destructor or *Class_Terminate* method.

The garbage collector supports an object finalizer method for necessary cleanup code.

```
Protected Overrides Sub Finalize()

    ' Perform whatever finalization logic we need.

    MessageBox.Show("In Finalize, my number = " + _
                    MyObjectNumber.ToString())

    ' Forward the call to our base class.

    MyBase.Finalize()

End Sub
```

Figure 2-26   Providing a Finalize function in an object.

Warning   Finalizers look simple, but their internal behavior is actually quite complex and it's fairly easy to mess them up. If you are planning on using them, you MUST read Jeffrey Richter's account of garbage collection in his book *Applied Microsoft .NET Framework Programming* (Microsoft Press, 2002). The fact that it took him a whole chapter to describe it should tell you something about the internal complexity of garbage collection, even if, or perhaps because, its connection to your program is so simple.

Using a finalizer has some disadvantages as well. Obviously it consumes CPU cycles, so you shouldn't use it if you have no cleanup to do. There is no way to guarantee the order in which the garbage collector calls the finalizers of garbage objects, so don't depend on one object finalizing before or after another, regardless of the order in which the last reference to each of them disappeared. Finalizers are called on a separate garbage-collector thread within your application, so you can't do any of your own serialization to enforce a calling order or you'll break the whole garbage collection system in your process. Since your object became garbage, the objects that you hold might have become garbage too unless you've taken steps to prevent that from happening. Don't plan on calling any other object in your application from your finalizer unless you've explicitly written code to ensure that someone is holding a reference to keep the other object from becoming garbage. Don't plan on throwing exceptions (see the section about structured exception handling later in this chapter) from your finalizer; no one is listening to

Using a finalizer can be trickier than it looks.

you any more, you garbage object, you. And make sure you catch any exceptions generated by your cleanup code so that you don't disturb the garbage collector's thread that calls your finalizer.

Finalizers are fine if we don't care when our cleanup gets done, if "eventually, by the time you really need it, I promise" is soon enough. Sometimes this is OK, but it isn't so good if the resources that a finalizer would recover are scarce in the running process—database connections, for example. Eventual recovery isn't good enough; we need this object shredded NOW so that we can recover its expensive resources that the generic garbage collector doesn't know about. We could force an immediate garbage collection, as discussed previously, but that requires examining the entire managed heap, which can be quite expensive even if there's nothing else to clean up. Since we know exactly which object we want to dismantle, we'd like a way of cleaning up only that object, as Julia often wipes off her favorite paring knife without having to clean up her entire kitchen (including taking out the garbage). This operation goes by the grand name of *deterministic finalization*. Objects that want to support deterministic finalization do so by implementing an interface called *IDisposable*, which contains the single method, *Dispose*. In this method, you place whatever code you need to release your expensive resources. The client calls this method to tell the object to release those resources right now. For example, all Windows Forms objects that represent a window in the underlying operating system support this feature to enable quick recovery of the operating system window handle that they contain.

Sometimes you will see an object provide a different method name for deterministic finalization in order for the name to make sense to a developer who needs to figure out which method to call. For example, calling *Dispose* on a file object would make you think that you were shredding the file, so the developer of such an object will provide deterministic finalization through a method with the more logical name of *Close*.

An object that wants to provide a deterministic way for a client to release its resources exposes a method called *Dispose*.

Deterministic finalization sounds like a good idea, but it also contains its own drawbacks. You can't be sure that a client will remember to call your *Dispose* method, so you need to provide cleanup functionality in your finalizer as well. However, if your client does call *Dispose*, you probably don't want the garbage collector to waste its time calling your object's finalizer, as the cleanup should have already been done by the *Dispose* method. By calling the function *System.GC.SuppressFinalize*, you tell the garbage collector not to bother calling your finalizer even though you have one. A Visual Basic object also needs to expressly forward the *Dispose* call to its base class if the base class contains a *Dispose* method, as the call won't otherwise get there and you will fail to release the base class's expensive resources. A C# destructor does this automatically. A sample *Dispose* method is shown in Figure 2-27.

This class is derived from *System.Object*, which doesn't contain a *Dispose* method, so I've omitted the code that would forward that call.

I've written a small sample program that illustrates the concepts of automatic memory management and garbage collection. You can download it from this book's Web site. A picture of the client app is shown in Figure 2-28. Note that calling *Dispose* does not make an object garbage. In fact, by definition, you can't call *Dispose* on an object that is garbage because then you wouldn't have a reference with which to call *Dispose*. The object won't become garbage until no more references to it exist, whenever that may be. I'd suggest that your object maintain an internal flag to remember when it has been disposed of and to respond to any other access after its disposal by throwing an exception.

> You have to write code to handle the case in which a client accesses your object after calling *Dispose* on it.

```
Public Class Class1
    Implements System.IDisposable

    Public Sub Dispose() Implements System.IDisposable.Dispose
        ' Do whatever logic we need to do to immediately free up
        ' our resources.

        MessageBox.Show("In Dispose(), my number = " + _
                        MyObjectNumber.ToString())

        ' If our base class contained a Dispose method, we'd
        ' forward the call to it by uncommenting the following line.

        ' MyBase.Dispose()

        ' Mark our object as no longer needing finalization.

        System.GC.SuppressFinalize(Me)
    End Sub

End Class
```

Figure 2-27   Sample *Dispose* method for deterministic finalization.

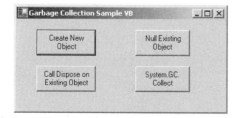

Figure 2-28   Memory management client application.

Microsoft decided on gar-
bage collection memory
management to make it
leak proof, even at the
cost of easy determinism.

While automatic garbage collection makes the simple operations of allo-
cating and freeing objects easier to write and harder to mess up than they
were in C++, it makes deterministic finalization harder to write and easier to
mess up than it was in Visual Basic 6. C++ programmers will probably consider this a great profit, while Visual Basic programmers, who are used to
their automatic, almost foolproof behavior also being deterministic, may at
first consider it a step back. The reason that Microsoft switched to garbage
collection is that Visual Basic's reference counting algorithm didn't correctly
handle the case of circular object references, as in the case where a child
object holds a reference to its parent. Suppose object A creates object B,
object B creates object C, and object C obtains and holds a reference to its
parent, object B. Suppose that object A now releases object B. Object B won't
be destroyed now because object C still holds a reference to it, and C won't
let go until B lets go of it. Unless a programmer writes code to break the circular reference before A lets go, both B and C are leaked away, orphans with
no references except their hold on each other, which keeps them both alive.
The garbage collection algorithm will automatically detect and handle this circular reference case, while reference counting will not. After much discussion
of alternatives and banging of heads against walls, Microsoft decided that
foolproof, automatic leak prevention in all cases was more important than
easy determinism. Some programmers will agree, others won't, but the choice
was carefully reasoned and not capricious. After an initial period of suspicion,
I'm coming around to this way of thinking. I find that I don't need deterministic finalization very often, and as a refugee from C++ memory leaks, I
REALLY love the fire-and-forget nature of garbage collection.

Interoperation with COM

The commercial success of any new software platform depends critically on
how well it integrates with what already exists while providing new avenues
for development of even better applications. For example, Windows 3.0 not
only allowed existing DOS applications to run, but it also multitasked them
better than any other product up to that point and provided a platform for
writing Windows applications that were better than any DOS app. The canvas
on which we paint is essentially never blank. How did God manage to create
the world in only six days? He didn't have any installed base to worry about
being backward compatible with. (My editor points out that He also skimped
on documentation.)

Windows has depended on COM for interapplication communication since 1993. Essentially all code for the Windows environment is neck-deep in COM and has been for an awfully long time in geek years. The .NET Framework has to support COM to have any chance of succeeding commercially. And it does, both as a .NET client using a COM server, and vice versa. Since it is more likely that new .NET code will have to interoperate with existing COM code than the reverse, I will describe that case first.

Backward compatibility is crucial in the development of any new system. Therefore, .NET supports interoperation with COM.

Using COM Objects from .NET

A .NET client accesses a COM server by means of a *runtime callable wrapper* (RCW), as shown in Figure 2-29. The RCW wraps the COM object and mediates between it and the common language runtime environment, making the COM object appear to .NET clients just as if it were a native .NET object and making the .NET client appear to the COM object just as if it were a standard COM client.

A .NET client accesses a COM object through a runtime callable wrapper (RCW).

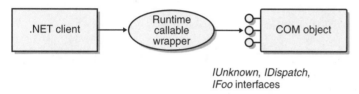

IUnknown, IDispatch,
IFoo interfaces

Figure 2-29   .NET client/COM object interaction via a runtime callable wrapper.

The developer of a .NET client generates the RCW in one of two ways. If you're using Visual Studio .NET, simply right-click on the References section of your project and select Add Reference from the context menu. You will see the dialog box shown in Figure 2-30, which offers a choice of all the registered COM objects it finds on the system. Select the COM object for which you want to generate the RCW, and Visual Studio .NET will spit it out for you. If you're not using Visual Studio .NET, the .NET SDK contains a command line tool called TlbImp.exe, the type library importer that performs the same task. The logic that reads the type library and generates the RCW code actually lives in a .NET run-time class called *System.Runtime.InteropServices.TypeLibConverter*. Both Visual Studio .NET and TlbImp.exe use this class internally, and you can too if you're writing a development tool or feeling masochistic.

You can generate an RCW with a variety of development tools.

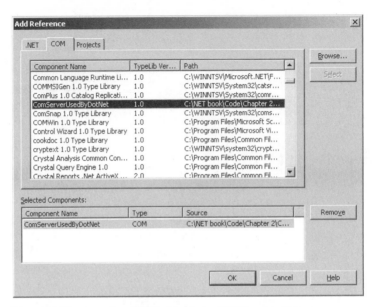

Figure 2-30 Locating COM objects for RCW generation.

Figure 2-31 shows a sample .NET client program that uses a COM object server. You can download the samples and follow along from the book's Web site. This sample contains a COM server, a COM client, and a .NET client so that you can compare the two. The source code is shown in Figure 2-32.

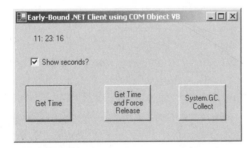

Figure 2-31 Sample .NET client using a COM server.

```
Protected Sub Button1_Click(ByVal sender As Object, _
                            ByVal e As System.EventArgs)

   ' Create an instance of the RCW that wraps our COM object.

   Dim RuntimeCallableWrapper As New ComUsedByDotNet.Class1()

   ' Call the method that gets the time.

   Label1.Text = RuntimeCallableWrapper.GetTimeFromCom(CheckBox1.Checked)

   ' Object becomes garbage when it goes out of scope,
   ' but is not actually released until next garbage collection.

End Sub
```

Figure 2-32   Code listing of a .NET client using an RCW.

After you generate the RCW as described in the preceding paragraph, you will probably want to import its namespace into the client program using the *Imports* statement, allowing you to refer to the object using its short name. You create the RCW object simply by using the *new* operator, as you would for any other .NET object. When it's created, the RCW internally calls the native COM function *CoCreateInstance*, thereby creating the COM object that it wraps. Your .NET client program then calls methods on the RCW as if it were a native .NET object. The RCW automatically converts each call to the COM calling convention—for example, converting .NET strings into the BSTR strings that COM requires—and forwards it to the object. The RCW converts the results returned from the COM object into native .NET types before returning them to the client. Users of the COM support in Visual J++ will find this architecture familiar.

The RCW magically converts .NET calls into COM and COM results to .NET.

When you run the sample COM client program, you'll notice (from dialog boxes that I place in the code) that the object is created when you click the button and then immediately destroyed. When you run the sample .NET client program, you'll find that the object is created when you click the Get Time button, but that the object isn't destroyed immediately. You would think it should be, as the wrapper object goes out of scope, but it isn't, not even if you explicitly set the object reference to nothing. This is the .NET way of lazy resource recovery, described previously in the section about garbage collection. The RCW has gone out of scope and is no longer accessible to your program, but it doesn't actually release the COM object that it wraps until the RCW is garbage collected and destroyed. This can be a problem, as most COM objects were not written with this life cycle in mind and thus might retain expensive resources that should be released as soon as the client is fin-

COM objects are actually destroyed when their RCWs are garbage collected.

ished. You can solve this problem in one of two ways. The first, obviously, is by forcing an immediate garbage collection via the function *System.GC.Collect*. Calling this function will collect and reclaim all system resources that are no longer in use, including all the RCWs not currently in scope. The drawback to this approach is that the overhead of a full garbage collection can be high, and you may not want to pay it immediately just to shred one object. If you would like to blow away one particular COM object without affecting the others, you can do so via the function *System.Runtime.InteropServices.Marshal.ReleaseComObject*.

The RCW mechanism described in the preceding paragraphs requires an object to be early-bound, by which I mean that the developer must have intimate knowledge of the object at development time to construct the wrapper class. Not all objects work this way. For example, scripting situations require late binding, in which a client reads the ProgID of an object and the method to call on it from script code at run time. Most COM objects support the *IDispatch* interface specifically to allow this type of late-bound access. Creating an RCW in advance is not possible in situations like this. Can .NET also handle it?

.NET also supports late binding without too much trouble.

Fortunately, it can. The .NET Framework supports late binding to the *IDispatch* interface supported by most COM objects. A sample late binding program is shown in Figure 2-33, and its code in Figure 2-34. You create a system type based on the object's ProgID via the static method *Type.GetTypeFromProgID*. The static method *Type.GetTypeFromCLSID* (not shown) does the same thing based on a CLSID, if you have that instead of a ProgID. You then create the COM object using the method *Activator.CreateInstance* and call a method via the function *Type.InvokeMember*. It's more work—late binding always is—but you can do it.

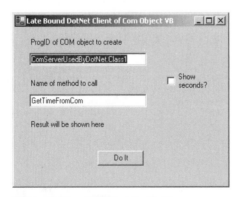

Figure 2-33   Sample late binding program.

```
Protected Sub Button1_Click(ByVal sender As Object, _
                            ByVal e As System.EventArgs)

    ' Get system type name based on prog ID.

    Dim MyType As System.Type
    MyType = Type.GetTypeFromProgID(textBox1().Text)

    ' Use an activator to create object of that type.

    Dim MyObj As Object
    MyObj = Activator.CreateInstance(MyType)

    ' Assemble array of parameters to pass to COM object.

    Dim prms() As Object = {checkBox1().Checked}

    ' Call method on object by its name.

    label2().Text = MyType.InvokeMember("GetTimeFromCom", _
        Reflection.BindingFlags.InvokeMethod, Nothing, MyObj, _
        prms).ToString()

End Sub
```

Figure 2-34   Sample late binding code.

Using .NET Objects from COM

Suppose, on the other hand, you have a client that already speaks COM and now you want to make it use a .NET object instead. This is a somewhat less common scenario than the reverse situation that I've previously described because it presupposes new COM development in a .NET world. But I can easily see it occurring in the situation in which you have an existing client that uses 10 COM objects and you now want to add an 11th set of functionality that exists only as a .NET object—and you want all of them to look the same to the client for consistency. The .NET Framework supports this situation as well, by means of a *COM callable wrapper* (CCW), as shown in Figure 2-35. The CCW wraps up the .NET object and mediates between it and the common language runtime environment, making the .NET object appear to COM clients just as if it were a native .NET object.

A COM client accesses a .NET object through a COM callable wrapper (CCW).

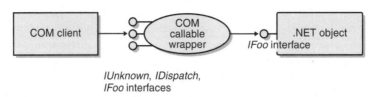

IUnknown, IDispatch,
IFoo interfaces

Figure 2-35   COM callable wrapper.

A .NET component must be signed, live in the GAC, and provide a default constructor to work with a COM client.

To operate with a COM-callable wrapper, a .NET component's assembly must be signed with a strong name; otherwise the common language runtime won't be able to definitively identify it. It must also reside in the GAC or, less commonly, in the client application's directory tree. However, as was the case previously when building the shared component's client, the component must also reside at registration time in a standard directory outside the GAC. Any .NET class that you want COM to create must provide a default constructor, by which I mean a constructor that requires no parameters. COM object creation functions don't know how to pass parameters to the objects that they create, so you need to make sure your class doesn't require this. Your class can have as many parameterized constructors as you want for the use of .NET clients, as long as you have one that requires none for the use of COM clients.

The SDK utility RegAsm.exe makes registry entries telling COM where to find the server for the .NET class.

For a COM client to find the .NET object, we need to make the registry entries that COM requires. You do this with a utility program, called RegAsm.exe, that comes with the .NET Framework SDK. This program reads the metadata in a .NET class and makes registry entries that point the COM client to it. The sample code provides a batch file that does this for you. The registry entries that it makes are shown in Figure 2-36. Notice that the COM server for this operation is the intermediary DLL Mscoree.dll. The *Class* value of the *InProcServer32* key tells this DLL which .NET class to create and wrap, and the *Assembly* entry tells it in which assembly it will find this class.

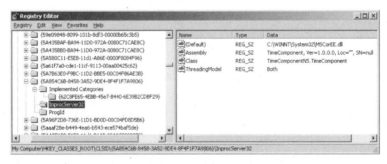

Figure 2-36   Registry entries made by RegAsm.exe.

A COM client accesses a .NET object as if it were a native COM object. When the client calls *CoCreateInstance* to create the object, the registry directs the request to the registered server, Mscoree.dll. This DLL inspects the requested CLSID, reads the registry to find the .NET class to create, and rolls a CCW on the fly based on that .NET class. The CCW converts native COM types to their .NET equivalents—for example, BSTRs to .NET *Strings*—and forwards them to the .NET object. It also converts the results back from .NET into COM, including any errors. The sample code for this chapter contains a COM client that accesses the shared time component assembly that we built previously in this chapter.

A .NET developer could reasonably want some methods, interfaces, or classes to be available to COM clients and others not to be. Therefore, .NET provides a metadata attribute called *System.Runtime.InteropServices.ComVisibleAttribute*. (The .NET Framework allows you to use the abbreviated form of attribute class names, in this case *ComVisible* rather than *ComVisibleAttribute*. I'll be using the short version from now on.) You can use this attribute on an assembly, a class, an interface, or an individual method. Items marked with this attribute set to False will not be visible to COM. The default common language runtime setting is True, so the absence of this attribute causes the item to be visible to COM. However, the Visual Studio .NET default behavior for assemblies is to set this attribute's value to False in the AssemblyInfo.vb file. Settings made lower in the hierarchy override those made higher up. In the sample program, I set this attribute to True on my class, thereby making it visible to COM, as shown in the code that follows. If I wanted everything in the assembly visible to COM, I'd change it in AssemblyInfo.vb.

```
<System.Runtime.InteropServices.ComVisible(True)> Public Class Class1
```

Transactions in .NET

Transactions are necessary to protect the integrity of data in distributed systems. Suppose we're writing an on-line bill paying application. Paying my phone bill requires us to debit my account in some database and credit the phone company's account, probably in a different database and possibly on a different machine. If the debit succeeds but the credit somehow fails, we need to undo the debit, or money would be destroyed and the integrity of the data in the system violated. We need to ensure that either both of these operations succeed or both of them fail. Performing both operations within a transaction does exactly that. If both operations succeed, the transaction com-

The sample code for this chapter contains a COM client using a .NET object.

Transactions ensure the integrity of databases during complex operations.

mits and the new account values are saved. If either operation fails, the transaction aborts and all account values are rolled back to their original values. (To learn more about transactions in general, I highly recommend *Principles of Transaction Processing* by Philip A. Bernstein and Eric Newcomer, published by Morgan Kaufmann, 1997.)

COM+ contains good automatic transaction support.

COM+, and its ancestor, Microsoft Transaction Server (MTS), provided automatic support that made it easy for programmers to write objects that participated in transactions. A programmer marked his objects administratively as requiring a transaction. COM+ then automatically created one when the object was activated. The object used COM+ Resource Managers, programs such as Microsoft SQL Server that support the COM+ way of performing transactions, to make changes to a database. The object then told COM+ whether it was happy with the results. If all the objects participating in a transaction were happy, COM+ committed the transaction, telling the Resource Managers to save all their changes. If any object was unhappy, COM+ aborted the transaction, telling the Resource Managers to discard the results of all objects' operations, rolling back the state of the system to its original values. To learn more about COM+'s implementation of transactions, read my book *Understanding COM+* (Microsoft Press, 1999).

Native .NET objects can participate in COM+ transactions by using pre-fabricated .NET Framework functionality.

Native .NET objects can also participate in COM+ transactions. The .NET Framework contains a layer of code that mediates between COM+ and native .NET objects, encapsulated in the base class *System.EnterpriseServices.ServicedComponent*. Objects that want to participate in COM+ transactions (or use any other COM+ services, for that matter) must inherit from this class. Just as with .NET components accessed from COM, your .NET class must contain only a default constructor (one that accepts no parameters), and you must sign it with a strong name. You specify your component's use of transactions by marking the class with the attribute *System.EnterpriseServices.Transaction*. The code in Figure 2-37 shows a class from my sample program that demonstrates COM+ transactions in a native .NET object.

```
Imports System.EnterpriseServices

' Mark our class as requiring a transaction

<Transaction(TransactionOption.Required)> Public Class Class1

    ' We need to inherit from ServicedComponent, which contains
    ' code for interacting with COM+
    Inherits ServicedComponent
    ' Mark this method to use .NET's automatic
    ' transaction voting (optional)
```

Figure 2-37   COM+ transactions in a native .NET object.

```
       <AutoComplete()> Sub AutoCompleteMethod()
           (program logic omitted)
       End Sub
End Class
```

Your .NET client creates a transactional object using the *new* operator, exactly as for any other .NET object. When you do this, the *ServicedComponent* base class from which your object inherits first looks to see if the component is registered with the COM+ catalog. If it's not, the base class registers the component with the COM+ catalog, creating a COM+ application for it and adding the .NET class to it as a COM+ component, as shown in Figure 2-38. The metadata in the .NET class specifies its transactional requirements, which the base class uses to set the .NET component's properties in the COM+ catalog. The base class sets not only the component's use of transactions, but also the other COM+ properties implied by the transaction, such as JIT activation and synchronization. If you want your component to set these or other COM+ properties explicitly, you will find that the namespace *System.EnterpriseServices* contains many other attributes, such as *ObjectPooling*, with which you decorate your class to specify its behavior. Once your object is created, your client calls methods on it exactly as for any other .NET object. You can watch the sample program's transactional operations in Component Services, as shown in Figure 2-39.

> The system base class registers your .NET component in the COM+ catalog.

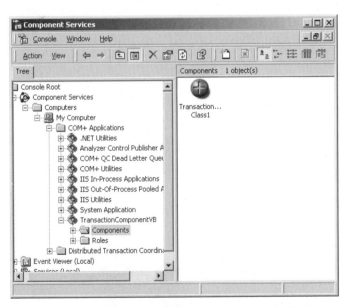

Figure 2-38 Transactional .NET component installed in Component Services Explorer.

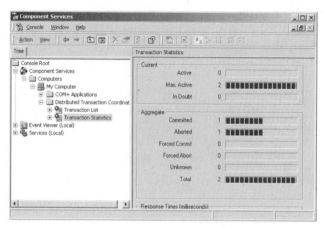

Figure 2-39 .NET component committing and aborting transactions.

A .NET transactional component can be configured so that it votes on its transaction automatically by throwing or not throwing an exception.

An object that participates in a transaction needs to vote on that transaction's outcome. Your .NET transactional object can do this in one of two ways. The easiest way is to use the automatic transaction voting in .NET. You mark your transactional-component method with the attribute *System.EnterpriseServices.AutoComplete*, as shown previously in Figure 2-37. In this case, a method that returns without throwing an exception automatically calls *SetComplete* internally, while a method that throws an exception to its caller automatically calls *SetAbort* internally. If your methods are self-contained (as they should be anyway for good transactional component design), and if they signal failure to their clients by means of exceptions (as they should do anyway for good .NET component design), this approach is probably the best choice.

A .NET transactional component can also vote on its transaction via explicit function calls.

Alternatively, your .NET object might want to vote on the outcome of its transaction by means of explicit function calls. In COM+ and MTS, an object fetched its context by calling the API function *GetObjectContext* and then called a method on the context to indicate its transaction vote. A .NET object will find its context on the system-provided object named *System.EnterpriseServices.ContextUtil*. This object provides the commonly used methods *SetAbort* and *SetComplete*, and their somewhat less common siblings, *EnableCommit* and *DisableCommit*. These methods set your object's happiness and doneness bits in exactly the same manner as they did in COM+. The context also contains everything else you would expect to find in a COM+ context, such as the properties *DeactivateOnReturn* and *MyTransactionVote*, which allow you to read and set these bits individually. If your object requires several function calls to accomplish its work within a single transaction, or you haven't yet converted your error handling code to use structured exception handling, this choice is probably best for you.

Structured Exception Handling

Every program encounters errors during its run time. The program tries to do something—open a file or create an object, for example—and the operation fails for one reason or another. How does your program find out whether an operation succeeded or failed, and how do you write code to handle the latter case?

Every program needs to handle errors that occur at run time.

The classic approach employed by a failed function is to return a special case value that indicated that failure, say, *Nothing* (or *NULL* in C++). This approach had three drawbacks. First, the programmer had to write code that checked the function's return value, and this often didn't happen in the time crunch that colors modern software development. Like seat belts or birth control, error-indicating return values only work if you use them. Errors didn't get trapped at their source but instead got propagated to higher levels of the program. There they were much more difficult to unravel and sometimes got masked until after a program shipped. Second, even if you were paying attention to it, the value of the error return code varied widely from one function to another, increasing the potential for programming mistakes. *CreateWindow*, for example, indicates a failure by returning 0, *CreateFile* returns –1, and in 16-bit Windows, *LoadLibrary* returned any value less than 32. To make things even more chaotic, all COM-related functions return 0 as a success code and a nonzero value to indicate different types of failures. Third, a function could only return a single value to its caller, which didn't give a debugger (human or machine) very much information to work with in trying to understand and fix the error.

Returning a special case value to indicate the failure of a function doesn't work well.

Different languages tried other approaches to handling run-time errors. Visual Basic used the *On Error GoTo* mechanism, which was and is a godawful kludge. *GoTo* has no place in modern software; it hasn't for at least a decade and maybe more. C++ and Java used a better mechanism, called *structured exception handling* (SEH), which uses an object to carry information about a failure and a handler code block to deal with that object. Unfortunately, like most features of any pre–common language runtime language, structured exception handling only worked within that particular language. COM tried to provide rich, cross-language exception handling through the *ISupportErrorInfo* and *IErrorInfo* interfaces, but this approach was difficult to program and you were never sure whether your counterpart was following the same rules you were.

No other technique works well across languages either.

The .NET common language runtime provides structured exception handling, similar to that in C++ or Java, as a fundamental feature available to all languages. This architecture solves many of the problems that have dogged error handling in the past. An unhandled exception will shut down

.NET provides structured exception handling as a fundamental feature available in and between all languages.

your application, so you can't ignore one during development. A function that is reporting a failure places its descriptive information in a .NET object, so it can contain any amount of information you'd like to report. Since the infrastructure is built into the runtime, you have to write very little code to take advantage of it. And as with all runtime functionality, .NET structured exception handling works well across all languages.

I've written a sample program that demonstrates some of the structured exception handling features in the common language runtime. Figure 2-40 shows a picture of it. You can download the code from the book's Web site and work along with me.

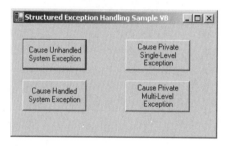

Figure 2-40   Sample program demonstrating structured exception handling.

A client program uses a *Try-Catch* block to specify its exception handling code.

A client program about to perform an operation that it thinks might fail sets up an *exception handler* block in its code, using the keywords *Try* and *Catch*, as shown in the Visual Basic .NET code listing in Figure 2-41. The exact syntax of structured exception handling varies from one language to another, but all the ones I've seen so far are pretty close to this.

```
Protected Sub btnHandled_Click(ByVal sender As Object, _
                               ByVal e As System.EventArgs)

    ' Entering this block of code writes an exception handler onto
    ' the stack.

    Try

        ' Perform an operation that we know will cause an exception.

        Dim foo As System.IO.FileStream
        foo = System.IO.File.Open("Non-existent file", IO.FileMode.Open)
```

Figure 2-41   Client application code showing structured exception handling.

```
        ' When an exception is thrown at a lower level of
        ' code, this handler block catches it.

    Catch x As System.Exception

        ' Perform whatever cleanup we want to do in response
        ' to the exception that we caught.

        MessageBox.Show(x.Message)
      End Try
  End Sub
```

When program execution enters the *Try* block, the common language runtime writes an exception handler to the stack, as shown in Figure 2-42. When a called function lower down on the stack throws an exception, as described in the next paragraph, the runtime exception-handling mechanism starts examining the stack upward until it finds an exception handler. The stack is then unwound (all objects on it discarded), and control transfers to the exception handler. An exception can come from any depth in the call stack. In the sample program, I deliberately open a file that I know does not exist. The system method *File.Open* throws an exception, and my client catches it and displays information to the user about what has happened.

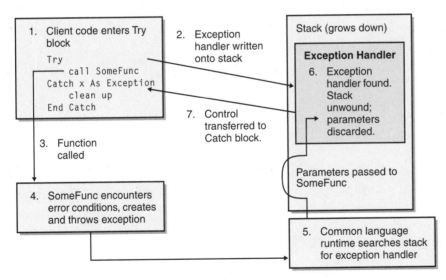

Figure 2-42   Structured exception handling diagram.

A piece of code that wants to throw an exception creates a *System.Exception* object, fills out its fields, and calls the system function *Throw*.

Any code that wants to can throw an exception. The common language runtime uses SEH for all of its error reporting, as shown in the previous example. For consistency, you therefore probably want to use SEH to signal errors from one part of your application to another. A piece of code that wants to throw an exception creates a new object of type *System.Exception*. You set the properties of this object to whatever you want them to be to describe the exception situation to any interested catchers. The common language runtime automatically includes a stack trace so that the exception handler code can tell exactly where the exception originated. Then you throw the exception using the keyword *Throw*, as shown in the code in Figure 2-43. This call tells the system to start examining the stack for handlers. The exception handler can live any number of levels above the exception thrower in the call stack.

```
Public Function BottomFunction() As String

    ' Create a new Exception object, setting its "Message" property,
    ' which can only be done in the constructor.

    Dim MyException _
        As New Exception("Exception thrown by BottomFunction")

    ' Set the new Exception's Source property, which can be
    ' done anywhere.

    MyException.Source = _
        "Introducing Microsoft .NET Chapter 2 ExceptionComponent"

    ' Throw the exception.

    Throw MyException

End Function
```

Figure 2-43   Throwing an exception in SEH.

You can enforce cleanup from an exception using a *Try-Finally* block.

When the common language runtime transfers control to an exception handler, the program stack between the thrower and the handler is discarded, as shown previously in Figure 2-42. Any objects or object references that existed on that stack are destroyed. Because of the .NET automatic garbage collection, you don't have to worry about objects being leaked away, which was a big concern when using C++ native exception handling. However, having the objects discarded in this manner means that you don't get a chance to call the *Dispose* methods of any that needed deterministic finalization. Their finalizers will be called eventually at the next garbage collection, but that might not be soon enough. You can handle this situation with a *Try-Finally* handler, as shown in Figure 2-44. Code in a *Finally* block is executed as the stack is unwound, so you can put your cleanup code there. You can combine a *Catch* and a *Finally* block in the same *Try* block if you want.

```
Public Function MiddleFunction() As String

    ' Entering this block causes a handler to be written onto the stack.

    Try
        BottomFunction()

        ' The code in this Finally handler is executed whenever
        ' execution leaves the Try block for any reason. We care most
        ' about the case in which BottomFunction throws an exception
        ' and the stack is unwound. Without the Finally handler, we'd
        ' have no chance to clean up from that exception.

    Finally
        MessageBox.Show("Finally handler in MiddleFunction")
    End Try

End Function
```

Figure 2-44 *Finally* handler in structured error handling.

SEH becomes even more powerful if throwers throw different types of exceptions to indicate different types of program failure. You do this by deriving your own class from the generic base class *System.Exception*. You can add any additional methods or properties to your exception class that you think would explain the situation to any potential catchers. Even if you don't add anything else, the mere presence of a particular type of exception will indicate what type of failure has taken place. In the example shown at the start of this section, when I attempted to open the nonexistent file, the system threw an exception of type *FileNotFoundException*. I wrote the handler shown in Figure 2-41 to catch any type of exception. If I wanted the handler to catch only exceptions of the type *FileNotFoundException*, I would change *Catch x As System.Exception* to *Catch x As System.IO.FileNotFoundException*. The common language runtime, when examining the stack, matches the type of exception thrown to the type specified in the *Catch* block, transferring control only if the type thrown matches exactly or is derived from the specified *Catch* type. A *Try* block can have any number of *Catch* handlers attached to it. The common language runtime will search them in the order in which they appear, so you want to put the most specific ones first.

You can throw and catch many different types of exceptions.

Code Access Security

Customers generally feel that software purchased from a store is safe for them to run.

At the beginning of the PC era, very few users installed and ran code that they hadn't purchased from a store. The fact that a manufacturer had gotten shelf space at CompUSA or the late Egghead Software pretty much assured a customer that the software in the box didn't contain a malicious virus, as no nefarious schemer could afford that much marketing overhead. And, like Tylenol, the shrink-wrap on the package ensured a customer that it hadn't been tampered with since the manufacturer shipped it. While the software could and probably did have bugs that would occasionally cause problems, you were fairly comfortable that it wouldn't demolish your unbacked-up hard drive just for the pleasure of hearing you scream.

However, most software today now comes from the Web.

This security model doesn't work well today because most software doesn't come from a store any more. You install some large packages, like Microsoft Office or Visual Studio, from a CD, although I wonder how much longer even that will last as high-speed Internet connections proliferate. But what about updates to, say, Internet Explorer? A new game based on Tetris? Vendors love distributing software over the Web because it's cheaper and easier than cramming it through a retail channel, and consumers like it for the convenience and lower prices. And Web code isn't limited to what you've conventionally thought of as a software application. Web pages contain scripts that do various things, not all of them good. Even Office documents that people send you by e-mail can contain scripting macros. Numerically, except for perhaps the operating system, your computer probably contains more code functions that you downloaded from the Web than you installed from a CD you purchased, and the ratio is only going to increase.

It is essentially impossible for a user to know when code from the Web is safe and when it isn't.

While distributing software over the Web is great from an entrepreneurial standpoint, it raises security problems that we haven't had before. It's now much easier for a malicious person to spread evil through viruses. It seems that not a month goes by without some new virus alert on CNN, so the problem is obviously bad enough to regularly attract the attention of mainstream media. Security experts tell you to run only code sent by people you know well, but who else is an e-mail virus going to propagate to? And how can we try software from companies we've never heard of? It is essentially impossible for a user to know when code downloaded from the Web is safe and when it isn't. Even trusted and knowledgeable users can damage systems when they run malicious or buggy software. You could clamp down and not let your users run any code that your IT department hasn't personally installed. Try it for a day and see how much work you get done. We've become dependent on Web code to a degree you won't believe until you try to live without it. The only thing that's kept society as we know it from collapsing is the relative scarcity of people with the combination of malicious inclination and technical skills to cause trouble.

Microsoft's first attempt to make Web code safe was its Authenticode system, introduced with the ActiveX SDK in 1996. Authenticode allowed manufacturers to attach a digital signature to downloaded controls so that the user would have some degree of certainty that the control really was coming from the person who said it was and that it hadn't been tampered with since it was signed. Authenticode worked fairly well to guarantee that the latest proposed update to Internet Explorer really did come from Microsoft and not some malicious spoofer. But Microsoft tried to reproduce the security conditions present in a retail store, not realizing that wasn't sufficient in a modern Internet world. The cursory examination required to get a digital certificate didn't assure a purchaser that a vendor wasn't malicious (like idiots, VeriSign gave *me* one, for only $20), as the presence of a vendor's product on a store shelf or a mail-order catalog more or less did. Worst of all, Authenticode was an all-or-nothing deal. It told you with some degree of certainty who the code came from, but your only choice was to install it or not. Once the code was on your system, there was no way to keep it from harming you. Authenticode isn't a security system; it's an accountability system. It doesn't keep code from harming you, it just ensures that you know who to kill if it does.

> The Authenticode system doesn't protect you from harm; it merely identifies the person harming you.

What we really want is a way to restrict the operations that individual pieces of code can perform on the basis of the level of trust that we have in that code. You allow different people in your life to have different levels of access to your resources according to your level of trust in them: a (current) spouse can borrow your credit card; a friend can borrow your older car; a neighbor can borrow your garden hose. We want our operating system to support the same sort of distinctions. For example, we might want the operating system to enforce a restriction that a control we download from the Internet can access our user interface but can't access files on our disk, unless it comes from a small set of vendors who we've learned to trust. The Win32 operating system didn't support this type of functionality, as it wasn't originally designed for this purpose. But now we're in the arms of the common language runtime, which is.

> We want to specify the levels of privilege that individual pieces of code can have, as we do with the humans in our lives.

The .NET common language runtime provides *code access security*, which allows an administrator to specify the privileges that each managed code assembly has, based on our degree of trust, if any, in that assembly. When managed code makes a runtime call to access a protected resource— say, opening a file or accessing Active Directory—the runtime checks to see whether the administrator has granted that privilege to that assembly, as shown in Figure 2-45. The common language runtime walks all the way to the top of the call stack when performing this check so that an untrusted top-

> The .NET common language runtime provides code access security at run time on a per-assembly basis.

level assembly can't bypass the security system by employing trusted henchmen lower down. (If a nun attempts to pick your daughter up from school, you still want the teacher to check that you sent her, right?) Even though this checking slows down access to a protected resource, there's no other good way to avoid leaving a security hole. While the common language runtime can't govern the actions of unmanaged code, such as a COM object, which deals directly with the Win32 operating system instead of going through the runtime, the privilege of accessing unmanaged code can be granted or denied by the administrator.

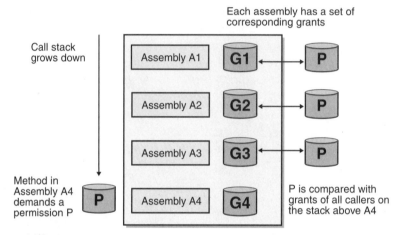

Figure 2-45 Access check in common language runtime code access security.

The administrator sets the *security policy*, a configurable set of rules that says which assemblies are and which aren't allowed to perform which types of operations. These permissions can be set at three levels: enterprise, machine, and user. A lower-level setting can tighten restrictions placed by settings at a higher level, but not the opposite. For example, if the machine-level permission allows a particular assembly to open a file, a user-level permission can deny the assembly that privilege, but not the reverse.

The administrator sets the code access security policy by editing XML-based configuration files.

An administrator sets the security policy by editing XML-based configuration files stored on a machine's disk. Any program that can modify an XML file can edit these files, so installation scripts are easy to write. Human administrators and developers will want to use the .NET Framework Configuration utility program mscorcfg.msc. This utility hadn't yet appeared when I wrote the first edition of this book, and I said some rather strong things about the lack of and the crying need for such a tool. Fortunately it now exists, whether because of what I wrote or despite it—or whether the development team even read it—I'm not sure. You can see the location of the security configuration files themselves in Figure 2-46.

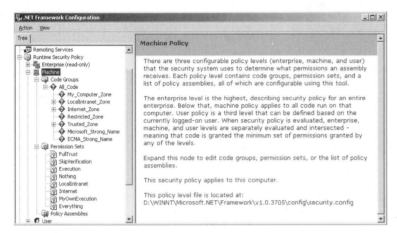

Figure 2-46   Security configuration files in the configuration utility.

Rather than grant individual permissions to various applications, an administrator creates permission sets. These are (for once) exactly what their name implies—lists of things that you are allowed to do that can be granted or revoked as a unit to an assembly. The .NET Framework contains a built-in selection of permission sets, running from Full Trust (an assembly is allowed to do anything at all) to Nothing (an assembly is forbidden to do anything at all, including run), with several intermediate steps at permission levels that Microsoft thought users would find handy. The configuration tool prevents you from modifying the preconfigured sets, but it does allow you to make copies and modify the copies.

The administrator constructs permission sets—lists of privileges that are granted and revoked as a group.

Each permission set consists of zero or more *permissions*. A permission is the right to use a logical subdivision of system functionality, for example, File Dialog or Environment Variables. Figure 2-47 shows the configuration tool dialog box allowing you to add or remove a permission to a permission set.

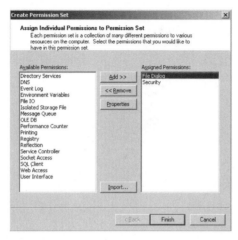

Figure 2-47   Assigning permissions to a permission set.

A permission set contains permissions, and a permission contains finer-grained properties.

Each permission in turn supports one or more *properties*, which are finer-grained levels of permitted functionality that can be granted or revoked. For example, the File Dialog permission contains properties that allow an administrator to grant access to the Open dialog, the Save dialog, both, or neither. Figures 2-48 and 2-49 show the dialog boxes for setting the properties of the File Dialog permission and the ambiguously-named Security permission.

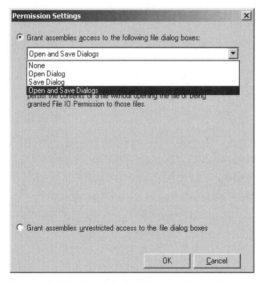

Figure 2-48   Setting properties of a single permission.

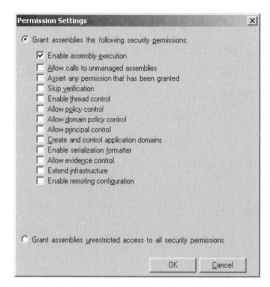

Figure 2-49   Setting properties of a different permission.

Now that you understand permission sets, let's look at how the administrator assigns a permission set to an assembly. A code-privilege administrator can assign a permission set to a specific assembly just as a log-in administrator can assign specific log-in privileges to an individual user. Both of these techniques, however, become unwieldy very quickly in production environments. Most log-in administrators set up user groups (data entry workers, officers, auditors, and so on), the members of which share a common level of privilege, and move individual users into and out of the groups. In a similar manner, most code-privilege administrators will set up groups of assemblies, known as *code groups*, and assign permission sets to these groups. The main difference between a log-in administrator's task and a code-privilege administrator's task is that the former will deal with each user's group membership manually, as new users come onto the system infrequently. Because of the way code is downloaded from the Web, we can't rely on a human to make a trust decision every time our browser encounters a new code assembly. A code-privilege administrator, therefore, sets up rules, known as *membership conditions*, that determine how assemblies are assigned to the various code groups. A membership condition will usually include the program zone that an assembly came from, for example, My Computer, Internet, Intranet, and so on. A membership condition can also include such information as the strong name of the assembly ("our developers wrote it"), or the public key with which it can be deciphered (and hence the private key with which it must have been signed). You set membership criteria using the .NET Framework Configuration tool, setting the properties of a code group, as shown in Figure 2-50.

An administrator assigns assemblies to various code groups based on membership conditions such as where the code came from and whose digital signature it contains.

The administrator then assigns a permission set to each code group.

Once you've set your membership criteria, you choose a permission set for members of that group, as shown in Figure 2-51. By default, .NET provides full trust to any assembly signed with Microsoft's strong name. I will be curious to see how many customers like this setting and how many do not.

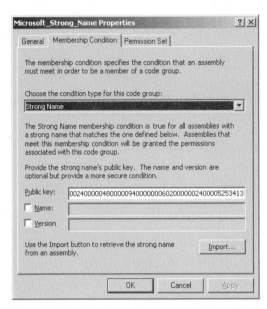

Figure 2-50   Setting code group membership conditions.

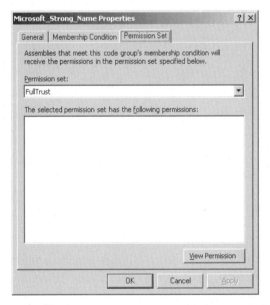

Figure 2-51   Assigning a permission set to a code group.

When the common language runtime loads an assembly at run time, it figures out which code group the assembly belongs to by checking its membership conditions. It is common for an application to belong to more than one code group. For example, if I purchased Microsoft Money by downloading it from the Web, it would belong to both the Microsoft group (because I can decode its signature with Microsoft's public key) and the Internet Zone group (because I downloaded it from the Internet). When code belongs to more than one group, the permission sets for each group are added together, and the resulting (generally larger) permission set is applied to the application.

While most of the effort involved in code access security falls on system administrators, programmers will occasionally need to write code that deals with the code-access security system. For example, a programmer might want to add metadata attributes to an assembly specifying the permission set that it needs to get its work done. This doesn't affect the permission level it will get, as that's controlled by the administrative settings I've just described, but it will allow the common language runtime to fail its load immediately instead of waiting for the assembly to try an operation that it's not allowed to do. A programmer might also want to read the level of permission that an assembly actually has been granted so that the program can inform the user or an administrator what it's missing. The common language runtime contains many functions and objects that allow programmers to write code that interacts with the code-access security system. Even a cursory examination of these functions and objects is far beyond the scope of this book, but you should know that they exist, that you can work with them if you want to, and that you almost never will want to. If you set the administrative permissions the way I've just described, the right assemblies will be able to do the right things, and the wrong assemblies will be barred from doing the wrong things, and anyone who has time to write code for micromanaging operations within those criteria is welcome to.

> If an assembly belongs to more than one code group, its permission set is the sum of the permission sets of the groups to which it belongs.

> The common language runtime contains many functions and objects for interaction with the code-access security system programmatically.

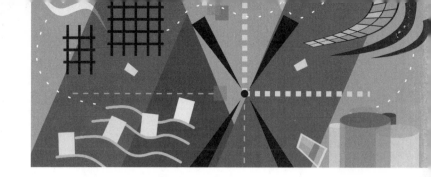

3

ASP.NET

Interdependence absolute, foreseen, ordained, decreed,
To work, Ye'll note, at any tilt an' every rate o' speed.
Fra skylight-lift to furnace-bars, backed, bolted, braced an' stayed,
An' singin' like the Mornin' Stars for joy that they are made;

> —Rudyard Kipling, writing on interoperation
> and scalability, "McAndrew's Hymn," 1894.

Problem Background

The Web was first used to deliver static pages of text and pictures. Programming a server to do this was relatively easy—just accept the URL identifying the file, fetch the file that it names from the server's disk, and write that file back to the client, as shown in Figure 3-1. You can do a lot with just this simple architecture. For example, my local art cinema has a small Web site that I can browse to see what's playing tonight (for example, *Happy, Texas*, in which two escaped convicts are mistaken for beauty pageant organizers in a small Texas town), learn about coming attractions, and follow links to trailers and reviews. They're using the Web like a paper brochure, except with richer content, faster delivery, and lower marginal cost—in a word, lower friction. (OK, two words, I was off by one.)[1]

The Web was initially used for viewing static pages, which was relatively easy to program.

---

1. One of the smartest, albeit geekiest, guys I know once said that there's only one bug in all of computing, and it's being "off by one." "Can't you be off by 25,000?" I asked him. "You've got to be off by one first," he replied.

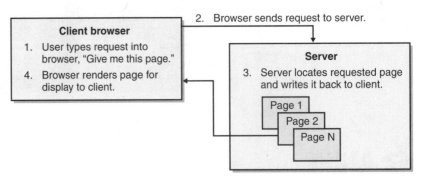

Figure 3-1   Server delivering static Web pages.

Web programmers today need to dynamically generate HTML pages in response to input received from the user, which poses new problems.

This approach worked well in the prehistoric days when all data on the Web was static (rendering the author's content verbatim, with no user input or programming logic) and public (available to anyone who knew or could find the magic address). But customers soon started asking, "If I can see what movie's playing tonight, why can't I see my current bank balance?" which the static page approach can't handle. A bank can't create a new page every day for every possible view of every account—there are far too many of them. Instead, the user needs to provide input such as the account number, and the bank's computer needs to create on demand an HTML page showing the user's account balance, as shown in Figure 3-2. This data is neither static nor public, which raises thorny new design problems

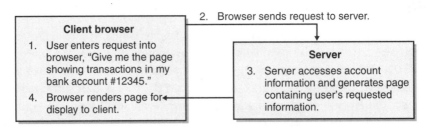

Figure 3-2   Server dynamically generating Web pages based on client input.

Our Web server application requires program logic that generates pages.

A Web server application that dynamically generates pages for a client needs several things. First, it needs a way of associating some sort of program logic with a page request. When a user requests a page, the server doesn't simply fetch the page from the disk; the page doesn't exist before the request. Instead, the server executes program logic that generates the page. In the bank example, we probably need to do a database lookup in the bank's central ledger to find out the customer's current balance and recent transactions. We'd like to be able to write this logic quickly and easily, using languages and tools with which we are already familiar. And we'd like it to run as quickly and efficiently as possible in production.

Second, our Web server needs a way to get input from the user into the server-side program logic and output from that program logic back to the user. The user's browser submits to the server an HTML form, whose input controls specify the data that he'd like to see on his page—for example, his account number and the range of dates for which he wants to see transactions. Parsing the interesting data values from this HTML is tedious and highly repetitive, so we'd like a prefabricated way of doing it that's quick and easy for us to program. Think how much easier the text box (edit control for you C++ geeks) makes reading character input in a Windows user interface compared to assembling character strings yourself from individual keystrokes. We'd also like a similar level of prefabrication in assembling the HTML page for output to the user. Raw HTML is difficult and tedious to write. Think how much easier the label control makes output in a Windows user interface compared to writing all the GDI calls needed to set font, color, text, and so on. We'd like something similar for the HTML output that a browser requires.

> Our Web server needs a convenient way of receiving input from and writing output to the user's browser.

Third, since at least some of our data is now private, our Web server needs to ensure that we know who a user is and that we only allow the user to see and do the things that he's allowed to. You'd like to see your bank account, but you really don't want your disgruntled former spouse looking at it, or, far worse, moving money out of it. This type of code is notoriously difficult and expensive to write—and proving to your wary customers that you've made the code bulletproof, so that they have the confidence to use it, is equally difficult and expensive. We need a prefabricated infrastructure that provides these security services to us.

> Our Web server needs security services to keep unauthorized users from seeing or doing things that they shouldn't.

Finally, our Web server needs a mechanism for managing user sessions. A user doesn't think of her interaction with a Web site in terms of individual page requests. Instead, she thinks of it in terms of a conversation, a "session," that takes place with multiple pages on your site over some reasonable amount of time. She expects the Web site to be able to remember things that she's told it a few minutes previously. For example, a user expects to be able to place items in an e-commerce site's shopping cart and have the cart remember these items until check out. Individual page requests don't inherently do this; we have to write the code ourselves to make it happen. Again, it's an integral part of most Web applications, so we'd like a prefabricated implementation of it that's easy to use. Ideally, it would work correctly in a multi-server environment and survive crashes.

> Our Web server needs a way to manage user sessions.

We need an entire Web
server programming and
run-time environment.

In short, our Web server needs a run-time environment that provides prefabricated solutions to the programming problems common to all Web servers. We'd like it to be easy to program as well as to administer and deploy. We'd like it to scale to at least a few servers, ideally more. And we don't want to pay a lot for it. Not asking for much, are we?

Solution Architecture

The original ASP was a
Web server run-time envi-
ronment that was easy to
use for simple tasks.

Microsoft released a relatively simple Web run-time environment called Active Server Pages (ASP) as part of Internet Information Server (IIS), itself part of the Windows NT 4 Option Pack, in the fall of 1997. IIS served up Web pages requested by the user. ASP allowed programmers to write program logic that dynamically constructed the pages that IIS supplied by mixing static HTML and scripting code, as shown in Figure 3-3. When a client requested an ASP page, IIS would locate the page and activate the ASP processor. The ASP processor would read the page and copy its HTML elements verbatim to an output page. In this case, the *style* attribute sets the text color to blue. It would also interpret the scripting elements, located within the delimiters <% %>. This code would perform program logic that rendered HTML strings as its output, which the ASP processor would copy to the location on the output page where the scripting element appeared. The resulting page, assembled from the static HTML elements and HTML dynamically generated by the script, would be written back to the client, as shown in Figure 3-4. ASP was relatively easy to use for simple tasks, which is the hallmark of a good first release.

```
<html style="color:#0000FF;">
    The time is:  <% =time %> on <% =date %>
</html>
```

Figure 3-3   Intermingling of code and HTML in ASP.

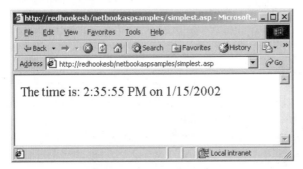

Figure 3-4   The Web page produced by ASP after processing the HTML/
code mixture in Figure 3-3.

As the Web spread and user demands increased, Web programmers required more sophistication from their Web run-time environment in two key areas: making it easier to program and making it run better. ASP.NET is a big improvement in both these areas. ASP.NET looks somewhat like the original ASP, and most code will port between the versions unchanged or very close to it. But internally ASP.NET has been completely redone to take advantage of the .NET Framework. You'll find that it runs better, crashes less, and is easier to program. These are good things to have. I discuss all of these features in more depth later in this chapter.

ASP's mingling of HTML output elements and scripting code may look logical, but it's the devil to program and maintain in any but the simplest cases. Because code and data could and did appear anywhere on the page, intelligent development environments such as Visual Basic couldn't make sense of it, so no one ever wrote a development environment that could handle ASP well. This meant that ASP code was harder to write than other types of code, such as a Visual Basic user interface application using forms. I know it drove me bats.

ASP.NET separates the HTML output from the program logic using a feature called *code-behind*. Instead of mixing HTML and code, you write the code in a separate file to which your ASP page contains a reference. You'd be astounded how much easier your code is to understand when you remove the distraction of HTML output syntax. It's like getting your three-year old to shut up while you're talking taxes on the phone with your accountant. Because of this separation, Microsoft was able to enhance the Visual Studio .NET programming and debugging environment so that you can use it while developing your Web applications.

Input and output in original ASP could be tricky, as the HTML environment was imperfectly abstracted. By this I mean that the programmer often had to spend time grappling with some fairly grotty HTML language constructs instead of thinking about her program logic, which isn't the best use of resources. For example, parsing data out of HTML forms required much more work than doing the same thing on a desktop app. Producing output required the programmer to assemble HTML output streams, which again isn't where you want your programmers to be spending their time. In Figure 3-3, our programmer had to know the proper HTML syntax for turning the text color blue.

ASP.NET supports *Web Forms*, which is a Web page architecture that makes programming a Web page very similar to programming a desktop application form. You add controls to the page and write handlers for their events, just as you do when writing a desktop app in Visual Basic. The ease of use that made Visual Basic so popular is now available for constructing Web applications. Just before the first edition of this book went to press, I

ASP.NET is a complete rewrite of the original ASP, keeping the best concepts.

ASP.NET disentangles your code from the HTML.

taught a class on the beta 1 release of ASP.NET to a seasoned bunch of ASP developers, and this is the feature that made them literally stand up and cheer.

ASP.NET contains prefabricated controls that do for HTML pages what Windows controls did for Windows applications.

As Visual Basic depended on Windows controls and third-party ActiveX controls, so does Web Forms depend on a new type of control, named *ASP.NET Server Controls*. For convenience, I refer to these as Web controls in this chapter. These are pieces of prefabricated logic dealing with input and output that a designer places on ASP.NET pages, just as he did with a Windows application form. The controls abstract away the details of dealing with HTML, just as Windows controls did for the Windows GDI. For example, you no longer have to remember the HTML syntax for setting the foreground and background color for a line of text. Instead, you'll use a label control and write code that accesses the control's properties, just as you did in any other programming language. Think of how easy controls make it for you to program a simple desktop app in Visual Basic. Web controls do the same thing for ASP.NET pages.

ASP.NET contains much good prefabricated support for securing your applications.

Original ASP included very little support for security programming. Security in ASP.NET is much easier to write. If you're running in a Windows-only environment, you can authenticate a user (verify that he really is who he says he is) automatically using Windows built-in authentication. For the majority of installations that are not Windows-only, ASP.NET contains prefabricated support for implementing your own authentication scheme. And it also contains prefabricated support for Microsoft's Passport worldwide authentication initiative, if you decide to go that route.

ASP.NET contains new session state management features that work on larger-scale Web farms.

Original ASP supported session state management with an easy-to-use API. Its main drawbacks were that the state management couldn't expand to more than one machine and that it couldn't survive a process restart. ASP.NET expands this support by adding features that allow it to do both automatically. You can set ASP.NET to automatically save and later restore session state either to a designated server machine or to Microsoft SQL Server.

ASP.NET contains many features, making it run better and making it easier to administer.

ASP.NET contains many useful new run-time features as well. Original ASP executed rather slowly because the scripting code on its pages was interpreted at run time. ASP.NET automatically compiles pages, either when a page is installed or when it's first requested, which makes it run much faster. Because it uses the .NET Framework's just-in-time compilation, you don't have to stop the server to replace a component or a page. It also supports recycling of processes. Instead of keeping a process running indefinitely, ASP.NET can be set to automatically shut down and restart its server process after a configurable time interval or number of hits. This solves most problems of memory leaks in user code. ASP.NET also has the potential of being easier to administer because all settings are stored in human-readable files in the ASP directory hierarchy itself. Unfortunately, the administrative tools that would make this job easier are still under development at the time of this writing.

Simplest Example: Writing a Simple ASP.NET Page

Let's look at the simplest ASP.NET example that I could think of. Shown in Figure 3-5, it displays the current time on the server, either with or without the seconds digits, in the user's choice of text color. You can download the code from this book's Web site, *www.introducingmicrosoft.net*, and follow along with the discussion. You will also find this page on the Web site, so you can open it in your browser and observe its behavior while I describe what I did to make it work that way.

An ASP.NET sample program begins here.

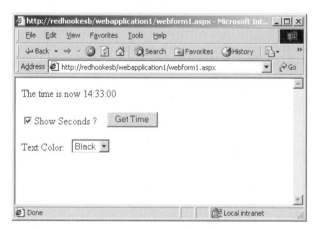

Figure 3-5   Simplest example of ASP.NET.

I wrote this sample using Visual Studio .NET. While I've tried to write my examples in a tool-agnostic manner, Visual Studio .NET contains so much built-in support for ASP.NET that not using it would have been like using Notepad to write a Visual Basic Windows desktop app. You can do it if you really, REALLY want to and probably get it to work eventually. But it will be much faster and less painful if you take the right approach from the beginning.

The key to understanding this example is to think of your Web page as a Visual Basic form. I use that analogy because I think that my readers are most familiar with it, but you could write this same code in any other Visual Studio .NET language—C#, C++, or JScript—if you want to. (I've provided C# version of all the code in the sample files.) I started by generating an ASP.NET Web Application project from Visual Studio .NET, as shown in Figure 3-6.

You put Web controls on your .ASPX pages, just as you do on a Visual Basic form.

Doing this creates, among other things, an ASP.NET page called WebForm1.aspx. I then used the Toolbox to drag Web controls onto the form, shown in Figure 3-7, adding a check box, a button, a drop-down list, and a couple of labels. I then set the properties of these controls using the Properties window in the lower right corner of the Visual Studio .NET window, specifying the text of each control, the font size of the labels, and the items in my drop-down list collection. I set the *AutoPostBack* property of the drop-down list control to *True*, meaning that it automatically posts the form back to the server when the user makes a new selection in the drop-down list. Setting user interface properties with a slick, familiar editor like this is so much easier than writing HTML strings in Notepad (which is what you had to do in ASP) that it isn't funny.

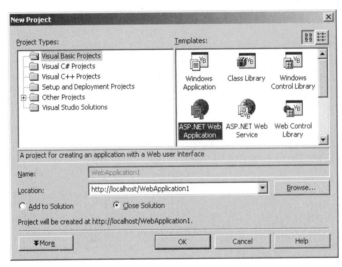

Figure 3-6   Choosing an ASP.NET Web Application in Visual Studio .NET.

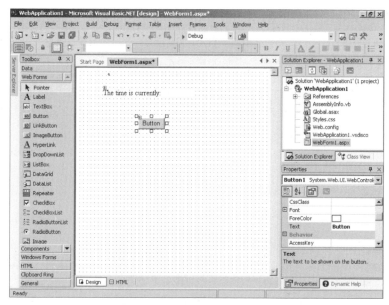

Figure 3-7   Using the Toolbox to drag Web controls onto the form.

Now that I've laid out my controls, I need to write the code that ties them together. When I generated the project, Visual Studio .NET also generated the class that represents the code behind my ASP.NET page. You view it by right-clicking on the page and selecting View Code from the shortcut menu, just as you do today with forms in Visual Basic 6.0. Web controls fire events to their forms, again just as in Visual Basic, so I need to write event handlers for them. I can add an event handler by choosing the control from the upper-left drop-down list and choosing the appropriate event from the upper-right drop-down list. I show excerpts from my Visual Basic class in Figure 3-8, and all of it is included with this book's downloadable sample code. In this simple example, when the button reports a *Click* event, I change the label's text property to hold the current time. I also added a handler for my drop-down list box's *SelectedIndexChanged* event. When the user makes a color selection from the list box, I set the label's color to the value selected by the user. When I build the project, Visual Studio .NET automatically publishes it to my machine's Web root directory.

You write event handlers for your controls' events, just as you do for a Visual Basic form.

```
Public Class WebForm1
    Inherits System.Web.UI.Page


    ' User clicked the button. Fetch the time and display it in the
    ' label control.

    Public Sub Button1_Click(ByVal sender As Object, _
            ByVal e As System.EventArgs) Handles Button1.Click
        If CheckBox1.Checked = True Then
            Label1.Text = "The time is now " + now.ToLongTimeString
        Else
            Label1.Text = "The time is now " + now.ToShortTimeString
        End If
    End Sub



    ' User has selected a different color from the list box.
    ' Change the label's color to reflect the user's choice.



    Protected Sub DropDownList1_SelectedIndexChanged(ByVal sender _
            As System.Object, _
            ByVal e As System.EventArgs) _
            Handles DropDownList1.SelectedIndexChanged
        Label1().ForeColor = _
            Color.FromName(DropDownList1().SelectedItem.Text)
    End Sub

End Class
```

Figure 3-8   Excerpts from the code behind the WebForm1.aspx page.

The event handler code
that you write runs on the
server.

The event handler code that you write runs on the server, not the user's browser. That's why Web Forms controls are often known as "server controls." When the user clicks the Get Time button or makes a selection from the drop-down list, the page is posted back to the server. ASP.NET catches the incoming page, detects which control event triggered the postback, and invokes the handler code for that event. This causes the page to be regenerated, with whatever changes the event handler code might have made to it, and written back to the client. You can read more about this process in the next section of this chapter, and still more in Chapter 11.

Now that I've finished writing my code, I'd like to see it in action. The easiest way to do this is to right-click on the page in Solution Explorer and select Build And Browse from the shortcut menu. This opens a browser window within the Visual Studio .NET environment. When this browser (or any other client) requests the .ASPX page, IIS loads it into the ASP.NET execution engine, which then parses the page. The first time the engine encounters the page it compiles its code "just-in-time." Subsequent requests for the same page will load and run the compiled code. The engine then executes the class's compiled code, creating the Web controls that I earlier placed on the form. The controls run only on the server side, rendering HTML that reflects their current state, which is incorporated in the page that gets sent to the client. The engine also executes the event handlers' code and renders the output HTML created by the code's interaction with the controls. The final HTML is written back to the client, which produces the page shown previously in Figure 3-5.

An execution engine executes the class associated with the ASP.NET page and renders HTML from its controls and code.

That's all I had to do to write an .ASPX page using Visual Studio .NET and Web controls. It's much easier than original ASP. It looks like and feels like writing Visual Basic code, which we're already familiar and comfortable with.

More on Web Controls

Web controls spring from the same philosophy that led to the creation of Windows user interface controls 15 years ago. That architecture made Bill Gates the world's richest man (even after last year's tech stock slide, according to Forbes.com). That's my definition of a successful architecture; don't know about yours.

Input and output operations are highly repetitive. Prefabricating them—rolling them up in a capsule for any programmer to use—is a great idea. You kids today don't know how lucky you are not to have to worry about writing your own button controls, for example, and painting the pixels differently to make the button look as if it's been clicked. This not only saves an enormous amount of expensive programming time, but also makes every program's user interface more consistent and thus easier for users to understand. Remember (I'm dating myself here) Windows 3.0, which didn't contain a standard File Open dialog box? Every application programmer had to roll her own. It cost a lot, and every application's implementation looked and worked a little (or a lot) differently. Windows 3.1 provided a File Open dialog box as part of the operating system, which made the lives of programmers and users much easier. A Web control, in the ASP.NET sense of the word, is any type of user-interface-related programming logic that is capable of a) exposing a standard programming model to a development environment such as Visual

Controls exist to encapsulate reusable program logic dealing with user interfaces.

Studio .NET, and b) rendering its appearance into HTML for display in a standard browser—more or less as a Windows control renders its appearance into Windows GDI function calls.

Web controls are richer, more numerous, and easier to program than standard HTML controls.

"But HTML already *has* controls," you say. "Buttons and checkboxes and links. I use them all the time. Why do I have to learn a new set?" HTML does support a few controls as part of the language, but these have severe limitations. First, they're not very numerous or very rich. A text box and a drop-down list box are about as far as they go. Compare their number to the controls advertised in *Visual Basic Programmers Journal* or their functionality to Visual Basic's data-bound grid control. We'd like to be able to package a lot more functionality than the few and wimpy existing HTML elements provide. Second, they are hard to write code for. The communication channel between an HTML control and its run-time environment isn't very rich. The Web Forms environment that Web controls inhabit contains an event-driven programming model similar to Visual Basic. It's much easier to program, there's much better support in development environments, and it abstracts away many of the differences from one browser to another. Web controls do more and are easier to program. Sounds decisive to me.

Web controls exist for many different functions.

ASP.NET comes with the set of basic Web controls listed in Table 3-1. I expect that third-party vendors will soon develop and market Web controls for every conceivable type of situation, as happened with ActiveX controls. You can also write your own, which isn't very hard. I discuss writing your own Web Forms controls in Chapter 11 of this book.

Table 3-1   Web Forms Server Controls by Function

Function	Control	Description
Text display (read only)	Label	Displays text that users can't directly edit.
Text edit	TextBox	Displays text entered at design time that can be edited by users at run time or changed programmatically.
		Note: Although other controls allow users to edit text (for example, Drop-DownList), their primary purpose is not usually text editing.
Selection from a list	DropDownList	Allows users to either select from a list or enter text.
	ListBox	Displays a list of choices. Optionally, the list can allow multiple selections.
Graphics display	Image	Displays an image.

Table 3-1   Web Forms Server Controls by Function

Function	Control	Description
	AdRotator	Displays a sequence (predefined or random) of images.
Value setting	CheckBox	Displays a box that users can click to turn an option on or off.
	RadioButton	Displays a single button that can be selected or not.
Date setting	Calendar	Displays a calendar to allow users to select a date.
Commands	Button	Used to perform a task.
	LinkButton	Like a Button control but has the appearance of a hyperlink.
	ImageButton	Like a Button control but incorporates an image instead of text.
Navigation controls	HyperLink	Creates Web navigation links.
Table controls	Table	Creates a table.
	TableCell	Creates an individual cell within a table row.
	TableRow	Creates an individual row within a table.
Grouping other controls	CheckBoxList	Creates a collection of check boxes.
	Panel	Creates a borderless division on the form that serves as a container for other controls.
	RadioButtonList	Creates a group of radio buttons. Inside the group, only one button can be selected.
List controls	Repeater	Displays information from a data set using a set of HTML elements and controls that you specify, repeating the elements once for each record in the data set.
	DataList	Like the Repeater control but with more formatting and layout options, including the ability to display information in a table. The DataList control also allows you to specify editing behavior.

(continued)

Table 3-1   Web Forms Server Controls by Function

Function	Control	Description
	DataGrid	Displays information, usually data-bound, in tabular form with columns. Provides mechanisms to allow editing and sorting.
Place holding	PlaceHolder	Enables you to place an empty container control in the page and then dynamically add child elements to it at run time.
	Literal	Renders static text into a Web page without adding any HTML elements.
	XML	Reads XML and writes it into a Web Forms page at the location of the control.

The execution engine creates and uses the controls on the server side. The controls render their own HTML for the client.

When I placed controls on my form in the preceding example, Visual Studio .NET generated the statements in the .ASPX page, shown in Figure 3-9. Every statement that starts with *<asp: >* is a directive to the ASP.NET parser to create a control of the specified type when it generates the class file for the page. For example, in response to the statement *<asp:label>*, the parser creates a label control in the class. When the page is executed, the ASP.NET execution engine executes the event handler code on the page that interacts with the controls (fetching the time and setting the text and background color, as shown previously in Figure 3-8). Finally, the engine tells each control to render itself into HTML in accordance with its current properties, just as a Windows control renders itself into GDI calls in accordance with its current properties. The engine then writes the resulting HTML to the client's browser. Figure 3-10 shows this process schematically. Excerpts from the actual HTML sent to the client are shown in Figure 3-11.

```
<%@ Page Language="vb" AutoEventWireup="false"
Codebehind="WebForm1.aspx.vb" Inherits="SimplestASPVB.WebForm1"%>
<!DOCTYPE HTML PUBLIC "-//W3C//DTD HTML 4.0 Transitional//EN">
<HTML>
    <HEAD>
        <title>WebForm1</title>
        <meta name="GENERATOR" content="Microsoft Visual Studio.NET 7.0">
        <meta name="CODE_LANGUAGE" content="Visual Basic 7.0">
        <meta name="vs_defaultClientScript" content="JavaScript">
        <meta name="vs_targetSchema"
            content="http://schemas.microsoft.com/intellisense/ie5"
```

Figure 3-9   Excerpts from .ASPX page created by Visual Studio .NET, showing control statements.

```
    </HEAD>
    <body MS_POSITIONING="GridLayout">
        <form id="Form1" method="post" runat="server">
          <asp:Label id="Label1"
         style="Z-INDEX: 101; LEFT: 32px; POSITION: absolute; TOP: 24px"
         runat="server">Time will be shown here</asp:Label>
          <asp:DropDownList id="DropDownList1"
        style="Z-INDEX: 102; LEFT: 136px; POSITION: absolute; TOP: 120px"
        runat="server" AutoPostBack="True">
              <asp:ListItem Value="Black">Black</asp:ListItem>
              <asp:ListItem Value="Red">Red</asp:ListItem>
              <asp:ListItem Value="Green">Green</asp:ListItem>
              <asp:ListItem Value="Blue">Blue</asp:ListItem>
          </asp:DropDownList>
          <asp:Button id="Button1"
        style="Z-INDEX: 103; LEFT: 184px; POSITION: absolute; TOP: 72px"
        runat="server" Text="Get Time"></asp:Button>
          <asp:CheckBox id="CheckBox1"
        style="Z-INDEX: 104; LEFT: 32px; POSITION: absolute; TOP: 72px"
        runat="server" Text="Show seconds?"></asp:CheckBox>
          <asp:Label id="Label2"
        style="Z-INDEX: 105; LEFT: 32px; POSITION: absolute; TOP: 120px"
        runat="server">Text color:</asp:Label>
        </form>
    </body>
</HTML>
```

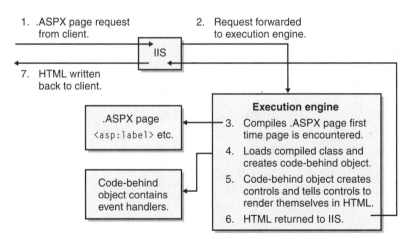

Figure 3-10   .ASPX page execution engine sequence.

```
<span id="Label1" style="color:Black;">
    (time will be displayed here)
</span>

<span>
<input type="checkbox" id="CheckBox1" name="CheckBox1" />
<label for="CheckBox1">Show Seconds ?</label>
</span>

<input type="submit" name="Button1" value="Get Time" id="Button1" />

<p>Text Color:

<select name="DropDownList1" id="DropDownList1"
        onchange="javascript:_ _doPostBack('DropDownList1','')">
    <option selected value="Black">Black</option>
    <option value="Red">Red</option>
    <option value="Green">Green</option>
    <option value="Blue">Blue</option>
</select>
```

Figure 3-11   Excerpts from the HTML generated by the controls.

Input controls can maintain their contents and selection from one round-trip to another. Display controls can also maintain their state from one round-trip to another.

Another great feature of the input controls in the Web controls package (list box, text box, check box, radio button, and so on) is that they can automatically remember the state in which the user left them when the page they are on makes a round-trip to the server. Microsoft calls this feature *postback data*. Observe the behavior of the check box control in the simplest example that I showed in the previous section. The check box correctly maintains its checked or unchecked state when the page is posted to the server for event handling and returned to the client browser afterward. I didn't have to write any code to get this behavior, as I would have had to in classic HTML. Input Web controls automatically remember their state. During the postback operation, the data actually resides in a dedicated field in the HTTP header of the page. This is an automatic feature that you can't turn off.

The display controls in the Web controls package, such as label, data list, data grid, and repeater, support their own version of property retention, called *view state*. Even though the user doesn't set them to specific values, they still remember the state in which the program left them in the previous round trip. The .ASPX page environment automatically places a hidden input control called __VIEWSTATE on each of its pages. Web controls automatically serialize their state into this hidden control when the page is being destroyed and then retrieve their state when the page is next created, which is what you want most of the time. If you don't want this, you easily can turn it off by setting the control's *MaintainState* property to *False*.

Why does Microsoft use two separate mechanisms for maintaining control state, one for input controls and the other for display controls? Probably to make it easier for programmers to comply with the Principle of Least Astonishment, which states simply that astonishing a human user is not a good thing, therefore you should do it as seldom as possible. When a user types something into a field, she expects to see what she typed stay there until she does something that changes it. If an input control didn't automatically maintain its state, a developer would have to write code to make it do so or astonish the heck out of his users. Since you have to do this all the time, Microsoft built it into the input control behavior and didn't provide an off switch. On the other hand, a display control often doesn't display what a user typed in. Instead, it usually shows the results of an internal computing operation. Sometimes you might want a display control to remember its state between operations, and sometimes you might not. Hence a different mechanism, this one with an off switch.

Web controls can also discover the specific browser on which the user will be viewing the page so that they can render their HTML to take advantage of different browser features if they want to. A good example of this is the range validator control, shown in Figure 3-12. Ensuring that a user-entered number falls between a certain maximum and minimum value is such a common task that Microsoft provides a Web control for it. You place the control on a form and set properties that tell it which text box to validate and what the maximum and minimum values are. When the control renders its HTML, it checks the version of the browser it's running on. If it's a newer browser that supports DHTML (specifically MSDOM 4.0 or later, and EcmaScript version 1.2 or later), the control renders HTML that includes a client-side script that will perform the numeric validation in the user's browser before submitting the form to the server, thereby avoiding a network round-trip if a control contains invalid data. If all the data passes validation on the client, the form is submitted to the server. Somewhat counterintuitively, the validation operation is then repeated on the server, even though it passed on the client. This guarantees that the validation is performed before your server-side code runs, even if the control somehow messed up the client-side script on a flaky browser. If the control detects an older browser that doesn't support DHTML, it automatically generates HTML code that performs a round-trip and validates on the server.

Web controls can detect the capabilities of the browser they are running on and render different code to take advantage of them.

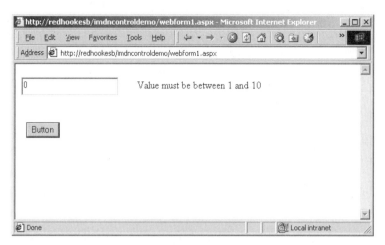

Figure 3-12   The range validator control.

You can write your own
Web controls without too
much trouble.

Writing your own Web controls isn't that hard because the .NET Framework contains prefabricated base classes from which you can inherit most of your control's necessary infrastructure (sort of like MFC on steroids). I show several examples in Chapter 11 of this book.

Managing and Configuring Web Application Projects: The Web.config File

A powerful run-time environment like ASP.NET requires excellent configuration management.

A powerful run-time environment like ASP.NET provides many prefabricated services. As you can imagine, an individual application has many, many options for its configuration. The configuration mechanism of an environment is as important as the underlying software that it controls. Cool features that you can't configure, or can't figure out how to configure, are about as useful as unsecured Enron bonds.

ASP.NET keeps its configuration information in individual files, each having the name web.config.

Previous run-time environments have used a central store for their configuration information. For example, classic COM used the system registry and COM+ added the COM+ catalog. ASP.NET takes a different, decentralized approach. Each application stores its ASP.NET configuration management information in a file named web.config, which is stored in the application's own directory. Each file contains configuration information expressed in a particular XML vocabulary. Excerpts from our sample program's web.config file are shown in Figure 3-13. This excerpt shows the compilation and custom error handling settings of this particular application. I will discuss other settings later in this chapter.

```
<?xml version="1.0" encoding="utf-8" ?>
<configuration>

    <system.web>

        <!--  DYNAMIC DEBUG COMPILATION
              Set compilation debug="true" to insert debugging symbols
              (.pdb information) into the compiled page. Because this
              creates a larger file that executes more slowly, you should
              set this value to true only when debugging and to false at
              all other times. For more information, refer to the
              documentation about debugging ASP.NET files.
        -->
        <compilation defaultLanguage="vb" debug="true" />

        <!--  CUSTOM ERROR MESSAGES
              Set customErrors mode="On" or "RemoteOnly" to enable
              custom error messages, "Off" to disable. Add <error>
              tags for each of the errors you want to handle.
        -->
        <customErrors mode="RemoteOnly" />

    </system.web>

</configuration>
```

Figure 3-13   Excerpts from the sample application's web.config file.

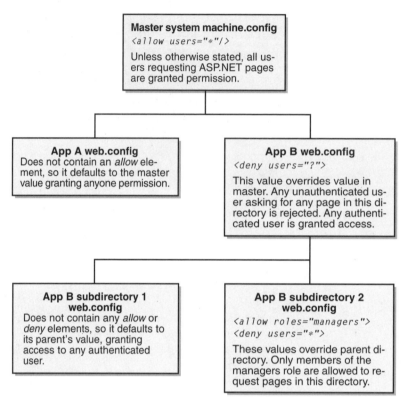

Figure 3-14   The hierarchical nature of web.config files.

A setting made in a web.config file overrides the settings made in directories above it.

Web.config files can also reside in various subdirectories of an application. Each web.config file governs the operation of pages within its directory and all lower subdirectories unless overridden. Entries made in a lower-level web.config file override those made in levels above them. Some users find this counterintuitive; some don't. The master file specifying the defaults for the entire ASP.NET system has the name machine.config and lives in the directory [system, e.g. WINNT]\Microsoft.NET\Framework\[version]\Config. Entries made in web.config files in the root directories of an individual Web application override entries made in the master file. Entries made in web.config files in subdirectories of an application override those made in the root. This relationship is shown in Figure 3-14.

Not all sections of the web.config file are configurable on all levels of subdirectory. The *<sessionstate>* section, for example, may not appear below an application's root directory. You'll have to examine the details of individual sections to find out the granularity of each.

At the time of this writing, this configuration scheme is difficult to use. You can edit the raw XML file using any editor, or Visual Studio .NET provides a slightly better tool as shown in Figure 3-15. But it still falls far below the ease of using the .NET Framework configuration utility described in Chapter 2, or any other administrative tool in the Windows 2000 environment—the COM+ Explorer, for example. The ASP.NET team acknowledges the need for a better tool but decided that it needed to finish working on the feature set of the product itself before writing the administrative tools, even though this causes the administrative tools to ship some time after the product release. While I disagree (respectfully but strongly) with this call, I can tell you that the problem is being worked on. I've seen some of the prototypes that the Microsoft developers are working on, and they're pretty cool. While major design choices are still under discussion and no schedule has been announced, I am now convinced that the ASP.NET team realizes that good administrative tools are critical to the product's success in the marketplace. I believe these tools will be shipped soon. I guarantee that the product won't take off until they do.

> Good administrative tools are still under construction.

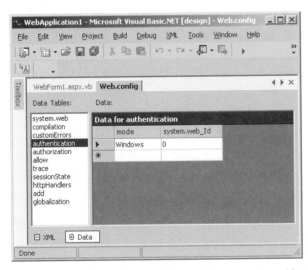

Figure 3-15   Visual Studio .NET provides a crude tool for editing configuration files.

ASP.NET State Management

Internet page requests from a single user didn't originally know about each other. Sometimes this is OK.

Web page requests are by default independent of each other. If I request page B from a server, the contents of page B don't know whether I have or haven't viewed page A a few minutes ago. This arrangement works well for simple read-only requests, such as the movie theater example I discussed in the opening paragraph of this chapter. It's easy to write a server that does this because you don't have to store any data from one page request to another.

Then again, as Web interactions get richer, sometimes it isn't.

As Web interactions get more sophisticated, however, this design no longer meets your users' needs. What I did on page A *does* affect the content that page B should show. For example, I book a lot of air travel directly on airline Web sites because they offer extra frequent flyer miles. It's not acceptable to me to search for an outgoing flight, write it down on paper, search for a return flight, write it down as well, and then manually type both of these flight numbers into yet another page for purchasing my ticket. I want the airline's site to automatically remember my outgoing flight selection while I choose a return flight and then remember both of these while I buy the ticket.

A Web programmer often must maintain separate data for many users simultaneously.

Remembering data from one form to another was never a problem for a desktop application, which targeted a single user. The programmer could simply store input data in the program's internal memory without worrying about which user it belonged to, since only one person used the program at a time. But keeping track of a user's actions over multiple pages is much more difficult in a Web application, used by (you hope) many different people simultaneously. A Web programmer needs to keep my data separate from all the other users' so that their flights don't get mixed with mine (unless they're headed to Hawaii in February, in which case, hooray!). We call this *managing session state*, and the Web programmer needs some efficient, easy-to-program way of doing it.

ASP.NET provides a set of data tied to a specific user. Called a *Session*, programmers can use this object to store data for a specific user.

Original ASP provided a simple mechanism for managing session state, which ASP.NET supports and extends. Every time a new user accesses an .ASPX page, ASP.NET creates an internal object called a *Session*. This object is an indexed collection of data living on the server and tied to a particular active user. The original ASP *Session* object could only hold strings, but the ASP.NET *Session* object can hold any type of .NET object. You can access items in the collection by means of a numerical index or a string name that you specify. The *Session* object can hold any number of items for each user, but since they all use server memory, I advise you to limit the amount of data you store in session state to the minimum necessary.

The *Session* object automatically remembers (placing a unique ID in a browser cookie or appending it to the URL) which user the data refers to, so the programmer doesn't have to write code to do that. For example, when I submit a form selecting a flight, the .ASPX page programmer can store that flight's information in the *Session* object. When I request the page to buy my ticket, the programmer reads the flight from my *Session* object. The .ASPX run time automatically knows who the user is (me), so the programmer's code automatically fetches my flights and not someone else's, as shown in Figure 3-16.

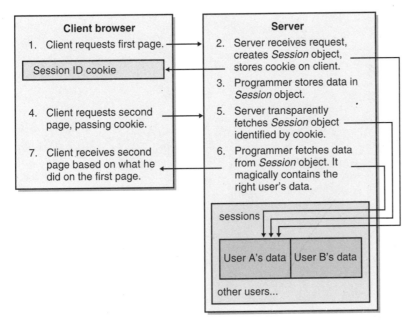

Figure 3-16   Managing session state.

This feature is easy for programmers to use, and hence quite popular. Each .ASPX page contains a property named *Session* that provides access to the session object for the current user. You place items in this object using an integer index or a string key, and retrieve them the same way. If you attempt to fetch an item that doesn't exist in the session object, you'll get a null object reference in return. A sample of the code that does this is shown in Figure 3-17. You will also find this sample on this book's Web site. The pages will look like Figure 3-18.

ASP.NET provides a simple API for setting and getting session state variables.

```
' Code that stores data in session state.

Protected Sub Button1_Click(ByVal sender As System.Object, _
                            ByVal e As System.EventArgs) _
                            Handles Button1.Click

    ' Store current text string in session state.

    Session("DemoString") = TextBox1().Text

    ' Redirect user to page for viewing state.

    Response().Redirect("WebForm2.aspx")

End Sub

' Fetch designated string from session state object
    ' Display to user in label

    Private Sub Page_Load(ByVal sender As System.Object, _
                          ByVal e As System.EventArgs) Handles MyBase.Load

        Dim str As String
        str = Session("DemoString")

        If (Not str Is Nothing) Then
            Label2.Text = str
        Else
            Label2.Text = ("(the item ""DemoString"" does not exist " & _
                           "in the session collection)")
        End If

    End Sub
```

Figure 3-17 Code for session state management.

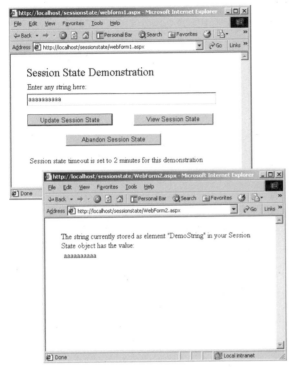

Figure 3-18 Session state management sample application.

Obviously, if a server were to maintain a permanent session for every user that ever viewed even one page on it, you'd run out of memory very quickly. The session mechanism is designed to maintain state only for active users—those who are currently performing tasks that require the server to maintain state for them. ASP.NET automatically deletes a user's *Session* object, dumping its contents, after it has been idle for a configurable timeout interval. This interval, in minutes, is set in the *<sessionstate>* section of the web.config file, shown in Figure 3-19. The default is 20 minutes. You can also dump the session yourself by calling the method *Session.Abandon*.

ASP.NET automatically deletes sessions after a configurable timeout interval.

```
<sessionState
        mode="inproc"
        stateConnectionString="tcpip=127.0.0.1:42424"
        sqlConnectionString="data source=127.0.0.1;user id=sa;password="
        cookieless="false"
        timeout="2"
    />
```

Figure 3-19 Session state management entries in the web.config file.

Session state can be stored in a separate process for robustness.

While the session mechanism in original ASP was easy to use, it had a number of drawbacks that hampered its expansion to large-scale systems. First, it stored session state in the worker processes that actually ran page scripts and called code living in programmer-written custom objects. A badly behaved object could and often did crash this process, thereby killing the session state of every user it was currently serving, not just the one whose call caused the crash. ASP.NET fixes this problem by providing the ability to store session state in a separate process, one that runs as a system service (see Figure 3-20), so badly behaved user code can't kill it. This means that worker processes can come and go without losing their session state. It slows down the access to the session state somewhat, as applications now need to cross process boundaries to get to their session state, but most developers figure that's worth it for reliability. To turn this feature on, set the *mode* attribute in the web.config file to *stateserver* and ensure that the state server process is running on the server machine.

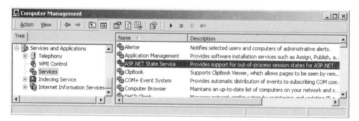

Figure 3-20 ASP.NET session state process running as a system service.

Session state can be easily stored on a different machine.

Original ASP always stored session state on the server machine on which it was created. This architecture didn't scale well to a Web farm in which every request is potentially handled by a different server. ASP.NET allows each application to specify the machine on which it wants its session state to be stored. You do this by setting the *stateConnectionString* attribute in the web.config file. In this way, any machine that handles a subsequent call can access the session state stored by a previous call handled by a different machine. Obviously, you now incur the overhead of another network round-trip, so maybe you'd rather set up your load balancer to route subsequent requests to the same machine. You can swap out that machine by simply changing its name in the configuration files of all the clients.

You can also store session state in SQL Server for better management of large collections. You do this by setting the *mode* attribute to *sqlserver* and providing a SQL connection string in the *sqlConnectionString* attribute. The current setup scripts create a temporary database for holding session state. This provides fast access because the data isn't written to the slow iron disk, but it also means that the session state won't survive a crash. If you want that durability and don't mind paying the performance penalty for it, you can change the database attributes yourself to use a permanent table.

You can also store session state in a SQL Server database.

ASP.NET also helps you manage application state, where an application represents a top-level IIS virtual directory and all of its subdirectories. Application-level state is stuff that changes from time to time, so you don't want to hard code it, but it applies to all users of the application and isn't tied to an individual user. An example of application state might be the current unadvertised special offer that every page would display. Each application contains one state object named *Application*, similar in use to the *Session* object, except that all accesses of the *Application* object operate on the same data regardless of the user on the other end.

ASP.NET also provides another state collection for data at an application level.

Security in ASP.NET

Security is vital to any type of distributed programming, and discussions of it are often highly charged with emotion. I will attempt to outline the problems that arise in this area and discuss how ASP.NET provides your Web application with prefabricated functionality that gives you the level of security you need without too much programming effort.

Security is vital to any distributed system.

The security requirements of a Web application are somewhat like those of a city hall. You have large numbers of people coming and going anonymously, accessing public areas such as the tourism office that dispenses maps. Because these areas aren't sensitive, you don't want to waste time and annoy users by subjecting them to strip searches, or else you won't get many customers and the businesses that sponsor the map giveaways will be angry. But other areas of the same city hall, such as the floor containing the mayor's office, are sensitive. You don't want to allow anyone in who can't prove their identity (authentication) and that they have business on the floor (authorization). And you might want to run them through a metal detector to make sure they can't hurt anybody.

Different areas of an application require different levels of security.

Authentication

The first problem in security is authentication—Who are you, and how do I know you really are that person? Authenticating a user usually takes the form of examining some sort of credential presented by the user, sometimes agreed upon directly between the two parties, such as a PIN or password; sometimes issued by a third party that both trust, such as a driver's license or passport. If the credentials are satisfactory to the server, the server knows who the user is and can use its internal logic to determine what actions she is allowed to perform. A user who is not authenticated is called an anonymous user. That doesn't necessarily mean that she can't have access to anything on the Web site. It means that she can have access only to the features that the designers have chosen to make available to anonymous users—perhaps checking an airline schedule but not redeeming a frequent flyer award.

Authentication has historically been the most difficult problem in security design. Most application designers don't want to deal with it because it's so important but so difficult to get right. You need a full-time team of very smart geeks who do nothing but eat, drink, and sleep security because that's what the bad guys have who are trying to crack your Web site and weasel free first-class upgrades (or worse). For example, you can't just send a password over the network, even if it's encrypted. If the network packet containing even an encrypted password doesn't somehow change unpredictably every time you submit it, a bad guy could record it and play it back. That's how I broke into the foreign exchange system of a certain bank whose name you would recognize—fortunately with the bank's permission—under a consulting contract to test their security. They were very proud of their password encryption algorithm, which I never even tried to crack, but it took me only 20 minutes with a packet sniffer to record a user ID/password packet and play it back to enter their server. Too bad I was charging them by the hour. Next time I'll vacation for a billable week before declaring success. If you'd like more information about the design problems of writing secure applications, I recommend the book *Writing Secure Code*, by Michael Howard and David LeBlanc (Microsoft Press, 2002). I never even imagined half the ways to crack a system that these guys discuss.

Because of the difficulty and importance of authentication, it's one of the first features that gets built into a (hopefully) secure operating system. ASP.NET supports three different mechanisms for authentication (four if you count "none"). They are shown in Table 3-2.

Table 3-2   ASP.NET authentication modes

Name	Description
None	No ASP.NET authentication services are used.
Windows	Standard Windows authentication is used from IIS.
Forms	ASP.NET requires all page request headers to contain a cookie issued by the server. Users attempting to access protected pages without a cookie are redirected to a login page that verifies credentials and issues a cookie.
Passport	Same idea as Forms, except that user ID info is held and cookies are issued by Microsoft's external Passport authentication service.

You need to think carefully about exactly where in your Web site authentication should take place. As with a city hall, you need to balance security versus ease of use. For example, a financial Web site will require authentication before viewing accounts or moving money, but the site probably wants to make its marketing literature and fund prospectuses available to the anonymous public. It is important to design your site so that areas that require security have it, but you don't want this security to hamper your unsecure operations. I have a hard time thinking of anything more detrimental to sales than making a user set up and use an authenticated account before allowing him to see a sales pitch, although some sites do just that.

> **Warning**   Unlike DCOM, which used its own wire format to support packet privacy, none of the authentication schemes available to ASP.NET provide for encryption of the data transmitted from client to server. This problem doesn't come from ASP.NET itself, but from the common Web transport protocol HTTP. If your Web site provides data that you don't want on the front page of *USA Today*, you need to use the Secure Sockets Layer (SSL) transport or provide some other mechanism for encrypting. Typically, you will do this only for the most sensitive operations because it is slower than unsecure transports. For example, an airline Web site will probably use encrypted transport for the credit card purchase page but not for the flight search page.

You need to think carefully about which of your site's resources require authentication for access and which don't.

Windows Authentication

ASP.NET supports what it calls *Windows-based authentication*, which basically means delegating the authentication process to IIS, the basic Web server infrastructure on which ASP.NET sits. IIS can be configured to pop up a dialog box on the user's browser and accept a user ID and password. These credentials must match a Windows user account on the domain to which the IIS host belongs. Alternatively, if the client is running Microsoft Internet Explorer 4 or higher on a Windows system and not connecting through a proxy, IIS can be configured to use the NTLM or Kerberos authentication systems built into Windows to automatically negotiate a user ID and password based on the user's current logged-in session.

Windows authentication works quite well for a Windows-only intranet over which you have full administrative control. For certain classes of installation—say, a large corporation—it's fantastic. Just turn it on and go. But it's much less useful on the wide-open Internet, where your server wants to be able to talk to any type of system, (say, a palmtop) using any type of access (say, not Internet Explorer), and where you don't want to set up a Windows login account for every user.

Windows authentication works well on a Windows-only intranet.

Forms-Based, or Cookie, Authentication

Most designers of real-life Web applications will choose *forms-based authentication*, otherwise known as *cookie authentication*. The user initially sets up an account with a user ID and password. Some Web sites, such as most airline sites, allow you to do this over the Web through a page open to anonymous access. Other Web sites, such as most financial services companies, require a signed paper delivered via snail mail.

Forms-based authentication starts with a user ID and password.

When the user first requests a page from a secure Web site, he is directed to a form that asks for his ID and password. The Web server matches these against the values it has on file and allows access if they match. The server then provides the browser with a cookie that represents its successful login. Think of this cookie as the hand stamp you get at a bar when they check your ID and verify that you really are over 21 years old. It contains the user's identification in an encrypted form. The browser will automatically send this cookie in the request header section of every subsequent page request so that the server knows which authenticated user it comes from. This relay keeps you from having to enter a user ID and password on every form submittal or page request. Figure 3-21 illustrates this process.

The server supplies the browser with a cookie, an admission ticket identifying the authenticated user.

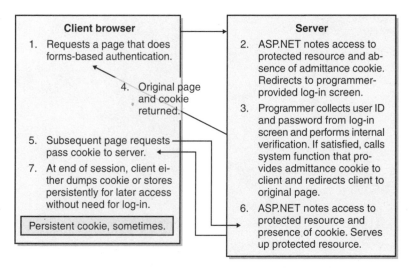

Figure 3-21   Forms-based authentication.

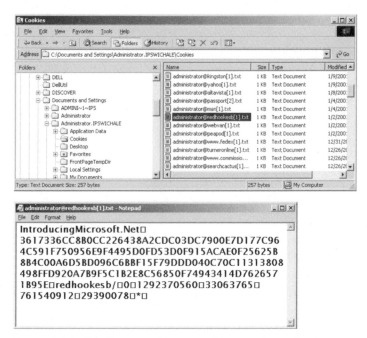

Figure 3-22   Persistent cookie created by sample application.

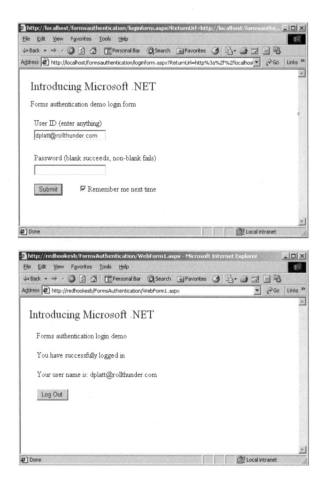

Figure 3-23 Sample application for forms-based authentication.

Cookies may be temporary or persistent.

When it supplies the cookie, the server specifies whether the cookie is to be thrown away when the browser session ends or should be saved on the user's hard disk so that he won't have to log in next time. Financial Web sites often require the former in order to be ultraprotective against unauthorized use that could cost thousands of dollars. The latter, however, is obviously much more convenient for users. Most Web sites whose data isn't very sensitive, on-line periodicals such as the *Wall Street Journal* for example, often provide the user with the capability to choose it. A sample persistent cookie is shown in Figure 3-22.

ASP.NET contains good prefabricated support for forms-based authentication.

ASP.NET contains good support for forms-based authentication. A sample application is available on this book's Web site and shown in Figure 3-23. You tell ASP.NET to use forms-based authentication by making an entry in the web.config file as shown in Figure 3-24. The *authorization* element tells ASP.NET to deny access to any unauthenticated users.

```
<authentication mode = "Forms" >
    <forms name="IntroducingMicrosft.NET" loginUrl="loginform.aspx"/>
</authentication>

<authorization>
    <deny users="?"/>
</authorization>
```

Figure 3-24   Web.config file for forms-based authentication.

This means that ASP.NET will require that any request for a page in that directory or its subdirectories must contain a cookie from the browser saying that you've authenticated the user and found him worthy. If the cookie is not present, as it won't be prior to your first login, ASP.NET directs the user to the page you have specified in the *loginUrl* attribute. You use this page to provide controls for the user to enter his ID and password. The page's handler contains whatever logic you need for checking that the user really is who he says he is. The sample code simply accepts a blank user password and rejects any that are nonblank. If the server accepts the incoming user, a simple function call (to *System.Web.Security.FormsAuthentication.RedirectFromLoginPage*) brings the user back to the page that he was trying to access when the authentication scheme shunted him to the login screen. If you'd like to send him somewhere else instead, you can use the function *Response.Redirect*. The code is shown in Figure 3-25.

```
Public Sub Button1_Click(ByVal sender As System.Object, _
                    ByVal e As System.EventArgs)

    ' Check for legal password (in this case, blank)

    If TextBox2.Text = "" Then
        System.Web.Security.FormsAuthentication.RedirectFromLoginPage( _
           TextBox1.text, CheckBox1.Checked)

    ' Reject a non-blank password. Don't need to make any system calls,
    ' just refrain from making the one that would grant access.

    Else
        Label5.Text = "Invalid Credentials: Please try again"
    End If

End Sub
```

Figure 3-25   Code for forms-based authentication form.

You can also set up ASP.NET to automatically perform forms-based authentication using user IDs and passwords stored in XML configuration files. This approach would probably work well for a small installation. Unfortunately, a demonstration is beyond the scope of this book, at least in this edition.

Passport Authentication

As Web sites proliferate, so do the user IDs and passwords that a user must remember. This is a growing menace to the security of all data.

The third authentication alternative is Passport-based authentication. The forms-based scheme described in the previous section sounds fine, and it's a lot easier to write today than it used to be as the result of ASP.NET's prefabricated support. But it suffers from the fatal problem of unchecked proliferation. Every Web site with anything the least bit sensitive needs some sort of login security. For example, I use five different airline Web sites for booking all the travel I have to do, and because they take credit cards, every one of them requires authentication. It is a colossal pain in the ass to keep track of all the user names and passwords I use on these different sites. On one of them my name is "dplatt"; on another one that ID was taken when I signed up so I'm "daveplatt". I've tried using my e-mail address, which no one else ought to be using and which I can usually remember. This occasionally works, but many sites won't accept the @ sign and others won't accept a string that long. For passwords, some use 4-character PINs for identification, others use a password of at least six (or sometimes eight) characters, and one insists that the password contain both letters and numbers. Many sites consider their data to be so sensitive (my frequent flyer record? get a life) that they won't allow a persistent cookie to remember my login credentials. The only way I can keep track of all my user names and passwords is to write them down and keep them near my computer, where any thief would look for them first. That's one way Nobel physicist Richard Feynman broke into classified safes and left goofy notes for fun while working on the atomic bomb project at Los Alamos during World War II. (See his memoirs, *Surely You're Joking, Mr. Feynman*, for the other two ways. I guess Los Alamos has had this problem for a while.) As a client told me a decade ago, the greatest threat to security isn't the packet sniffer, it's the Post-It® note.

Microsoft Passport is a one-step secure login service.

Microsoft .NET Passport (*http://www.passport.com*) is an attempt to provide a universal one-step secure login procedure. It's very much like the forms-based authentication mechanism described in the preceding section, except that Microsoft's Passport Web servers handle the storing and verifying of user IDs and passwords. A user can go to the Passport Web site and create a passport, essentially a user ID and password stored on Microsoft's central server farm. When the user requests a page from a site that uses Passport authentication, that site looks for a Passport cookie in the request. If it doesn't find one, it redirects the request to Passport's own site, where the user enters her ID and password and receives a Passport cookie. Subsequent browser requests to any Passport-compliant site will use that cookie until the user logs out. The process is illustrated in Figure 3-26. A user can thus use the same user ID and password pair at any participating site. This scheme could greatly simplify the proliferation problem and make many users' lives easier, with a net gain in security.

Passport also allows a user to store personal information that he wants to easily provide to the Web sites that he visits. For example, a user's passport can contain snail mail addresses to allow Web sites to automate the procedures of filling out delivery forms; even credit card numbers for making purchases. The idea seems to be to make Amazon.com's fantastically successful (and patented) one-click ordering available to any willing site. You can see a Passport Express Purchase button on sites such as Crutchfield.com or RadioShack.com.

Passport can also contain information such as addresses and credit cards.

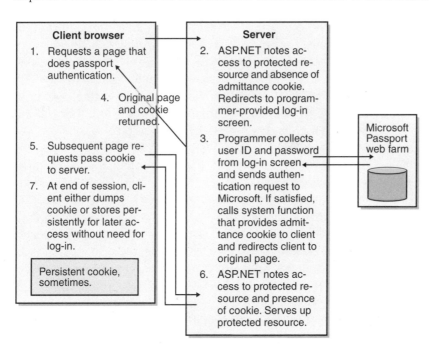

Figure 3-26   Passport authentication.

Acceptance by businesses depends on acceptance by consumers, in a circular fashion.

Will users find the convenience of Passport compelling enough to get one? It depends on how many sites accept a Passport, which in turn depends on how many customers have them. It's essentially impossible to deal with Microsoft on line without acquiring one. In addition to automatically assigning Passports to all MSN.com and Hotmail users, Microsoft just last week insisted that I supply them with my Passport ("click here to sign up if you don't have one") before they would play me a "Sounds-like" radio station based on an online music clip. While Microsoft claims a user base of 165 million Passport accounts today, no one outside of Microsoft is sure how many of these accounts are active, or what percentage of them contains express purchase information. What about customers who hold a religious loathing for Microsoft? I don't think Larry Ellison will ever request a Passport, nor will Janet Reno. Are these customers few enough that sites are willing to ignore them, or perhaps support Passport side by side with a non-Passport login?

Passport has been slow to catch on outside of Microsoft.

You would think that such a useful idea would be wildly popular, but Passport hasn't quite caught on yet outside of Microsoft. According to Passport's own Web site, only 51 sites support Passport authentication at the time of this writing (February 10, 2002), of which 16 belong to Microsoft. The same site lists only 71 online merchants that accept Passport express purchase, up from 65 when I wrote the previous edition of this book a year ago. And of these sites, almost a quarter of those I examined (5 of 22, specifically Pro-Flowers, Smart Bargains, South Bay Software, Spencer Gifts, and Starbucks) either didn't have their Passport implementations running yet or had hidden them so cleverly that I couldn't find them. (Victoria's Secret's site doesn't use the Passport icon, hiding the capability behind a small text link, but I found it after a VERY careful search taking me to every page on their site.)

The future of Passport depends on acceptance by the business community.

Clearly, Passport hasn't crossed over to the mainstream yet. Part of the problem might be that Microsoft requires a licensing agreement to use Passport and charges fees for some of its services. Although the fees are currently waived for basic authentication, businesses might be worried about committing to such a scheme and seeing prices rise later. They might also be worried about outsourcing such an important piece of their online software presence. Since it's not under their control, how can they be sure it won't crash, or even slow below acceptable limits? How many would fear a repetition of January 23, 2001, when a boneheaded Microsoft technician made an incorrect DNS entry that blocked access to most Microsoft sites, including Passport, for almost a day? (I wonder if that technician had to use Notepad to edit a raw XML file, in which case the problem might have been avoided with a dedicated configuration tool.) And what about a falling out later? How could a Web company tell Microsoft to go to hell if Microsoft holds its login data?

The basic problem hindering the advance of Passport is customers' willingness (or lack thereof) to allow Microsoft to hold their authentication data. I discussed Passport while teaching a class on .NET in a European country in September 2001. (Before.) I asked if any of the students' companies had considered using Passport for basic authentication. Students representing three separate banks said that they had looked at it for their customer Web sites, but decided not to use it. The student with the best English explained, the others nodding agreement, that "As banks, the basic commodity we sell is trust. Would you trust your brother to hold your money? No, [he must know my brother] but you trust us [he must NOT know my bank, whom I trust only because I owe them far more money in loans than they owe me in deposits]. We did research and focus groups, and found that an uncomfortable [he wouldn't quantify it] percentage of our customers would feel that we had betrayed their trust if we let Microsoft hold their authentication data instead of keeping it ourselves. They worry about it getting hacked, and they worry about it being used without their permission. I'm not necessarily saying that they're correct to worry about this, and I'm not necessarily saying that we're any better on our own, but like it or not, that IS how our customers told us they feel. So if we don't want them to think that we've done to them the worst thing that a bank can do, betray their trust, we can't use it, and that's the end of that."

Public distrust of Microsoft hinders widespread acceptance of Passport.

Microsoft seems finally to be getting the message. Bill Gates sent a company-wide e-mail on January 15, 2002, announcing that what he called "Trustworthy Computing" was Microsoft's highest priority. Trustworthy Computing, he wrote, was composed of availability, security, and privacy. "… ensuring .NET is a platform for Trustworthy Computing is more important than any other part of our work. If we don't do this, people simply won't be willing—or able—to take advantage of all the other great work we do." I've said for years that Microsoft needed to change priorities; that spending one single developer day, nay, one single developer minute, on a paper clip's blinking eyes before plugging every possible security hole and fixing every possible crash is to worship false gods. I'm ecstatic (OK, I'm a geek) that they finally seem to be doing it. How far and how quickly Trustworthy Computing (TC?) will go, and how much and how quickly the market will believe it, we'll just have to wait and see. Because of its late-breaking nature, I'll discuss this more in my chapter on .NET My Services, available on this book's Web site. But I see a major turn in the right direction, and I'm glad of it. Now tell those airlines, OK?

Bill Gates has declared "Trustworthy Computing" to be Microsoft's top priority.

Passport is an interesting idea, and the market will determine its success or failure, as it should. I would not choose it as my sole authentication mechanism today, but I'd give serious thought to offering it as an option side by

ASP.NET includes prefabricated support for Passport authentication.

side with non-Passport alternatives. It will make the lives of some unknown (until you do it) percentage of your users easier, which should bring you more money, especially if your competitors don't do it. You'll find that the prefabricated support in ASP.NET makes it quite easy. You set the authentication mode to Passport in the web.config file. You will have to download the Passport SDK, sign a licensing agreement, and then write some simple code that delegates the authentication process to Passport.

Authorization

Once we've authenticated the user, we need to check whether the user is authorized to do what he's trying to do.

Once the authentication process is complete, we know who the user is or know that the user is anonymous. We now need to decide whether the user should be allowed to see the page he is requesting. This is called *authorization*. You can perform authorization administratively by restricting access to pages in your ASP.NET application, or you can perform it programmatically at run time.

You can administratively specify which users are allowed to view various pages by making entries in the web.config files for specific pages or directories.

ASP.NET contains good support for controlling access to .ASPX pages. You can administratively limit access to pages by making entries in your application's web.config files, as shown in Figure 3-27.

```
<!-- Authorization

    This allows a user named Simba, and any users belonging to the
    role Doctors, to access pages in this directory (and any
    subdirectories that don't override this setting in their own
    web.config files).
-->

<authorization>
    <allow users="Simba" roles="Doctors" />
    <deny users="*" />
</authorization>
```

Figure 3-27   Authorization entries in a web.config file.

The *<authorization>* section contains *<allow>* and *<deny>* elements that respectively allow and deny[1] the specified users and members of the specified roles (groups of users) access to pages in the directories to which the web.config files apply. These elements can also accept a *verb* attribute (not shown) so that you can allow some users to view the page with a get operation but forbid them to post anything back to the server. Although

---

1. Well, duh!

web.config files apply to an entire directory (and its subdirectories unless overridden lower down), you can administratively restrict access to a single file by using the *<location>* element (not shown).

When a user requests a page, ASP.NET applies the rules specified in the web.config file in the order in which they appear until it finds a rule that tells it whether to grant or deny the requesting user access to the requested page. If ASP.NET can't tell from the entries made in that file, it will look in the web.config file in that directory's parent and so on until it reaches the master ASP.NET machine.config file discussed previously. That file, by default, grants access to all requests. So if you don't want people to see a certain file, you'll have to explicitly put in a *<deny>* element. In the example shown in Figure 3-27, ASP.NET will first apply the *<allow>* element. If the user is named "Simba" or is a member of a role named "Doctors," access is granted and the checking process ends. If neither of these tests is true, ASP.NET applies the next rule, which says to deny access to everybody (the * character). ASP.NET will fail the request, and the checking process will end. In this way, only Doctors and Simba can view the pages of this subdirectory. Note that when using Windows authentication on a domain, you must prepend the domain name onto the role or user name in order for ASP.NET to recognize it, as shown in Figure 3-28.

> ASP.NET applies the administrative access rules in the order in which they appear.

```
<!-- Authorization

    This does the same thing as the previous example, except
    user ID and role names are prefixed with the domain name so as to
    work correctly with Windows authentication on a domain.
-->

<authorization>
    <allow users="REDHOOKESB0\Simba"/>
    <allow roles="REDHOOKESB0\Doctors"/>
    <deny users="*" />
</authorization>
```

Figure 3-28   Web.config file showing authorization entries for domain users using Windows authentication.

Since it is likely that our Web site will be used by many anonymous users—those who have not been authenticated—we need a way of specifying what they are allowed to do. The question mark character (?) denotes anonymous users. You use it exactly like any other name or the * character. You can see an example in Figure 3-24, the web.config file used for forms-based authentication. It says that unauthenticated users aren't allowed to

> The "?" character allows you to set permissions for unauthenticated users.

view pages in that directory, thereby forcing them to the login form to become authenticated.

Most real-life authorization works with roles, which are groups of users.

ASP.NET allows you to authorize either individual users or entire roles. Most real-life installations perform little or no authorization on an individual user basis; it's almost always done on a group basis. For example, a hospital prescription application might allow physician's assistants to prescribe Tylenol, but only licensed doctors to prescribe controlled narcotics. An administrator will set permissions for each role, and add individual users to or remove them from role membership as required.

ASP.NET automatically determines role membership when you use Windows authentication.

When you use Windows authentication, ASP.NET automatically recognizes a role as any standard Windows user group set up by the administrator. Every user assigned to that group is a member of the role. You don't have to program anything, recognition just automatically happens. When you use forms or Passport authentication, however, the definition of a role becomes much more difficult. ASP.NET doesn't know how your user data is stored or what constitutes role membership in your application. You therefore have to write your own code and plug it into the ASP.NET environment to tell it which role(s) a user belongs to when it asks.

I've written a sample program that does this, which you can download from the book's Web site. The application file Global.asax contains handlers for application-level events. I've added code to the handler for the *AuthenticateRequest* event. Somewhat confusingly named, this event gets called at the beginning of each page request when ASP.NET has already discovered the user's identity and authenticated it by whatever means you have told it to use. This is your code's chance to make any changes, and where you have to place the code that tells ASP.NET the roles to which a user belongs. The code is shown in Figure 3-29. We check to see if the user has been authenticated by ASP.NET. If so, we create a new object of type *GenericPrincipal*, which contains the user's ID that we've been given as well as the roles to which we have decided the user belongs, and set it into ASP.NET.

How do we know at this juncture what roles this user belongs to? I could certainly do my own lookup from within the event handler, based on the user ID I've been given. But this could involve an expensive database lookup and possibly a network round-trip happening every time a page request comes in, so we'd like a faster way. The sample program accomplishes this by placing the role strings in the cookie itself when it's first issued, at login time. The code is shown in Figure 3-30. The function *MyOwnGetRole* looks up user names and comes back with a role string. I've hardwired users named Seuss and Kevorkian to members of the role Doctors, and users named Ratched and Houlihan to members of the role Nurses. In order to store this information in the cookie, I have to manually create my admission ticket, placing the role string into an element called *UserData* that exists for this purpose. The sample code demonstrates the degree of control that I have over the admission ticket cookie, setting its persistence and expiration time. As I described previously, my *AuthenticateRequest* event code reads the user data from the cookie, thereby providing me the list of roles to which my user belongs. Since every forms authentication program that wants to use role-based security needs to write this code, I wish Microsoft had provided a pre-fabricated implementation of it. Maybe in the next version.

```
Sub Application_AuthenticateRequest(ByVal sender As Object, _
                                    ByVal e As EventArgs)

    ' If ASP.NET has figured out who the user is

    If (Not HttpContext.Current.User Is Nothing) Then

        ' If the user has been authenticated by means of forms,
        ' and thus contains the admission ticket in a cookie

        If (TypeOf (HttpContext.Current.User.Identity) _
            Is System.Web.Security.FormsIdentity) Then

            ' Fetch the object giving the identity of the user

            Dim id As System.Web.Security.FormsIdentity
            id = HttpContext.Current.User.Identity

            ' Fetch the authentication ticket from this identity object

            Dim ticket As System.Web.Security.FormsAuthenticationTicket
            ticket = id.Ticket

            ' Create a new object identifying the user. Pass the role
            ' strings that we placed in the UserData section of the
            ' ticket back in the logon form where we issued it.

            Dim NewPrincipal As New _
                System.Security.Principal.GenericPrincipal( _
                id, New String() {ticket.UserData})

            ' Place the new principal object, carrying the roles, into
            ' the context to identify the user in subsequent processing
            ' of this request.
```

Figure 3-29   Global.asax.vb code to set role membership on a user's page request.

Figure 3-29 *(continued)*

```
            HttpContext.Current.User = NewPrincipal

        End If
    End If
End Sub
```

```
Private Sub Button1_Click(ByVal sender As System.Object, _
                     ByVal e As System.EventArgs) _
                     Handles Button1.Click

    If (TextBox2.Text = "") Then

        ' Create new ticket

        Dim ticket As New System.Web.Security.FormsAuthenticationTicket( _
            1, TextBox1.Text, Now, Now.AddYears(10), True, _
            MyOwnGetRole(TextBox1.Text))

        ' Get the encrypted representation suitable for placing
        ' in an HTTP cookie

        Dim cookieStr As String = _
            System.Web.Security.FormsAuthentication.Encrypt(ticket)

        ' Place ticket in cookie

        Dim cookie As New _
            HttpCookie( _
            System.Web.Security.FormsAuthentication.FormsCookieName, _
            cookieStr)
        Response.Cookies.Add(cookie)

        ' redirect to the URL user asked for

        Dim returnURL As String = Request("ReturnURL")
        Response.Redirect(returnURL, False)

    Else
        Label4.Text = "Invalid credentials, try again"
    End If
End Sub
```

Figure 3-30 Code to place role membership in authentication cookie for later use.

Administratively restricting access on a per-page basis is fine, but sometimes your application requires finer granularity. For example, several classes of user might need access to a prescription form page. Suppose that members of the role Doctors can prescribe morphine, but members of the role Nurses can only prescribe aspirin. You could provide two separate pages, administratively restricting access to the morphine page to doctors, but this would require constant page redesign as drugs change their prescription status. It would be much easier to check in the middle tier. Your page code can find out who a user is by accessing the member variable *Page.User*. This object contains a method called *IsInRole*, which you can call to see if the currently authenticated user is a member of the specified role. The page is shown in Figure 3-31, and the code in Figure 3-32. If you'd like finer granularity, you can access the object *Page.User.Identity*, which contains the user's name.

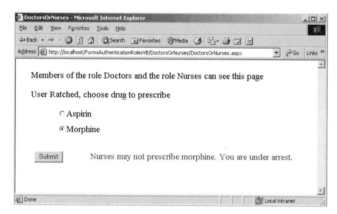

Figure 3-31   Sample application for forms role authentication.

```
Private Sub Button1_Click(ByVal sender As System.Object, _
                    ByVal e As System.EventArgs) _
                    Handles Button1.Click

    ' User wants to prescribe aspirin. Our business logic allows this for
    ' the roles Doctors and Nurses. Since these are the only two roles
    ' allowed to see this page, the prescription is automatically approved

    If (RadioButton1.Checked) Then

        Label3.Text = "Doctors and Nurses can both prescribe " & _
                    "aspirin. Prescription approved."
    Else
```

Figure 3-32   Code to discover the role a user belongs to.

```
' User clicked button to prescribe morphine. Doctors are allowed
' to do this, but Nurses are not. Check the role of the user.
' Approve prescription if user is a Doctor, fail if it's a Nurse.

If User.IsInRole("Doctors") Then
    Label3.Text = "Because you are a member of the role " & _
                        "'Doctors', your prescription is approved"
Else
    Label3.ForeColor = Color.Red
    Label3.Text = "Nurses may not prescribe morphine. " & _
                        "You are under arrest."
End If


    End If
End Sub
```

Identity

Your Web site is usually the middle tier of a three-tier system, mediating access to a data tier.

Your Web pages usually represent the middle tier of a three-tier system, mediating access to a database behind it (the data tier). The middle tier performs business logic, such as determining whether the user attempting to prescribe morphine is a licensed doctor. If this business logic is successful, the middle tier will communicate with the data tier to subtract morphine from the pharmacy inventory and to add another item to the patient's billing statement. If not, the middle tier will probably generate a fascinating game to keep the user occupied while it calls the police.

The security identity of the Web server process is important.

The back-end data tier almost certainly has its own security mechanisms. All commercial databases allow administrators to set access permissions of various granularity, specifying which users are allowed access to various databases and tables and which are not. Even the NTFS file system allows an administrator to specify which users or groups of users are allowed to perform which operations on which files and directories. The operation of these back ends depends critically on what the data tier considers to be the identity of the user making the request for services.

The data tier usually trusts the middle tier to perform authorization.

One security mechanism, and probably the one that you'll wind up using, is called the *trusted user* model. In this model, the server process runs with a particular identity, say, PharmacyApp, known as the trusted user. The data tier is configured to allow this user to do anything in the database that it might need to in order to get its work done. For example, the trusted user identity used for the pharmacy application will have permission to make entries in the pharmacy inventory tables and the patient billing tables but probably not the patient census tables or the employee payroll records. The data tier trusts the middle tier server to have done all the authorization checking that needs to happen—for example, to have checked that the doctor's license is current—so the data tier doesn't perform a second authorization. You trust your spouse to go through your wallet, so you don't bother asking what the money is for. This relationship is shown in Figure 3-33. You specify the identity of your server process via the *<identity>* element in your application's web.config file, as shown in Figure 3-34.

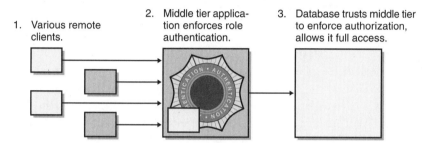

1. Various remote clients.

2. Middle tier application enforces role authentication.

3. Database trusts middle tier to enforce authorization, allows it full access.

Figure 3-33   Trusted user model of authorization.

```
<identity impersonate="false"
          userName="MyDomain\MyUsername
          password="MyPassword" />
```

Figure 3-34   Web.config file specifying server process identity.

Not every database installation is comfortable with this approach. Many databases were designed and database administrators trained before three-tier programming became popular. Particularly with legacy systems, it often happens that the database layer contains security checks or audit trails that depend on the actual database entry being made under the network identity of the base client.

> Sometimes the trusted user model doesn't fit.

In this case, if you're using Windows authentication, you can fall back on the older *impersonation-delegation* model, as used by original ASP. In this model, the .ASPX page code takes on the identity of ("impersonates") the authenticated user (or uses a special identity designated for anonymous users). The page code then attempts to access the data-tier resource, and the resource itself, say, SQL Server, performs the authorization, checking to see whether the user is allowed access. This case is shown in Figure 3-35.

> In this case, the Web server can impersonate the client, if you're using Windows authentication.

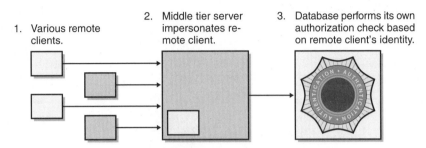

1. Various remote clients.

2. Middle tier server impersonates remote client.

3. Database performs its own authorization check based on remote client's identity.

Figure 3-35 Impersonation/delegation model of authorization.

The impersonation-delegation model is expensive in terms of performance.

While this approach may sound attractive, it is expensive in terms of performance. It requires two authentications instead of one: the first when ASP.NET authenticates the user prior to impersonating him, and the second when the database authenticates the server object's current impersonating identity. Furthermore, when authorization rejects a user, it does so rather late in the process. You've already gone down three tiers instead of two and made two network hops instead of one. It's better that you notice that you forgot your wallet when you arrive at the supermarket instead of after you've shopped and waited in the checkout line. It's better still to notice it when you first get in your car.

A Web server can impersonate a client programmatically, if using Windows authentication.

The Web server impersonates a client in one of two ways. Original ASP automatically impersonated the client every time a request was made. ASP.NET does not do this by default, but you can turn on this functionality in the web.config file by setting the *impersonation* attribute shown in Figure 3-36 to True. Alternatively, you can impersonate the client programmatically by calling the function *System.Security.Principal.WindowsIdentity.GetCurrent().Impersonate.*

```
<identity>
    <impersonation enable="true" />
</identity>
```

Figure 3-36 Web.config setting for automatic impersonation.

Process Management

One of the main features that we want in a Web server is unattended 24/7 operation. This level of service is a problem developers never really had to address in writing desktop applications. For example, memory leaks in a Solitaire game that runs for 5 minutes at a time (OK, 2 hours) probably won't waste enough memory to hurt anything. But if I kept the Solitaire game running for a year, redealing instead of closing it, any memory leaks would eventually exhaust the process's address space and cause a crash.

Robustness under load is a very important feature of a Web server.

That sort of robustness is very hard to develop, partly because it takes a long time to test. The only way to find out whether something runs for two weeks under load is to run it under load for two weeks. And when the crash does happen, it's often caused by a banana peel dropped days earlier, which is essentially impossible to find at the time of the crash.

It's also extremely difficult to develop. That figures.

I once (13 years ago) worked on an application that ran in a major bank. It was a DOS-based system (remember DOS?) that would usually run all day, but it just couldn't run for a week without crashing and we couldn't wring it out so that it could. I had the bright idea of putting a watchdog timer card into the machine that our software would periodically reset while it ran. If the timer ever actually expired without being reset, it would automatically reboot the system, sort of a "dead-geek" switch. The bank balked at installing such a god-awful kludge (we probably shouldn't have told them; we probably should have just done it and smiled) and instead agreed to have the administrator reboot the system every night.

Most software needs periodic restarting.

Original ASP kept a user process running indefinitely. Any bugs or memory leaks in any of the user code would accumulate and eventually cause crashes. ASP.NET recognizes that user code probably isn't going to be perfect. It therefore allows an administrator to configure the server to periodically shut down and restart worker processes.

ASP.NET supports process recycling to continue working robustly in the face of imperfect user code.

You configure process recycling using the *<processModel>* element of the machine-level machine.config file, as shown in Figure 3-37. I wish Microsoft had allowed process model configuration on a per-application basis, but they haven't at the time of this writing. You can tell ASP.NET to shut down your worker process and launch a new one after a specified amount of time (*timeout* attribute), a specified number of page requests (*requestLimit* attribute), or if the percentage of system memory it consumes grows too large (*memoryLimit* attribute). While not removing the need to make your code as robust as possible, this will allow you to run with a few memory leaks without rebooting the server every day or two. You can see that the process model contains other configurable capabilities as well.

You configure process recycling in the machine.config file.

```
<processModel
        enable="true"
        timeout="infinite"
        idleTimeout="infinite"
        shutdownTimeout="0:00:05"
        requestLimit="infinite"
        requestQueueLimit="5000"
        memoryLimit="80"
        webGarden="false"
        cpuMask="0xffffffff"
        userName=""
        password=""
        logLevel="errors"
        clientConnectedCheck="0:00:05"
        />
```

Figure 3-37 Machine.config file showing process recycling settings.

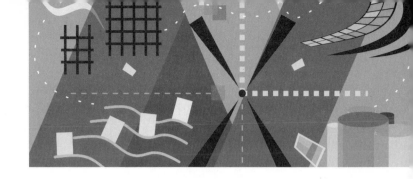

4

.NET Web Services

Now, a' together, hear them lift their lesson—theirs an' mine:
"Law, Order, Duty an' Restraint, Obedience, Discipline!"
Mill, forge an' try-pit taught them that when roarin' they arose,
An' whiles I wonder if a soul was gied them wi' the blows.

> —Rudyard Kipling, writing on the mental toughness needed
> to work with high technology, "McAndrew's Hymn," 1894.

Problem Background

The primary user interaction model described so far in this book hasn't changed since the Web was created at CERN in Geneva for browsing boring physics reports. A human (or, in a famous cartoon, a dog) uses an all-purpose browser program to request a page from a server, the server decodes the request and supplies the page, the browser renders it for human viewing, and the human attempts to stay awake long enough to read it. Improved content (sports scores, pornography, Weird Al Yankovic music videos[1]) has largely solved the problem with boredom, but the final consumer of the requested data is still a human being rather than a computer program.

> The current structure of the Internet is designed to render pages for humans to read, not to provide data for client programs to process.

The great thing about the Internet, though, is that it's everywhere. Every intelligent device on the planet is connected to it, or soon will be. Users could reap great benefits if Web servers could provide data to programs running on all these devices as easily as they do pages for humans to look at. For example, developers could greatly enhance the user experience by writing an excellent, dedicated user interface that runs on a client machine rather than

> We could reap enormous benefits if dedicated client programs could use, request, and understand data from the Internet as easily as humans can.

---

1. See his hilarious spoof of Star Wars at www.sagabegins.com.

relying on a mediocre browser interface provided by the server. Think how much easier it is to process e-mail in Microsoft Outlook's dedicated user interface than it is in Hotmail's generic browser-based interface. (Of course, we could also screw up this opportunity by writing stupid UIs—death to the dancing paper clip!) The development of dedicated UIs would also improve server performance by moving the formatting of presentations to the client machine, having 1000 clients doing their own formatting instead of one server doing it for 1000 clients. Providing data from the Internet to a range of devices would also allow programs that don't have any user interface, such as a bank auditing program, to use the ubiquitous connectivity of the Internet without having to divide their program logic into page requests. Likewise, we'd allow the forthcoming generation of non-PC Internet devices, such as a telephone that uses the Internet instead of standard phone lines, to do the same thing.

Dedicating hardware and software to specific tasks makes them easier to use than a single generic device for everything.

The situation today, with Internet access primarily available through a generic browser program, is similar to the early part of the twentieth century, when electricity first started arriving in United States households. Then, electric motors weren't usually built into household appliances. Sears, for example, sold a stand-alone electric motor (for $8.75) that you could connect to different appliances, such as your sewing machine, mixer, or fan.[1] This situation was difficult because you had to connect and configure the motor before you could use any appliance. You could probably afford only one motor, so you had to choose between sewing and fanning if your clothes needed mending on a hot day. And since the motor had to run with all kinds of different appliances, it didn't serve any of them particularly well. As motors got smaller and cheaper, they were built into individual appliances, to the point that today it's difficult to buy a toothbrush or a carving knife that doesn't contain at least one. Modern appliances are easy to use because the motor and its infrastructure (power supply, linkages, and so on) are optimized for each specific task and hidden from you. You don't think about the motors; you just turn your appliance on and use its dedicated human interface.

The same sort of seismic shift is just now beginning in Internet programming. Just as motors got built into appliances, so Internet access will soon be built directly into every program anyone ever writes. You won't use a generic browser except when you feel like browsing generically. Instead, you will use dedicated programs that are optimized for accomplishing specific tasks. You won't think about the program's Internet access, as you don't really think about the motors in your appliances (except when they break, and the same will apply to dedicated Internet access programs). An early example of this

---

1. You can see a picture of this Sears catalog offering on page 50 of *The Invisible Computer*, by Donald Norman (MIT Press, 1999).

type of program is Napster, which allows you to search the hard drives of thousands of participating users for music files that meet specified criteria, and then download the ones you like. A screen shot of this program, showing a search for songs freely and publicly released on the Internet by the artists, is shown in Figure 4-1. The dedicated user interface of a multiplayer game is another example of hidden Internet access. And the latest edition of Microsoft Money does a good job of seamlessly blending Web (current stock quotes, latest balances) and desktop content (financial plans you create locally).

Easy programmatic Web access would mean that developers could compose their applications from services available on the Web, as they now compose applications from prebuilt components available on their local PCs. The designer of a word processor, which most people today would consider strictly a desktop application, might not provide a spelling checker with the application or might supply only a rudimentary one. For more sophisticated spelling or definition services, the word processor could use the online edition of the *Oxford English Dictionary*, whose Web site, *oed.com*, modestly admits that it is "the most authoritative and comprehensive dictionary of English in the world."[1] This site charges a subscription fee and is currently available only to humans with generic browsers. If the OED provided seamless access to programs, they'd probably sell a lot more subscriptions. Maybe the word processor vendor could get a cut of the subscription fee. If they were really smart, they'd provide a seamless free trial for a few months so you got dependent on it and then take it away if you didn't start paying.

Application designers will compose their applications from services available on the Web, as they compose them today from prebuilt components on a user's machine.

---

1. I am currently trying to get the OED to accept a word that I coined in my Byte.com column of August 23, 1999. The word is MINFU, patterned after the military acronyms SNAFU and FUBAR, which have crossed into general usage. In polite company, MINFU stands for MIcrosoft Nomenclature Foul-Up, and it happens a lot. For example, referring to in-place activation of an embedded object as "visual editing" (to distinguish it from tactile editing, I guess, or olfactory editing) is a MINFU. The whole COM-OLE-COM-ActiveX-COM nomenclature debacle was and to this day remains a giant MINFU. When I wrote to the OED, they politely said, in part, "...we will be looking for more general currency before we could consider including it in the OED." So far, I've gotten a couple of authors to use it, most notably David Chappell. I hope you'll all use it in your writing and send me a link to it, which I'll forward to the OED. You don't have to credit me, just use it. If I can get it into the Microsoft Press style guide, I'll have it made.

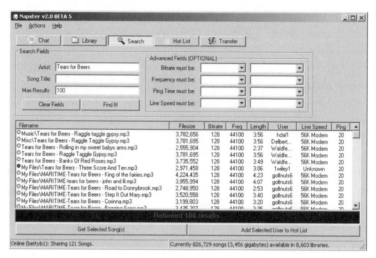

Figure 4-1   User interface of Napster, an application containing dedicated Internet access.

Most existing communication technologies only work with other instances of themselves.

To develop programs of this type, programmers need to be able to quickly and easily (which in turn means cheaply) write code that communicates with other programs over the Internet. The idea isn't new; any number of techniques exist for this type of communication, such as RPC, DCOM, and MSMQ. Each of these techniques is cool in itself, and they all seemed like good ideas two or three years ago. However, they all share the fatal shortcoming that they only work from one similar system to another—MSMQ talks only to MSMQ, a DCOM client only to a DCOM server, and so on.

We need universal, program-to-program, function-based communication over the existing Internet pathway.

What we really need is universal programmatic access to the Internet—some way for a program on one box to call a function on any other box written by anyone. This access has to be independent not only of the operating system but also of the program's internal implementations. (C++ or Basic? Which vendor? Which version? We can barely solve this problem on a single desktop.) And it has to be easy to use, or no one will be able to afford the programming time to take advantage of it.

Solution Architecture

International air traffic control faces a problem similar to universal Internet access.

The problem of universal programmatic access to the Internet is similar to the problem faced by designers of the international air traffic control system. A randomly changing set of heterogeneous nodes (different types of aircraft) needs to talk to fixed servers (control towers) and each other. Their internal programming (the flight crews' thoughts) works in all kinds of different, incompatible languages (Thai, Norwegian, Californian). Communication between the flight crews, aircraft, and control towers has to work right or terrible things happen, such as on March 27, 1977, at Tenerife, when two 747s collided during takeoff because of misunderstood tower communications and 583 people died.

Solving the problem requires agreement among all parties operating aircraft. Given the size (all aircraft operators in the world) and heterogeneity (rich and poor passenger airlines, cargo carriers, general aviation, military, smugglers, and so on) of this group, the only approach that stands any chance of working is to standardize on the lowest common denominator in two critical areas. First, as the mechanism for physically transmitting information from one party to another, aircraft use VHF radios on designated frequencies. Second, air traffic control requires a standardized way of encoding the information transmitted. By international agreement, all pilots and control towers are required to use only English, even Air France landing at Charles de Gaulle International Airport in Paris (which annoys the heck out of them).

> The air traffic control problem was solved by agreeing on a lowest common denominator, the English language.

Like the solution for the air traffic control problem, the only way to deal with the enormous numbers of heterogeneous entities on the Internet is to use the lowest common denominator. When we decide how to transfer bytes from one box to another, we need to use something that every box on the Internet has, analogous to the VHF radio that every aircraft carries. The most common Internet transfer protocol is HTTP (Hypertext Transfer Protocol), which is used today by essentially all Web browsers to fetch the pages they display. We also need a lowest common denominator for encoding the information that we transfer with HTTP. As air traffic control uses English, our universal scheme will use XML (eXtensible Markup Language) for encoding the data sent from one party to another.

> The lowest common denominator on the Internet is HTTP and XML.

Microsoft put these ideas together and came up with the concept of *XML Web services*. An XML Web service is a seamless way for objects on a server to accept incoming requests from clients using the Internet's lowest common denominator of HTTP/XML. To create an XML Web service you don't have to learn a new way to program. You simply write a .NET object as if it were being accessed directly by local clients, mark it with an attribute that says you want it to be available to Web clients, and ASP.NET does the rest. ASP.NET automatically hooks up a prefabricated infrastructure that accepts incoming requests through HTTP and maps them to calls on your object, as shown in Figure 4-2. When you roll your objects into an XML Web service, they can

> An XML Web service seamlessly connects your .NET objects to incoming HTTP requests.

work with anyone on the Web that speaks HTTP and XML, which should be everybody in the universe, no matter what type of operating system and runtime environment they're running in. You don't have to write the infrastructure that deals with Web communication; the .NET Framework provides it for you.

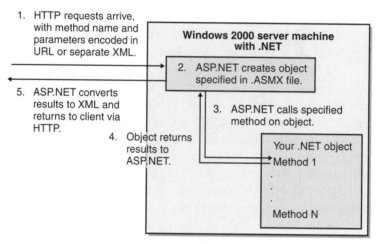

1. HTTP requests arrive, with method name and parameters encoded in URL or separate XML.

Windows 2000 server machine with .NET

2. ASP.NET creates object specified in .ASMX file.

5. ASP.NET converts results to XML and returns to client via HTTP.

3. ASP.NET calls specified method on object.

4. Object returns results to ASP.NET.

Your .NET object
Method 1
.
.
.
Method N

Figure 4-2   Server-side view of XML Web services.

.NET also provides proxy classes that make it easy to write an XML Web service client by hiding the details of Internet communications.

On the client side, .NET provides proxy classes that allow easy, function-based access to the XML Web services provided by any server that accepts HTTP requests, as shown in Figure 4-3. A developer tool reads the description of the XML Web service and generates a proxy class containing functions in whatever language you use to develop the client. When your client calls one of these functions, the proxy class creates an HTTP request and sends it to the server. When the response comes back from the server, the proxy class parses the results and returns them from the function. This allows your function-based client to seamlessly interact with any Web server that speaks HTTP and XML, which, again, should be everybody.

0.   At programming time, a developer generates proxy
     object code from a description of an XML Web service.

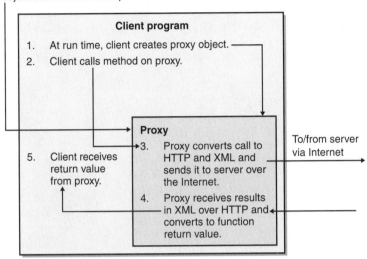

Figure 4-3   Client-side view of XML Web services.

Simplest Example: Writing an XML Web Service

As I always do when trying to learn or explain a new piece of technology, I've written the simplest sample program that I could think of to demonstrate XML Web services. The program exposes a single method, called *GetTime*, that provides the current time on the server machine in the form of a string, either with or without the seconds digits. You can download the sample code for this service from this book's Web site (*www.introducingmicrosoft.net*) and follow along with this description.

An XML Web service example begins here.

I wrote this XML Web service in the form of an ASP.NET page. I first installed the .NET Framework SDK, a free download from *http:// msdn.microsoft.com*. I then used the normal Windows 2000 Internet Information Services (IIS) administrative tools to set up a virtual directory pointing to the folder in which I would do my XML Web service file development. Then I wrote my ASP.NET code in a file named TimeServiceVB.asmx (or TimeServiceCS.asmx) on my server. You don't need Visual Studio for this; in fact, I did the whole thing in Notepad. The program is shown in Figure 4-4.

You don't need Visual Studio to write an XML Web service; I wrote this one in Notepad.

```
<%@ WebService Language="VB" Class="TimeService"%>

' The previous header line tells ASP.NET that this file contains
' a Web service written in the Visual Basic language
' and that the name of the class providing that service
' is TimeService.

' Import the namespaces (think of them as references)
' required for a Web service.

Imports System
Imports System.Web.Services

' Declare a new class for our new service. It must inherit
' from the system-provided base class WebService.

Public Class TimeService : Inherits WebService

' Place our functions in the class.
' Mark them as WebMethods.

Public Function <WebMethod()> GetTime (ShowSeconds as Boolean) _
    As String

    ' Perform the business logic of our function.
    ' Find current time, format as requested, and
    ' return the string.

    If (ShowSeconds = TRUE) Then
        return DateTime.Now.ToLongTimeString
    Else
        return DateTime.Now.ToShortTimeString
    End if

End Function

End Class
```

Figure 4-4   A basic XML Web service.

Your ASP.NET page specifies which .NET object class to use for the XML Web service.

While this program is quite simple, it contains a few constructs that are probably new to you, so let's go over it section by section. The program starts with the standard ASP.NET salutation, <%@ %>. In it we have the directive *WebService*, which tells ASP.NET that the code on the page should be exposed as an XML Web service. The *Language* attribute tells ASP which language compiler to use for the code on the page. I've used Visual Basic because it's familiar to the greatest number of my readers (although you'll also find a C# version with the sample files). ASP.NET will use Visual Basic .NET to compile the code. You don't have to install Visual Studio; all the language compilers come with the .NET Framework SDK. The *Class* attribute tells ASP.NET which object class to activate for incoming requests addressed to this service.

The rest of the page contains the code that implements the class. I used the *Imports* directive, a new feature of Visual Basic .NET, which tells the compiler to "import the namespaces," as I described in Chapter 2. *Namespace* is a fancy way to refer to the path that leads to a description of a set of prefabricated functionality. It is conceptually identical to a reference in your Visual Basic 6 projects. Since ASP.NET will compile this example's code "just-in-time" when a request arrives from a client, I don't have a project in which to set these references. I have to explicitly add them to the code. The names following *Imports* tell the engine which sets of functionality to include the references for. In this case, *System* and *System.Web.Services* are the ones containing the prefabricated plumbing used in XML Web services. Stop me if I get too technical.

> ASP.NET will automatically compile your Visual Basic code the first time a request comes in for it.

The next line defines the name of our class. You've seen and written many classes in Visual Basic, and this one is very similar. My program uses a new keyword at the end of the line that reads *Public Class TimeService : Inherits WebService*. One of the main enhancements to Visual Basic .NET is its support for an object-oriented programming technique called *inheritance*, which I described in Chapter 2 and which you will grow to like. When I say that my new *TimeService* class inherits from the *WebService* class, I am telling the compiler to take all the code from the system-provided class named *WebService* (known as the *base class*) and include it in the *TimeService* class (known as the *derived class*). Think of inheritance as cutting and pasting without actually moving anything. In fact, deranged C++ and Java geeks often refer to physically cutting and pasting code as "editor inheritance." The *WebService* class is provided by the new .NET run-time library, just as many Visual Basic 6 objects were provided by the operating system. This class contains all the prefabricated plumbing required to handle the incoming HTTP requests and route them to the proper methods on your object.

> Visual Basic now supports inheritance, which allows you to easily access prefabricated system features.

Students often ask me what the difference is between importing the namespace and declaring inheritance; that is, the difference between the *Imports* and *Inherits* keywords. *Imports* brings in only the description of a set of functionality; it doesn't actually make use of it. As I said before, it's like setting a reference. *Inherits* actually takes part of the code referred to in the description and uses it. It's like *Dim As* on steroids.

You tell ASP.NET to expose your method as an XML Web service by adding an attribute to the code.

Now that we've defined our class, we need to define the methods and functions of the class. Again, doing this is very similar to the way you do this in Visual Basic 6, with one new twist: you have to add the new attribute *<WebMethod( )>* to every method that you want exposed to Web clients. This attribute tells ASP.NET that the method in which it appears is to be exposed to clients as an XML Web service. You've seen plenty of attribute-like elements in Visual Basic 6, such as *Public*, *Private*, and *Const*. Visual Basic .NET and the .NET Framework use many more of them, hence the new syntax for specifying them. Just as your class can contain public and private methods, it can contain some methods that are exposed to Web clients and others that are not.

You write your business logic in Visual Basic classes, pretty much as you've always done.

Finally, we get down to the internals of our method. The handling of times might be a little new to you; it was to me. Don't worry about it today; it's just how Visual Basic .NET deals with dates and times.

Now let's access our XML Web service from a client. ASP.NET contains good prefabricated support for this as well. If you fire up Internet Explorer 5.5 and request the ASP.NET page we just wrote, you will see the page shown in Figure 4-5.

Figure 4-5   Default screen generated by ASP.NET when you request the XML Web service base page.

ASP.NET detects the access to the XML Web service page itself (as opposed to one of the methods within the service) and responds with a page showing the list of functions supported by the service—in this case, only *GetTime*. If you click on the name of the function, ASP.NET will respond with a page that provides a test capability for this method, as shown in Figure 4-6. Enter TRUE or FALSE to tell *GetTime* whether to show the seconds digits, click Invoke, and the test page will call the specified method and return the results, as shown in Figure 4-7. You can see in the Address box that the parameters are passed in the URL and the results returned as XML. Also note that you must open the page in a way that goes through IIS, typing in a URL such as *http://localhost/[your virtual directory name]/TimeServiceVB.asmx*. If you simply double-click the page in Internet Explorer's view of your hard disk, you'll bypass IIS and ASP.NET and simply receive the text of the .ASMX page, which isn't what you're looking for.

The convenient logistical and deployment features of .NET objects, described in Chapter 2, apply to my XML Web service as well. For example, ASP.NET does not need registry entries to locate my object as COM did; instead, the URL specifies the location of my object. Updating the code is quite easy; I just copy the new file over the old one. (Try this with the sample code on your local machine.) It isn't locked as a COM server would be. I don't even have to restart my IIS server to make it notice the new file. It automatically detects the fact that the file has changed, compiles it just-in-time if necessary, and uses the new version for future object requests.

> The XML Web service is as easy to administer and deploy as other .NET objects.

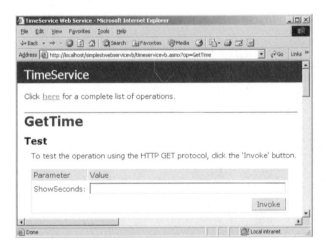

Figure 4-6   ASP.NET responds with a page like this.

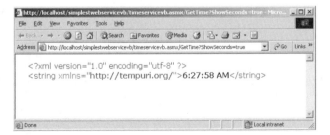

Figure 4-7   Results returned by the XML Web service.

That's all I had to do to write my XML Web service. It took only 12 lines, counting *Else* and *End If*. How much easier does it get?

Self-Description of XML Web Services: The WSDL File

XML Web services need to provide a description of their functionality to interested clients.

For programmers to develop client applications that use our XML Web service, we need to provide a description of what our service does and what a client has to say to the service to make the service perform its task. For example, a client of our XML Web service would like to know the methods the service exposes, the parameters those methods require, and the protocols they support—information conceptually similar to the type library that a standard COM component would carry. The problem with type libraries, however, is that they are Microsoft COM specific, and we want non-Microsoft systems to be able to become clients of our XML Web service. We also want to be able to write descriptions of non-Microsoft services running on non-Microsoft systems so that our Microsoft-built client applications can use those services. What we need is a universal approach, not restricted to the Microsoft world, of describing a service. (Did you ever think you'd read these words in a Microsoft book? Me neither. Different world today.) And we need this approach to be machine-readable so that intelligent development environments can make use of it (again, like type libraries).

The description of an XML Web service is provided in the form of a WSDL file. The .NET infrastructure can generate this description from your code.

The ASP.NET infrastructure can generate just such a description by examining the metadata (see Chapter 2) in the code that implements the service. The description is stored in an XML file that uses a vocabulary called WSDL (Web Service Description Language).[1] The WSDL file for an XML Web service is sometimes known as its *contract* because it lists the things that the service is capable of doing and tells you how to ask for them. You obtain the WSDL file from ASP.NET by requesting the .ASMX file with the characters *?WSDL* attached to the URL. For example, on my local machine, I obtained the file for my sample XML Web service by requesting the URL *http://localhost/ simplestwebservicevb/TimeServiceVB.asmx?WSDL*. That's what the Service Description link on the page shown in Figure 4-5 does.

---

1. You will note that many of the acronyms used in .NET aren't the TLAs (Three-Letter Acronyms; TLA itself is a TLA) you're used to seeing in most computing projects. That's because only 17,576 unique TLAs exist, and Microsoft ran out of them halfway through the project. I foresaw this problem three years ago and offered the solution of folding TLAs into CCTs (Clever Compound TLAs; CCT itself is a CCT). While the XML world seems to have adopted this idea (for example, XSL, XML Stylesheet Language, or SAX, Simple API for XML, a semisaturated CCT), Microsoft seems to have spurned it, opting instead to increase the word length to produce acronyms such as SOAP, WSDL, and UDDI. These nomenclature objects haven't been named yet, so I hereby declare them to be FLAPs, which stands for Four-Letter Acronym Packages. And, naturally, FLAP itself is a FLAP.

When you wrote COM components in Visual Basic 6 and Visual C++ 6, sometimes you wrote the component first and then wrote a type library to describe it. Other times you started with a type library describing an interface and wrote code that implemented it. WSDL can work in both of these ways as well. You can write the code first, as I've done in this sample, in which case ASP.NET will generate a WSDL file for interested clients. Alternatively, I could have written the WSDL file first, or gotten it from a third party, describing what the service should do, and then used the SDK utility program Wsdl.exe to generate a template file that implements the service that the WSDL file describes. (This approach is similar to using the *Implements* keyword in Visual Basic 6.)

Alternatively, you can write the description first and generate the code from it.

The WSDL file is somewhat complex, so I've extracted just one portion, shown in Figure 4-8, to illustrate the sorts of things that it contains. The *<schema>* element holds subelements that describe the function calls that a client can make and the responses it will receive from the server. You can see that there's an element named *GetTime*, containing a Boolean element named *ShowSeconds* that must appear exactly once. You can see that the response (return value) is in the form of a string, which is optional. Just as you usually interact with a type library by means of an interpretive viewer instead of picking apart its binary constituents, you will probably not deal with raw WSDL files unless you are writing a programming tool that digests them. Instead, you will use WSDL files through interpretive tools, such as the test page provided by ASP.NET. I'll describe some of these tools and how they help you write XML Web service clients next.

A sample excerpt of a WSDL file is shown here.

```
<s:schema elementFormDefault="qualified"
  targetNamespace="http://tempuri.org/">
    <s:element name="GetTime">
      <s:complexType>
        <s:sequence>
          <s:element minOccurs="1" maxOccurs="1" name="ShowSeconds"
            type="s:boolean" />
        </s:sequence>
      </s:complexType>
    </s:element>
    <s:element name="GetTimeResponse">
      <s:complexType>
        <s:sequence>
          <s:element minOccurs="0" maxOccurs="1" name="GetTimeResult"
            type="s:string" />
        </s:sequence>
      </s:complexType>
    </s:element>
    <s:element name="string" nillable="true" type="s:string" />
</s:schema>
```

Figure 4-8 An excerpt from a WSDL file.

In addition to the testing capacity shown previously in Figure 4-6, the same page interprets the WSDL file to show you the protocols it supports and the manner in which you must employ them in order to access the service. The screen shot in Figure 4-9 shows the portion of the page describing how to access our time service through the SOAP protocol.

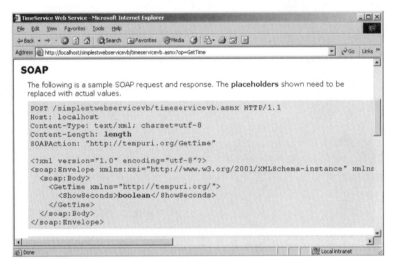

Figure 4-9   Accessing time service through SOAP.

Writing XML Web Service Clients

I found writing a client as easy as writing the service itself. The ASP.NET listener that funnels incoming requests to XML Web service objects accepts three different ways of packaging the incoming requests. These are HTTP GET, HTTP POST, and SOAP. This is conceptually similar to an aircraft control tower speaking three dialects of English, say U.S., British, and Strine (Australian). The first two approaches are present primarily for backward compatibility. New development projects will find it easier and more powerful to use SOAP, particularly when you see the prefabricated support for this protocol that Visual Studio .NET and other toolkits provide. Because of this, I'll only discuss SOAP-based clients in this book, though I'll leave HTTP GET and HTTP POST samples on the Web site.

SOAP, which stands for Simple Object Access Protocol, is an XML vocabulary that describes function calls and their parameters. A client of our sample XML Web service will format a SOAP request packet, as shown in Figure 4-10 (namespaces omitted for clarity) and send it to our XML Web service by means of an HTTP POST operation. The XML Web service will parse the packet, create the object, call the method with the specified parameters, and return a SOAP response packet, as shown in Figure 4-11. I learned the required formatting of the SOAP packets for this XML Web service by looking at the test page for this method, shown previously in Figure 4-9.

To demonstrate that you don't have to use .NET at all to write a SOAP-based XML Web service client, I've written one using Visual Basic 6. Figure 4-12 shows a screen shot of it. The sample program assembles and reads the SOAP packets using Microsoft's COM-based XML parser, and it uses the Microsoft Internet Transfer Control (again, COM-based) to do the actual HTTP communication. The code is somewhat unwieldy, so I haven't listed it in this book, but you will find it in the sample code on the book's Web site. Simply by running it, you can see the client program converting the user's input to SOAP, sending the SOAP to the server and receiving SOAP in reply, and parsing meaning from the SOAP and displaying it to the user.

XML Web service SOAP request and response packets are shown in the following figures.

```
<soap:Envelope>
  <soap:Body>
    <GetTime>
      <ShowSeconds>0</ShowSeconds>
    </GetTime>
  </soap:Body>
</soap:Envelope>
```

Figure 4-10   SOAP request packet.

```
<soap:Envelope>
  <soap:Body>
    <GetTimeResponse>
      <GetTimeResult>9:34</GetTimeResult>
    </GetTimeResponse>
  </soap:Body>
</soap:Envelope>
```

Figure 4-11   SOAP response packet.

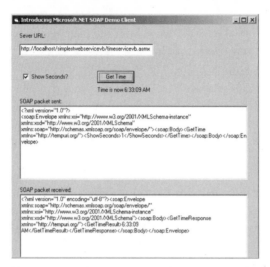

Figure 4-12 Sample application showing SOAP access to the XML Web service.

A client-side SOAP proxy class makes client applications much easier to write.

The SOAP example is quite tedious to write. It reminds me of manually writing an *IDispatch* client in classic COM in the sense that there's an awful lot of boilerplate packaging that's critical to get correct (one character off and you're hosed) but which varies little from one method to the next. As Visual C++ provided wrapper classes that took the pain out of accessing Automation objects (many Visual Basic programmers never knew it *was* painful for the C++ geeks, and the rest either didn't care or actively approved), many vendors provide tools that generate proxy wrapper classes that make writing a SOAP client for your XML Web service a trivial operation. These generators read the WSDL file that describes an XML Web service and produce a class in a high-level language containing type-safe methods for accessing the XML Web service. For example, the IBM Web Service Toolkit provides a utility that reads WSDL and produces a proxy class written in Java. The Microsoft SOAP toolkit produces COM-based proxy classes that can be used from non-.NET Microsoft code. SourceForge produces proxy classes written in Python, and SOAP::Lite produces proxy classes for Perl.

The .NET Framework SDK provides a proxy class generator.

As you might imagine, .NET comes with its own tool for generating proxy wrapper classes for the use of .NET Framework programs. The command-line utility program Wsdl.exe, which comes with the .NET Framework SDK, reads the description of the XML Web service from a WSDL file and generates a proxy for accessing its methods from the language you specify. It currently supports Visual Basic, C#, and JavaScript, but not C++. You can ask for proxies that use any of the supported transport protocols, but the default is SOAP.

I've written a sample program that demonstrates the use of the Visual Studio proxy generator. A screen shot is shown in Figure 4-13.

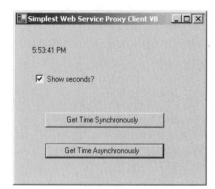

Figure 4-13   Proxy generator example.

I created a standard Windows Forms project. I then right-clicked References in Solution Explorer and selected Add Web Reference from the context menu, and the Add Web Reference dialog box appeared. I entered the address of my XML Web service page, as shown in Figure 4-14. This caused the internal browser to request the page, returning its WSDL description, shown previously in Figure 4-8. I then clicked the Add Reference button, and Visual Studio ran Wsdl.exe internally, asking for a SOAP-based proxy in the language of the project, in this case, Visual Basic. Visual Studio then displayed the namespace of the proxy class in Solution Explorer. The most informative view of it is the Class View, as shown in Figure 4-15.

Visual Studio .NET uses the proxy class generator internally.

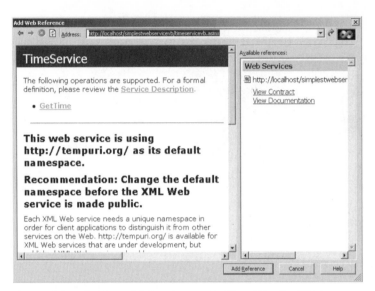

Figure 4-14   Adding a Web reference in Visual Studio .NET.

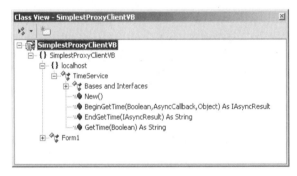

Figure 4-15   Class view of the TimeService reference.

When my client wants to access the XML Web service, I simply create an object of the proxy class and call the desired method on it, as shown in Figure 4-16. Even though it's an XML Web service call, it looks and feels as though you're creating and using any other .NET object.

```
Private Sub Button1_Click(ByVal sender As System.Object, _
                         ByVal e As System.EventArgs) _
                         Handles Button1.Click

    'Create new object of proxy class

    Dim foo As New localhost.TimeService()

    ' Call function on proxy, which accesses Web service
    ' via SOAP. Place result in label for user to see.

    Label1.Text = foo.GetTime(CheckBox1.Checked)

End Sub
```

Figure 4-16   Code accessing XML Web service by means of a proxy.

The proxy class file, named *Reference.vb*, doesn't appear in Solution Explorer, but it lives in a project subdirectory where you can examine it. Figure 4-17 shows selected portions of the code from our time service proxy. You can see that it inherits from the base class *System.Web.Services.Protocols.SoapHttpClientProtocol*. From this base class it inherits a property called *Url*, which specifies the URL of the server to which the call is directed. This property contains a default value, which it gets from the original WSDL file, but the sample program demonstrates how you can change it at run time if you want. When the client calls the named method on the proxy, the proxy calls the generic method *Invoke*, which, again, it has inherited from the base class. This method creates a SOAP packet containing the method name and parameters of the desired XML Web service method and sends it to the server over HTTP. When the SOAP response packet comes back from the server, the base class parses out the return value and returns it to the proxy, which then returns it to the client. Another useful proxy property is *Timeout*, which is the number of milliseconds that the proxy will wait for the response from the server before throwing up its hands and returning an error.

```
<System.Diagnostics.DebuggerStepThroughAttribute(), _
 System.ComponentModel.DesignerCategoryAttribute("code"), _
 System.Web.Services.WebServiceBindingAttribute(Name:="TimeServiceSoap", _
 [Namespace]:="http://tempuri.org/")> _
Public Class TimeService
    Inherits System.Web.Services.Protocols.SoapHttpClientProtocol

    <System.Web.Services.Protocols.SoapDocumentMethodAttribute( _
      "http://tempuri.org/GetTime", _
      RequestNamespace:="http://tempuri.org/", _
      ResponseNamespace:="http://tempuri.org/", _
      Use:=Syst_u109 ?.Web.Services.Description.SoapBindingUse.Literal, _
      ParameterStyle:= _
      System.Web.Services.Protocols.SoapParameterStyle.Wrapped)> _
    Public Function GetTime(ByVal ShowSeconds As Boolean) As String
        Dim results() As Object = _
            Me.Invoke("GetTime", New Object() {ShowSeconds})
        Return CType(results(0),String)
    End Function
End Class
```

Figure 4-17   Proxy code generated by Visual Studio.

Note that the attributes block in the function name (the characters between the angle brackets) contains information that tells the base class how to package the call, such as the names of methods. Visual Studio .NET makes extensive use of these metadata attributes as a way of passing information to the prefabricated functionality of system code. In earlier days, this would probably have been done through member variables of the base class, where it would have been difficult to differentiate immutable run-time attributes from those that can change during program execution. The new arrangement is harder to mess up, which is generally a good idea.

Calls from a client to an XML Web service usually want to run asynchronously.

The Internet can be a lot of fun, but it's almost always so crowded that you have no hope of enjoying it without a clever strategy for managing its chronic overload—sort of like Disney World. Even the simplest call to an XML Web service might take 5 or 10 seconds to complete, depending on network and server traffic, and the time can go up to anything from there. You can't leave a user with a frozen interface for more than a second or two, if that. Accordingly, our proxy provides both synchronous and asynchronous mechanisms for calling the methods of the XML Web service. In addition to the *Get-Time* method that we called, you'll notice that the proxy contains methods called *BeginGetTime* and *EndGetTime*. The proxy generator creates *Begin[name]* and *End[name]* methods for each method in the XML Web service. The *Begin* method starts the call, hands it off to a background thread, and returns immediately. The *End* method harvests the result when the call is finished. You can either poll periodically to see if the operation is complete or you can be notified by a callback function. The sample program demonstrates the latter technique. This asynchronous operation isn't limited to XML Web service proxies but instead is available to any function call in .NET. I discuss its operation in more detail in Chapter 8.

XML Web Service Support in Visual Studio .NET

The XML Web service example I showed earlier demonstrated that writing XML Web services does not depend on fancy programming environments. But since developer time is the second-greatest constraint in software development (boneheaded managers who don't know which end of a soldering iron to hold being number one), it makes sense to write our XML Web services using tools that will help us crank them out faster. Since our old friend Notepad lacks such useful features as an integrated debugger, Visual Studio .NET is usually a better choice for writing XML Web services. I'll show you how to write a similar service using the final release version of Visual Studio .NET.

When you select File/New/Project from the Visual Studio main menu, it offers you the dialog box shown in Figure 4-18. I selected Visual Basic Projects in the left pane and the ASP.NET Web Service icon in the right pane, entered a project name in the edit control, and clicked OK. Visual Studio .NET generated a new solution containing the files shown in Figure 4-19.

An XML Web service example in Visual Studio .NET starts here.

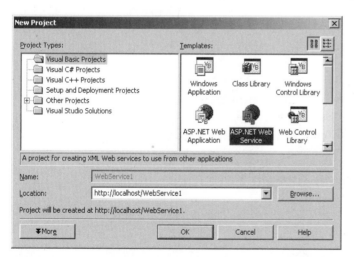

Figure 4-18   Creating a new project in Visual Studio .NET.

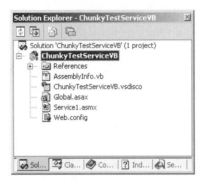

Figure 4-19   Visual Basic .NET solution based on the ASP.NET Web Service template.

A wizard generates the basic project.

You'll see a number of files that are similar to those generated in an ASP.NET application project. That's because XML Web services run on top of ASP.NET. The Web.config and Global.asax files do exactly the same thing as they do in ASP.NET. The .vsdisco file contains information for discovery of the XML Web service by proxy generators; you will probably never touch it.

The .ASMX file is the target for client requests.

The .ASMX file is the target for client requests. Unlike this chapter's simplest example, in which the code lived in this file, the ASMX page in this example contains a callout to code that lives elsewhere, as did the ASPX pages we saw in Chapter 3. The interesting programming takes place in the code behind file Service1.asmx.vb, in which the code that implements your XML Web service actually lives. Features such as auto-complete make the code much easier to write with Visual Studio .NET than it was with Notepad.

When you build your project, Visual Studio .NET automatically publishes it to the Web server you specify (in this case, the system default). To test the XML Web service, simply start the debugger from the Visual Studio main menu. It pops up a testing page similar to the one we saw previously in Figure 4-5, which is a very smooth way to handle things. You can set breakpoints in your XML Web service and debug anything. It's smooth, quick, and—dare I say it—fun application development.

XML Web Service Design Considerations

When I asked Keith Ballinger, the Microsoft project manager who wrote the foreword to this book, what I should tell readers about designing their XML Web services, he said, "Two things—make them chunky, and think carefully about their state." In this section of the chapter, I'll discuss what he meant and why he said it, and throw in a few more suggestions for writing robust, high-performance XML Web services quickly.

Make Them Chunky

The simplest sample service shown in this chapter returns a single string. While an XML Web service method can return only one object as its return value, the object is not limited to being a simple type such as the string shown here. It can be any .NET object that can be serialized into XML. I discuss the requirements for XML serialization in Chapter 7, but basically it's any type of object that contains a default constructor (one that requires no parameters), which means almost every type of object in existence. This means that you can return any amount of data from your XML Web service methods. In Chapter 6, for example, you'll see a sample XML Web service that returns a *DataSet* representing the results of a database search.

An XML Web service can return almost any type of .NET object.

The overhead of making an XML Web service call is fairly high. A lot of work goes on at low levels even though you don't have to write the code for it, as I've discussed earlier in this chapter. You want to incur this overhead as seldom as possible, which means bundling as much information as you think you're going to want into each call. For example, you don't want to make one call to get a customer's first name, another to get his last name, and a third to get his middle initial. You'd rather make one call to obtain a customer object containing all this information. Even if the customer object contained some information that you didn't care about in this particular case, maybe the prefix and suffix fields of the customer's name, you still make a performance profit by avoiding multiple calls. On the other hand, you probably don't want to transfer the customer's entire 25-megabyte buying history record when all you want to do is send him a birthday card. It's sort of like the shipping charges on Amazon.com, which they've cleverly structured to encourage you to buy more than one item per order.

The overhead of an XML Web service call can be significant.

I wondered where the break-even point for chunkiness was, so I wrote a sample program, which you can see in Figure 4-20. The XML Web service method accepts an integer parameter and returns an array containing that number of bytes. The user specifies the number of calls to make and the number of bytes to fetch per call. The client program makes that series of calls and reports the elapsed time.

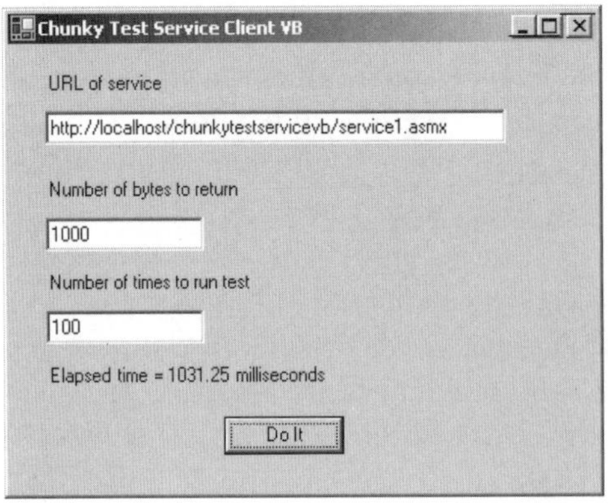

Figure 4-20 Sample program demonstrating the break-even point for chunkiness.

The time required for a call itself is roughly equal to the time required to transfer a few thousand bytes.

Going from one machine to another machine on a 100-MB/sec Ethernet in my own office with authentication turned off and nothing else happening on the network or on either machine, I measured the results shown in the following table. The basic overhead (the cost of Amazon.com shipping an empty box) is about 6 milliseconds per call. Transferring data took about 1.5 milliseconds per kilobyte (the extra shipping cost based on the weight of your package's contents). This means that it's worth transmitting about 4000 bytes of unneeded data to avoid one unnecessary call. Your mileage, of course, will vary significantly. Authentication will raise the per-call overhead; network congestion will raise the per-kilobyte transmission cost; faster machines and networks will lower them both. You'll have to repeat this measurement on your target system to know exactly where the break-even point is for your project. But in general, Keith is right, make them chunky.

Bytes transferred per call	Elapsed time per call, milliseconds
1	6
100	6
1000	7
4000	12

Think Carefully About Their State

XML Web services are stateless by default.

XML Web service objects in their natural state are stateless (groan). That means that ASP.NET constructs a new instance of the XML Web service object for each incoming call and destroys it at the end of the call. None of the data from one call is available to the next call unless you go out of your way to make it so. This situation is somewhat analogous to just-in-time activation of objects in COM+.

Sometimes this behavior is what you want; sometimes it isn't. For my time service shown in this chapter, it probably is. Whether a client wants to show the seconds digit has no bearing on what the next client wants or should get. Each function call is sufficient unto itself; there's no reason to remember anything from one to the next. In the classic sense of an object as a combination of data and the code that operates on the data, you might argue that there's no object here. The client is simply making a call that has no relation to anything else, and that's not an object, that's a function. You can waste your time arguing religious semantics; I've got a product to ship.

When this behavior isn't what you want, an object can maintain state between one call and another. The physical instance of an object is still created and destroyed on demand, but you can maintain the data that it was working on in its previous life, as you might leave instructions in your will for your descendants. There are basically two ways to do this, each with its advantages and disadvantages.

First, we can use the internal state collections in ASP.NET. In Chapter 3 I discussed the *Session* and *Application* state collections available to objects used on ASP.NET pages. The same state management options are available to your XML Web service objects, as they run on top of ASP.NET. The base class *WebService*, from which your XML Web service is derived, contains two collections for holding state, called *Session* and *Application*. You put data into them and take data out by accessing the collections through string names of items, just as ASP.NET page code does. However, XML Web service code has one large difference from ASP.NET page code. Because of its overhead, *Session* state is turned off by default in an XML Web service. If you want to use it, you have to explicitly turn it on by passing a parameter to the *WebMethod* attribute declaration, as shown in Figure 4-21. You must do this in every method that you want to access session state. If you don't, the *Session* object will be *Nothing*, and accessing it will cause an exception. I've written a sample service and client to demonstrate session state and exception handling in the next section. The screen shot is shown in Figure 4-22.

> XML Web services can store state in the session-level and application-level state containers in ASP.NET.

```
<WebMethod(EnableSession:=True)> _
Public Function IncrementAndReturnSessionHitCount() As String
```

Figure 4-21   Turning on session state using the WebMethod attribute.

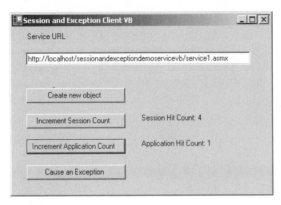

Figure 4-22   Sample service demonstrating session state and exception handling.

Using ASP.NET *Session* state requires server CPU cycles and storage space.

That sounds easy to program, and it is. However, excessive use of the *Session* collection can hinder your service's scalability for several reasons. First, it takes time on each XML Web service call to create the session object, restore its state, and attach it to the XML Web service context. You also pay a space price to store the state information between calls. So don't just store session state for the sake of storing it; think carefully about exactly how much you need and why. Make sure to omit it from methods that don't require it.

The indeterminacy of *Session* state lifetime can cause algorithm problems.

The indeterminacy of the *Session* state lifetime is a subtler problem. Suppose a client calls method A on an XML Web service that stores some state in the *Session* object. Suppose the client then calls method B, whose functionality is dependent on that state, some time later. If the session state timeout interval has expired, then the state on which method B depends will no longer exist. You'll have to program both client and server to handle that eventuality. You could increase the session state timeout interval, but this might mean keeping lots of state information around for XML Web service clients that have finished their business and gone away. Session state is a good idea in pages viewed by casual human users, but this indeterminacy is a bigger problem in functions called by other computer programs. If you go this route, think about having some sort of logout method that the client can call to clean up and dump the session state.

Alternatively, all state can live on the client side, which has its own set of problems.

The alternative to storing object state in the *Session* collection is to maintain all state on the client. The client calls method A on an XML Web service, which returns some sort of object containing internal state information. The client then passes this object back to the service when it calls method B, and the server picks the state information out of the parameter and picks up where it left off. The advantages are obvious: neither party has to worry about session state timing out, and the server doesn't have to buy space to store state for its thousands of clients. The disadvantages are also obvious: all the required state information has to travel over the network on each call, increasing the bandwidth requirements. Also, the client can examine and potentially change the state information between calls, so you'll have to encrypt it if it contains any sensitive information. This is how Web Forms controls maintain their view state from one round trip to another, as I'll describe in Chapter 11

Handling Exceptions

I discussed error handling at great length in Chapter 2, explaining the problems of communicating an error from method to caller and why .NET structured exception handling was such an advance. However, structured exception handling only works in .NET because all programs use the same MSIL implementation internally. The whole point of XML Web services is to receive and service calls from clients that are *not* running on the .NET Framework, so how can we signal errors to them?

Signaling errors to XML Web service clients can be a problem.

    The one commonality that client and server have in XML Web services is SOAP. The SOAP specification provides for error handling with an element called *<Fault>*. When the XML Web service throws an exception of any type, ASP.NET catches it. ASP.NET then copies the exception's message into a SOAP *<Fault>* element, and passes it back that way.

XML Web service exceptions are transmitted to clients by a SOAP <Fault> element.

    I've written a sample program that causes an exception by accessing a non-existent session property (I didn't turn on the session state, as I discussed in the previous section). Accessing the state object throws a NULL reference exception, which ASP.NET catches and converts into a SOAP *<Fault>* element, as shown in Figure 4-23.

```
<soap:Envelope>
  <soap:Body>
    <soap:Fault>
      <faultcode>
        soap:Server
      </faultcode>
      <faultstring>Server was unable to process request--&gt;
       Object reference not set to an instance of an object
      </faultstring>
      <detail />
    </soap:Fault>
  </soap:Body>
</soap:Envelope>
```

Figure 4-23   SOAP <Fault> example.

It is up to the client to map the SOAP *<Fault>* element into its own programming language.

Once the SOAP fault returns to the client, it's entirely up to the client to determine how to proceed with it. Any proxy generator worthy of the name will read the SOAP fault and translate it back into the language of the proxy. For example, a Java proxy will turn the SOAP fault into some kind of Java exception. The .NET proxy generator code turns it into a .NET exception of type *System.Web.Services.Protocols.SoapException*. Our client program catches it, as it would any other type of exception, and tries to make sense of it. The *Message* element of the exception contains the original message from the server with the location of the error on the server. All the rest of the fields of the exception refer to where it originated on the client, which doesn't tell us anything about the source of the error on the server side. So if you want the client to understand the cause of the error, to be able to differentiate, say, a login failure from a file-not-found error, you'll have to come up with some sort of encoding system to place that information in this string.

What if the client hasn't accessed the service with SOAP? Then throwing an exception from your XML Web service code causes ASP.NET to send back an uninformative HTTP error screen. If we want to be able to signal useful error information to HTTP clients, we have to use special-case return values. Deciding whether or not this is cost effective is a marketing call. I'd suggest probably not.

Replacing the Namespace URI

You've probably seen the message on the XML Web service test page that says, "This web service is using http://tempuri.org/ as its default namespace. Recommendation: Change the default namespace before the XML Web service is made public." In the wild and woolly world that is the Web, it's entirely possible that other vendors will create services with the same object and method name as yours, such as *Service1.GetTime*. We'd like to have some way of definitively marking our service so that callers who care are certain that they have ours and not someone else's. You can argue that the URL at which a client accesses a service definitively differentiates yours from another's, but we'd like a way of identifying the service itself regardless of its location. When the secret police kick down your door at 4:00 AM shouting, "KGB! You are Ivan Ivanovich?" you'd very much like to be able to say, "No, he lives down the hall."

An XML Web service contains a namespace URI to distinguish it from other XML Web services.

You do this by placing a *namespace URI* on your service by means of a .NET programming attribute. A namespace URI is nothing more nor less than a big, long, fancy string that is the unique family name of your service and all other services that you create. You are promising callers that any service and method name within this namespace is unique, that you are in control of the development of services marked with this namespace URI, and that you've made sure that there aren't any conflicts. A proxy wanting to access an XML Web service can specify the namespace URI in addition to the service and method name to make even more sure that he's gotten what he asks for. The server will compare the requested URI with the URI that it actually has, and throw an exception if they don't match.

The namespace URI can be anything at all that you'd like it to be, as long as it's unique in the universe—for example "PoliticalFamilyFromHyannisport-MassWithMoreMoneyThanBrains." It often begins with your Web address because you own it and no one else should be using it, just as you often use your e-mail address as a login ID. Nothing prevents someone else from using yours just to mess you up, but they probably won't. No one accesses the namespace URI as a Web address during an XML Web service call, so there doesn't have to be anything there and often isn't. However, some vendors do indeed put product or service information at the Web address used as a namespace URI so that potential customers who see the code know where to contact them.

Once you've chosen a namespace URI, you place it on your XML Web service by using the attribute *Namespace* on your XML Web service class declaration, as shown in Figure 4-24. The namespace URI appears in your XML Web service's WSDL file, and thus makes its way into generated proxy clients.

> You assign a namespace URI to your service with a .NET programming attribute.

```
<WebService(Namespace:="http://www.rollthunder.com/")> _
Public Class Service1
```

Figure 4-24   Placing a namespace on your XML Web service.

Note that specifying the namespace of the service the server is accessing does not provide any real check on the identity of the server. It only specifies who the server must claim to be, without requiring proof that the server really is that particular one—sort of like a limousine driver carrying a sign with the expected passenger's name on it, but not asking for a picture ID. If your client really cares about authenticating the server (as opposed to the other way around, which is much more common), then you'll have to work with some sort of trust provider certificate program.

XML Web Service Security

XML Web services have many of the same security considerations as ASP.NET pages. Some XML Web services are public and anonymous, such as an airline schedule browsing program. Others are private, such as a financial company's mutual fund trading program. Most will require at least some degree of authentication and authorization, more in the case of medical or financial

> Most XML Web services will require some sort of security.

records, less in the case of $20/year magazine subscriptions. There is no One True security design for XML Web services. Even more than for ASP.NET pages, you have to look carefully at the specific details of every case.

We've seen that XML Web services are layered on top of ASP.NET. Since we get services such as state management from the underlying layer, it would only make sense that we would get our security from it as well. While this happens in some situations, it doesn't always solve our problems. XML Web services differ from Web Forms because the client of an XML Web service may not be a human being; it could easily be another computer program. In ASP.NET forms authentication, we redirected an unauthenticated user to a Web form and required her to type in her authentication credentials. That won't work for XML Web services, so we have to come up with some automatic way for the user to present authentication credentials. Passport authentication suffers from the same problem; it is likewise human-centric.

Our XML Web services can get automatic authentication from ASP.NET today if we select Windows authentication. But as I explained in Chapter 3, this approach works well only in Windows-only environments. That's fine for a corporate intranet, where you have control over all the software and machines. Security-conscious designers can do things such as restrict the IP addresses from which clients are allowed to access the service, require the clients to present X509 certificates issued by their own certificate authority or by a third party, or install encrypted network cards in all their computers. But to my mind, that's exactly what XML Web services are *not* about. The whole point of XML Web services is to be open to everyone on the amorphous Internet, from anybody, to anybody. We need a security mechanism that works no matter what hardware and software environments the clients are using. We don't currently have a point-and-click mechanism in .NET, but as I'll show you, we can use .NET utility objects to roll our own without too much trouble.

I wrote a sample XML Web service that simulates a magazine publisher that allows paying clients to request the text of articles from its server. Users must purchase a subscription, which is done outside the XML Web service, perhaps on the human-readable Web site with a credit card. The user is then given a user ID and password, which is good for unlimited requests for some period of time.

The XML Web service has two methods, one called *Login* and one called *RequestArticle*. The first takes a user ID and password and returns an admission ticket, a "session key" if you will. The second requires this admission ticket and an article number, and returns the article. Figure 4-25 shows the workflow in this system.

XML Web services can't depend on a human user to enter credentials.

Windows authentication only works well in a Windows-only network, which the Internet is not.

An Internet XML Web service security example starts here.

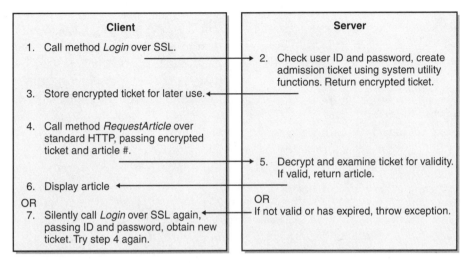

Client	Server
1. Call method *Login* over SSL.	2. Check user ID and password, create admission ticket using system utility functions. Return encrypted ticket.
3. Store encrypted ticket for later use.	
4. Call method *RequestArticle* over standard HTTP, passing encrypted ticket and article #.	5. Decrypt and examine ticket for validity. If valid, return article.
6. Display article	OR
OR	If not valid or has expired, throw exception.
7. Silently call *Login* over SSL again, passing ID and password, obtain new ticket. Try step 4 again.	

Figure 4-25   XML Web service security example workflow.

I really don't want anyone to steal a user ID and password. Anyone who did that could use my system for free for the duration of that user's account. They couldn't hurt anything with it, as I don't store any sensitive information about my users, but I don't want the bad publicity that a theft would bring. So my client would use Secure Sockets Layer (SSL) for making the call to my service's *Login* method. That's easy to do—simply change HTTP to HTTPS in the request URL. This causes the client to request the server's public key, use that to negotiate a session key, and use the session key to encrypt the call transmitting the user ID and password. That way no one with a packet sniffer can record the user ID and password to break in later. The drawback is that the handshaking and encryption require a significant amount of extra time and CPU cycles. (Note: the sample program supplied with this book uses HTTP instead of HTTPS, because most readers will find it difficult to set up their servers to handle HTTPS.)

The *Login* method on the server checks to see if the user is in my subscriber database and if the subscription is current. My sample program simulates that with hardwired names. If the user ID or password is not valid, the server throws an exception and it's up to the client to deal with it. The server then creates an admission ticket, using the forms authentication utility functions that I demonstrated in Chapter 3. The ticket contains the user's name, the roles to which the user belongs, and an expiration time. I encrypt the ticket using other system utility functions and return it to the client in the form of a string. The client retains this string for use in future calls.

The XML Web service accepts a user ID and password over SSL to avoid eavesdropping, and returns an encrypted admission ticket.

The client presents the admission ticket over clear HTTP in subsequent service requests.

When the client wants to request an article, he calls the *RequestArticle* method, passing the encrypted admission ticket and the desired article number. The server decrypts the admission ticket using the system utility functions. My server now knows who the user is, what roles he belongs to, and whether the ticket's expiration time has passed. If a client presents an expired ticket in an article request, the server throws an exception and the client has to send the user ID and password again (over SSL). My sample program does this internally without bothering the user.

I don't use SSL to prevent eavesdropping on non-login service calls because my data isn't sensitive and my admission tickets expire frequently.

I didn't use SSL for requesting an article because I didn't want to take the performance hit. Anyone who might be sniffing packets could read the clear text of the articles being retrieved, though since the user's name is encrypted in the ticket, they won't know who is reading which article. If the data were sensitive in itself, such as medical or financial records, I'd probably use SSL throughout regardless of time cost, but in this case, it's just an article that the snooper didn't select. If a snooper records the ticket string and plays it back in a spoof request, he'd be able to request articles without paying for a subscription, but only for the duration of the ticket's validity, which I set to half an hour when I create it.

You have to balance security programming effort and cost against the cost of a security failure.

This security architecture was relatively easy for me to implement. Without spending too much developer time and money, I've made the cost of cracking my system significantly higher than the cost of buying a subscription, and limited the damage done in case someone does crack it. If some frustrated geek has nothing better to do on a lonely Saturday night than sniff my packets to hijack free article retrieval for an average time of 15 minutes per break-in, welcome to it, say I.

You can see the design decisions that I've made, trading off development time against security against runtime efficiency. I hope you see why I think I have about the right balance for this particular system. Different systems will require different trade-offs. Pick the one that makes you the most money, as I've done.

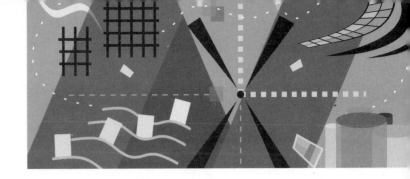

5

Windows Forms

Problem Background

This book has until now primarily discussed using Microsoft .NET for writing server-side code, and .NET is very good for that. However, what operating system is running on all the desktop PCs at your business, the good one in your home that you use for take-home work, and the old one you let the kids hack with (or the other way around)? The laptop of the guy next to you on the airplane? Except for a few religious Macintosh adherents and some geeky Linux hobbyists, it's Microsoft Windows. It seems to me that developers often forget that Windows runs on many more client machines than it ever will on servers, probably by a factor of 100 or more. Did those users choose Windows for its transaction throughput or scalability to server farms? No. They chose it because it has a good user interface and lots of available desktop software. It's the largest software market in the world and will be for the foreseeable future. We'll be writing different types of desktop applications from what we wrote a decade ago. Spreadsheets and word processors have been pretty much beaten into the ground, but we'll still be writing for the Windows

> The Windows desktop software market is the largest in the world and will remain so for the foreseeable future.

desktop. For example, we'll be writing more rich front ends for Internet applications, such as the Napster music search program that I showed you in Chapter 4.

Some of the architectural problems that desktop developers face are different from those of server developers. For example, a desktop developer deals with a single human being who reacts slowly compared to a computer, so the developer generally has plenty of CPU cycles available and doesn't have to worry about scalability the way a server developer does. On the other hand, many of the problems that desktop developers face are the same. For example, both types of developers care about reusing code that other developers wrote. They might reuse different types of code—say, code for database access vs. graphical animation—but they both face the economic necessity of leveraging the efforts of other developers. They both care about versioning. They both care about abstracting away distinctions between different language implementations. They both care about interoperating with COM. Desktop developers have largely ignored security until now, considering it only a server-side problem, but now that a lot of code is delivered over the Web, desktop developers face the twin problems of authentication and authorization that have long deviled their server-side colleagues. Welcome to the real world. Developers writing desktop apps need prefabricated solutions to these problems just as server developers do.

In addition to the problems they share with server developers, desktop developers have their own set of problems. I remember writing Windows desktop apps in C about a decade ago. I spent most of my time writing code for user interface features that all Windows applications needed. Prefabricated status bars and toolbars didn't exist then, so I had to write code for my own and so did every other developer who wanted to implement these features in an application. I had to write my own command handlers for receiving messages from controls. I still have nightmares about the time I foolishly promised a client that I'd add a print preview feature to his program for a fixed fee. For every programmer to write her own implementation of all these common user interface items makes no sense, either economically (all that duplicated, triplicated, octuplicated programmer effort) or ergonomically (every toolbar works differently, which drives users barking mad). We need prefabricated solutions for these common UI design problems.

Seizing the opportunity to provide standards that developers could reuse, different development environments provided different approaches to prefabricated user interfaces. Visual Basic offered a programming model based on events and forms that became quite popular for its ease of use. Visual C++ offered the Microsoft Foundation Classes (MFC), which used C++ inheritance to provide prefabricated functionality, such as the print preview feature I banged my head against so long ago. The code-based design in Visual C++ was harder to use than Visual Basic's forms-based model, but its underlying language was much more powerful. Programmers had to choose between a powerful language and rapid GUI design features. I'd often choose Visual Basic to write a front end because I liked its form editor and the ease of connecting with controls, but the wimpy language, with its arcane syntax for COM objects, its idiotic error handling, and the difficulty of calling API functions to do common tasks such as manipulate the registry would send me through the ceiling. Or I'd choose Visual C++ for its powerful language, in which case its lower-level of abstraction—for example, the difficulty of handling and firing connection point events—would send me through the ceiling.

Like everybody else in the world, desktop developers want everything, all at once, and we don't want to trade anything else away to get it. We want prefabricated solutions to the problems we share with server developers. We want rapid GUI development, but we want it to work with a powerful programming language, ideally the powerful programming language of our choice. For consistency's sake, we want it all to use the same programming model. And we want it to cost relatively little. As long as we're writing to Santa Claus, it couldn't hurt to at least *ask* for a pony.

> As usual, we want everything but our business logic done for us (and I wouldn't mind if someone did that, too)

Solution Architecture

As you've seen in this book, .NET provides good prefabricated functionality for solving the problems common to desktop developers as well as those that server developers deal with. I covered the problems that are common to both in Chapter 2. Desktop developers will use and like the common language runtime code-reuse model, its versioning and memory management capabilities, its easy deployment of private assemblies, its organization of the system namespace, its security features, and its interoperation with COM. XML Web services, described in Chapter 4, will give desktop developers something to design products for and a way of connecting to the server back end.

> Many .NET common language runtime features help both server and desktop developers.

Microsoft .NET also provides a rich set of functionality to desktop developers, which goes by the stunningly uninformative name of Windows Forms. Windows Forms provides .NET classes that contain prefabricated user interface components for many of the features common to most desktop apps. If you think of a cross between Visual Basic and MFC, implemented in .NET and thus available to any language, you'll have about the right mental model. Windows Forms provides support for such features as menus, toolbars, and status bars; printing and print preview; hosting of ActiveX controls; and easy access to databases and XML Web services. It is such a large, rich set of functionality that this chapter can only provide the barest skim of its surface.

> Windows Forms is a package that provides prefabricated user interface elements as part of the common language runtime.

Doing justice to Windows Forms would require an entire book devoted solely to it, and Charles Petzold has written exactly that. Although it's entitled *Programming Microsoft Windows with C#* (Microsoft Press, 2001), its 1300+ pages are devoted almost entirely to Windows Forms in their various permutations. Programmers who learned their Windows programming from Petzold in C, as did I, back when the world was new (remember *TranslateMessage()* and *DispatchMessage()?*), will find his approach familiar and comfortable, like eating chicken noodle soup while wearing a soft, well-worn flannel shirt.

Warning   The user interface tools in Windows Forms are double-edged, as are all powerful tools. You can use them to write excellent user interfaces or terrible ones. As war is too important to be left to generals, so user interface design is too important to be left to programmers. Anyone who designs a user interface without reading the fundamental texts, *About Face* by Alan Cooper (IDG, 1995) and *The Design of Everyday Things* by Donald Norman (Doubleday, 1990), is committing malpractice. And reading *Web Pages That Suck*, by Vincent Flanders and Michael Willis (Sybex, 1998) and its sequel *Son of Web Pages That Suck* by Flanders alone (Sybex, 2002) might save you from producing some.

Simplest Example

A Windows Forms sample, written in Visual Basic using Notepad, begins here.

As I've done with the other topics in this book, I started my exploration of Windows Forms by writing the simplest example I could think of, shown in Figure 5-1. You can download the code from this book's Web site (*http://www.introducingmicrosoft.net*) and work along with me. Visual Studio .NET is a great tool for creating this type of project, and I have used it in other examples in this chapter, but to underline the tool and language independence of Windows Forms, I wrote this Visual Basic example in Notepad. The app will seem trivial, and I wrote very little code for it, but you will see that it demonstrates several of the most basic and important features of Windows Forms.

Figure 5-1   A simple Windows Forms sample.

Figure 5-2 shows the code for my sample app. You'll notice that I didn't import any namespaces in this example. (See Chapter 2 for an explanation of namespaces.) I never have to do that if I don't want to; it's simply a matter of convenience when I want to call objects by their short names instead of their fully qualified names. I decided to do the latter in this case so that you can see exactly where each object comes from. You do need to include some system DLLs in the compilation by reference, which you can see in the compilation batch file in the downloaded source code. Visual Studio .NET automatically does this if you use it for a Windows Forms project.

The sample doesn't bother to import namespaces.

A top-level window in Windows Forms is called a *form*, and every application needs to have at least one. This requirement will be familiar to Visual Basic programmers. C++ programmers should think of this form as their application's main window. Windows Forms provides a prefabricated implementation of the basic functionality that every top-level window needs to have in the common language runtime base class *System.Windows.Forms.Form*. This base class provides such features as hosting controls, supporting the docking of child windows, and responding to events.

We derive our own form class from a common language runtime base class that provides basic prefabricated form functionality.

I start this simple app by deriving a new class, called *SimplestHelloWorld*, from this base class. By using this inheritance notation, I tell the compiler to take all the functionality of the base class that Microsoft wrote and include it by reference in my new derived class. (See Chapter 2 for a further discussion of inheritance.)

Now that we have our new class representing our own top-level window, we need to write code that says how our object differs from the base class. In this case, we override the base class's *New* method (known as a constructor, you'll remember from Chapter 2), which is called whenever an instance of our object is created. In this method, we first call our base class's constructor, thereby allowing the base class to complete its initialization

We override the base class's constructor to tack on new functionality when our form is created.

before we attempt anything in our derived class. Failing to do this is a common cause of bugs in object-oriented programming. This call is not made automatically by the .NET Framework because occasionally you want to omit it or point it somewhere else; for example, in cases where you are completely replacing some part of the base class's functionality instead of piggy-backing on it as we are doing here. The base class contains a property named *Text*, which represents the string in the form's title bar. We set that property to a distinctive title that we will recognize.

```
Namespace IMDN.SimplestHelloWorld

' Declare a new class that derives from the runtime base
' class System.Windows.Forms.Form.

Public Class SimplestHelloWorld : Inherits System.Windows.Forms.Form

    ' Class constructor. Forward call to the base class for
    ' its initialization, and then set our window's caption.

    Public Sub New()
        MyBase.New
        Me.Text = "Introducing Microsoft .Net: Hello World"

    End Sub

    ' This function is the entry point for a Windows Forms
    ' application. Create a new instance of our form
    ' object, and then pass that to the system function that
    ' runs the application.

    Shared Sub Main()
        System.Windows.Forms.Application.Run(New SimplestHelloWorld())
    End Sub

End Class

End Namespace
```

Figure 5-2   Simplest sample app's code listing.

We create an instance of our form object and tell the loader to run it.

We now need to hook up our top-level form so that the system loader will know which form to show when the program starts running. Visual Studio .NET would add this code to the project for us automatically if we were using it. Since we're not, it's up to us to add the code. When a program starts up, the loader looks for a function called *Main*, which you will see I've placed in our object. Only your startup form can contain this method, and the loader will call it only once. The qualifier *Shared* means that there is only one instance of this function shared among all objects of the class (*static* for you C++ geeks). The runtime loader calls this function to start the application. It is up to you to put in this function whatever code you need to make the application go. A Windows Forms application requires a thread to run a message loop that receives user interface messages (such as keystrokes and mouse clicks) from the operating system and routes them to the correct event handlers. The static runtime function *System.Windows.Forms.Application.Run* creates and starts exactly such a thread. We pass this function a new instance of our form object to tell it which form to send the messages to.

More Complex Example: Controls and Events

Our simplest application demonstrated a few necessary features, but other than that it's extremely boring. Our form doesn't even have an OK button. I will now demonstrate a less trivial example, a screen shot of which is shown in Figure 5-3. I've switched to Visual Studio .NET for this example, even though I didn't have to, because its editor makes manipulating the controls much easier.

A more complex Windows Forms example starts here.

Figure 5-3   A more complex form created with Visual Studio .NET.

You will find that the Windows Forms programming model closely resembles the Visual Basic 6.0 programming model, although it's available to any common language runtime language. That's a good idea because Visual Basic's programming model was and is immensely popular. It's the language behind it that many programmers couldn't stand, myself included. Now we can use any runtime-compliant language that we want, in addition to which Visual Basic has gotten much smarter so I like it better. Besides, the C++ guys won most of the arm wrestling over the object programming model discussed in Chapter 2. An optimist would say that Microsoft was blending the best fea-

The Windows Forms programming model resembles the familiar Visual Basic 6.0 programming model.

tures of two design philosophies. A pessimist would say that Visual Basic programmers needed a consolation prize.

Controls on a form are created by common language runtime function calls.

Forms usually contain controls to obtain input from and display output to the user. The common language runtime Windows Forms package contains a rich set of controls, just as Visual Basic 6.0 does. In writing this sample program, I dragged controls from the Visual Studio .NET toolbox onto my form, as shown in Figure 5-4. When I did this, Visual Studio .NET generated code in my form that makes runtime calls that create the controls, set their properties, and place them at the proper position when the form is first created. An excerpted version of this method is shown in Figure 5-5.

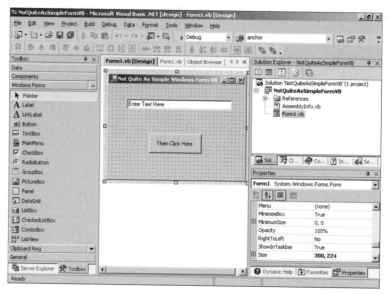

Figure 5-4 The Visual Studio .NET toolbox.

```
'NOTE: The following procedure is required by the Windows Form Designer.
'It can be modified using the Windows Form Designer.
'Do not modify it using the code editor.

Friend WithEvents Button1 As System.Windows.Forms.Button
Friend WithEvents TextBox1 As System.Windows.Forms.TextBox

Private Sub InitializeComponent()

    ' Create controls.
```

Figure 5-5 Excerpted version of the *InitializeComponent* method showing control creation.

```
Me.Button1 = New System.Windows.Forms.Button()
Me.TextBox1 = New System.Windows.Forms.TextBox()

' Set button properties.

Me.Button1.Location = New System.Drawing.Point(88, 104)
Me.Button1.Size = New System.Drawing.Size(112, 40)
Me.Button1.TabIndex = 1
Me.Button1.Text = "Then Click Here"


' Set text box properties.

Me.TextBox1.Location = New System.Drawing.Point(40, 32)
Me.TextBox1.Text = "Enter Text Here"
Me.TextBox1.TabIndex = 0
Me.TextBox1.Size = New System.Drawing.Size(224, 20)

' Set form properties.

Me.Text = "Not Quite As Simple Windows Form VB"

Me.Controls.AddRange(New System.Windows.Forms.Control() _
    {Me.TextBox1, Me.Button1})

End Sub
```

For the editor's logistical convenience, this code lives in a private method called *InitializeComponent*, which is called from the form's constructor. In Visual Basic .NET, the controls on a form are created by code that you can actually see, instead of by some invisible hand behind the scenes, as they were in Visual Basic 6.0. The newly created controls are added to a collection called *Controls*, which our form inherited from its base class. This collection allows a form to keep track of all of its controls.

The controls fire events to their containers in response to their interaction with the human user. For example, a button control fires an event signaling a click. We need to write event handler functions that will get called when the control signals an event. We do this by adding a method called *<Control_name>_<Event_name>* to the form class, in this case, *Button1_Click*, shown in Figure 5-6. Visual Studio .NET does this for us when

Controls fire events to handlers in your code.

we click on the button control in the editor, but anyone writing code in Notepad could simply add the method to the form class's code. When the control fires an event, the CLR's event mechanism looks for a handler function sporting the proper name for that event from that control and calls it if it finds one. You can also add an event handler dynamically as your code executes via the Visual Basic function AddHandler, not described here. I describe event handlers and the event process in detail in Chapter 8.

```
' User clicked the button. Display a message box containing the
' text currently in the text box.

Private Sub Button1_Click(ByVal sender As Object, _
                          ByVal e As System.EventArgs) _
                          Handles Button1.Click
    MessageBox.Show("You entered: " + TextBox1.Text)
End Sub
```

Figure 5-6   Event handler for a button click.

A form supports the *Dispose* method for deterministic finalization.

Forms support deterministic finalization, which I discussed in the section about garbage collection in Chapter 2. The base class *System.Windows.Forms.Form* contains a method called *Dispose* that allows a client to immediately liquidate a form and free its resources without having to wait for or cause a complete garbage collection. This is especially important in Windows Forms because every form contains an operating system window handle for each control it contains, plus one for the form itself. These window handles are somewhat scarce in Windows 98 (don't get me started), and deterministic finalization allows a client to release these resources as soon as it is finished with a form. You will see when you examine the source code that Visual Studio .NET automatically overrides this method, adding code that calls the *Dispose* method of all the controls that the form contains.

Hosting ActiveX Controls in Windows Forms

Windows Forms can host ActiveX controls.

I've written previously of the enormous popularity of ActiveX controls. If .NET couldn't use them, many developers wouldn't use .NET, which would mean that ActiveX developers wouldn't have a large enough market to merit converting their controls, and the whole .NET concept would be stillborn on the client side. Therefore, the developers of Windows Forms wisely decided to include support for hosting ActiveX controls. Since ActiveX controls work by means of COM, I'd strongly suggest that anyone interested in pursuing this topic go back to Chapter 2 and read the section about interoperation between COM and .NET.

A Windows Forms application does not inherently know how to use an ActiveX control. It only understands controls written with its own native Windows Forms architecture. For a Windows Forms application to host an ActiveX control, you need to generate a wrapper class that will contain the ActiveX control, mediate between its COM-based world view and the .NET world view of its container, and present it to Windows Forms as if it were a native Windows Forms control. You essentially need a monster runtime callable wrapper, as described in Chapter 2, that consumes all the COM interfaces that an ActiveX control provides, while also providing the COM interfaces that an ActiveX control requires from its host. This architecture is shown in Figure 5-7. If you think that sounds like a hell of a lot of work, you're right, but don't worry because the common language runtime provides a prefabricated class that does it all for you, called *System.Windows.Forms.AxHost*.

A Windows Forms application hosts an ActiveX control by generating a wrapper class similar to the runtime callable wrapper that wraps a COM object.

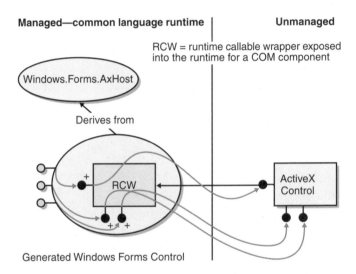

Figure 5-7   Windows Forms architecture for hosting ActiveX controls.

You need to derive a separate wrapper class from *AxHost* for each class of ActiveX control that your application wants to host. This class will contain the class ID or program ID used to create the ActiveX control and will expose in a native .NET format the properties, methods, and events of the internal ActiveX control. This will feel familiar to anyone who has ever imported an ActiveX control into Visual C++ or Visual J++. You generate this wrapper class using a command-line utility call AxImp.exe that comes with the .NET Framework SDK. If you are using Visual Studio .NET, you can simply right-click on

You create the wrapper class using Visual Studio .NET or a command-line utility.

the toolbox, pick Customize Toolbox from the shortcut menu, and you will see the dialog box in Figure 5-8, which offers the list of what Microsoft now calls *COM Controls*. (So long "ActiveX," and good riddance. One less MINFU in the world.)

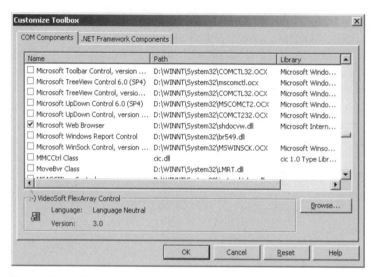

Figure 5-8   Dialog box offering choice of ActiveX controls to import into your project.

When you select a control from this list, Visual Studio .NET runs AxImp.exe internally and generates this wrapper class for you. It's built into a separate DLL as part of your project. You can't see the source code directly, at least not currently, but you can view its methods and properties in the Object Browser, shown in Figure 5-9. The new control will appear on your toolbox, and you can use it in the familiar manner.

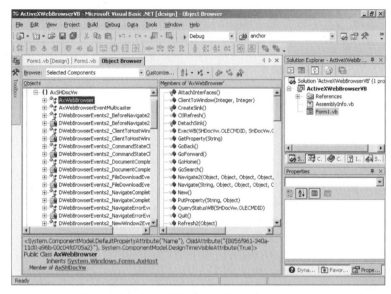

Figure 5-9   Visual Studio .NET Object Browser showing methods and properties of generated wrapper class for Web Browser ActiveX control.

I've written a sample Windows Forms program that uses the Microsoft Web Browser ActiveX control. Figure 5-10 shows a screen shot of it, displaying the Web page of the first edition of this book.

Figure 5-10   Windows Forms application using Web Browser ActiveX control.

I imported the ActiveX control into Visual Studio .NET as described previously. I then placed the control on my form and wrote the code shown in Figure 5-11. When the user clicks the Fetch button, I call the wrapper class's *Navigate* method, passing the URL that the user has entered. The wrapper class transforms this call into a COM call and passes it to the wrapped ActiveX control.

```
' Call method on RCW of Web Browser ActiveX control to
' fetch the requested page.

Private Sub Button1_Click(ByVal sender As System.Object, _
                       ByVal e As System.EventArgs) _
                       Handles Button1.Click
    AxWebBrowser1.Navigate(TextBox1.Text)
End Sub
```

Figure 5-11   Windows Forms ActiveX sample code.

Form Enhancements

A (relatively) advanced form example starts here.

Most developers think of forms as simply containers for controls, which do the actual work of interacting with the user. Sometimes this view is accurate, particularly in small applications. But more often, the form does a lot of significant work on its own that must, or at least should, be handled in its top-level central location. This section briefly describes the sorts of things that you can do while getting your hands dirty with forms. It refers to the sample application shown in Figure 5-12, called FancySchmancyFormVB (C# version in the sample code, as always).

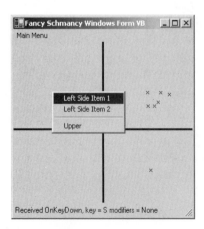

Figure 5-12   The FancySchmancyFormVB sample application.

Drawing

A form is responsible for maintaining its own appearance. The operating system window manager sends the form an *OnPaint* notification when it determines that a previously unshown portion of the window has become visible, for example, due to the movement or resizing of the form or of other windows. The newly uncovered area of the form is said to be *invalid*. Its appearance was not maintained by the OS. Instead, it is up to you to write code that paints the portion of the form that needs it, as shown in Figure 5-13.

A form is responsible for drawing its own appearance in response to the OnPaint notification.

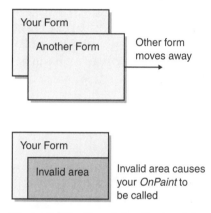

Figure 5-13   Repainting the invalid area of a form.

You can place your form's *OnPaint* code in one of two places. You can either override the *OnPaint* method of your form's base class directly, or you can add an event handler for the form's *OnPaint* event. While they seem identical from the programming environment's point of view, they actually differ significantly under the hood. The former approach, which is the preferred method, connects directly to the operating system's notification of your form. The latter approach uses a delegate and a handler, requiring a certain amount of runtime effort on the part of your program, as we'll discuss in Chapter 8. By overriding *OnPaint* rather than hooking up an event handler, you burn fewer microseconds. The event actually gets fired to any listeners when you pass the *OnPaint* call to your form's base class, which you do by calling *MyBase.OnPaint*. (Note that IntelliSense may not show this method, but it does exist and you usually want to call it.) This means that by overriding *OnPaint*, you have the flexibility to run your painting code at different times: before invoking the set of registered *OnPaint* event handlers, after invoking them, some of your code before and some after, or even instead of them by not calling the base class at all.

You place your form's code in the overridden OnPaint method of the base class.

Your *OnPaint* code draws on the screen by calling methods of the *Graphics* object it gets passed.

The *OnPaint* method of my sample program is shown in Figure 5-14. The operating system passes a parameter of type *PaintEventArgs* to this method. I create output on the screen by calling the methods of the *Graphics* object that this parameter contains. Petzold managed to fill hundreds of pages describing the interesting things you can do with this object, so I won't even bother trying to list its methods; but whatever type of drawing you want to do, this is where you go. My sample program draws a vertical line and a horizontal line dividing the form into quadrants. Drawing a line requires using a pen, a graphics object that I create when my program starts. (See the complete sample code.) The form's member variable *ClientSize* tells me the width and height of the form's client area, the area inside the borders and below the caption bar. Note that the client size doesn't take into account any other controls on the form, such as toolbars, menus, or status bars. If your form carries these, you'll have to add your own adjustments for the space they take up. My sample program ignores them.

```
Protected Overrides Sub OnPaint( _
    ByVal e As System.Windows.Forms.PaintEventArgs)

    ' Draw vertical line

    e.Graphics.DrawLine(MyPen, CInt((Me.ClientSize.Width / 2)), 0, _
        CInt((Me.ClientSize.Width / 2)), Me.ClientSize.Height)

    ' Draw horizontal line

    e.Graphics.DrawLine(MyPen, 0, CInt((Me.ClientSize.Height / 2)), _
        Me.ClientSize.Width, CInt((Me.ClientSize.Height / 2)))

    ' Invoke base class.

    MyBase.OnPaint(e)

End Sub
```

Figure 5-14   Overriden *OnPaint* method of a form.

PaintEventArgs also contains a *ClipRect* structure. This is a rectangle that tells me which parts of the form need painting. A real-life application would probably check it and touch up only the parts of the window that need it, particularly if your drawing code is complex. Mine wasn't, so I didn't bother taking the time.

Invalidation doesn't occur only when windows move. It can also be done programmatically. My sample application wants to keep the lines centered on the screen in order to form even quadrants. So every time my window's size changes I need to erase my lines and redraw them. Simply changing my window's size doesn't cause that to happen. Dragging the window to make it smaller doesn't trigger an *OnPaint*, because no new portion of the window has been exposed, so the window manager thinks that nothing has been made invalid. If I drag the window to make it larger, only the newly exposed portions are considered invalid, so the rest of the window isn't erased and the lines don't look right. In order to make the invalidation behavior the way I want it for this sample, I overrode the *OnResize* notification, which is called when my form's size changes for any reason. In this method (not shown), I call the method *Form.Invalidate()*. This causes the entire form to be invalidated, erasing the background, invoking my *OnPaint*, and triggering my drawing code. This process makes my window look the way I want it to.

Invalidating a window can also be done programmatically.

Mouse Handling

The graphical nature of Windows user interfaces means that your form will probably want to track and respond to the user's mouse behavior in some manner. While this is often done through the use of other controls (such as buttons and checkboxes), your form will at least occasionally want to handle mouse input on its own. The operating system calls methods on your form's base class whenever the mouse enters, leaves, moves, or clicks within your form. As with painting, you can handle these situations by overriding the base class's method or by installing an event handler, and you will probably want to choose the former.

The operating system calls methods on your form to tell it about mouse happenings.

My sample program contains an override of the base class's *OnMouse-Down* method, which gets called when a mouse key is depressed (poor thing). The code is shown in Figure 5-15. The operating system passes my handler function an object of type *MouseEventArgs*, describing the state of the mouse at the time the call was made. The object contains such items as the mouse button that the user clicked and the X and Y locations on the form in which the click took place. In the sample program, I check to see if the button is the left one. If so, I draw a little X right at the click location. This drawing is done outside the *OnPaint* handler, so it is erased when the form is. I get the *Graphics* object to use for drawing by calling the base class's *Create-Graphics* method.

The operating system passes a MouseEvent-Args object to tell your code what the user did with the mouse.

```
Protected Overrides Sub OnMouseDown( _
    ByVal e As System.Windows.Forms.MouseEventArgs)

    ' If user clicked left mouse button, then draw a little X at the point

    If (e.Button = MouseButtons.Left) Then

        Dim gr As Graphics = CreateGraphics()
        gr.DrawLine(Pens.Black, e.X - 2, e.Y - 2, e.X + 2, e.Y + 2)
        gr.DrawLine(Pens.Black, e.X - 2, e.Y + 2, e.X + 2, e.Y - 2)

        ' If user clicked right mouse button, then make adjustments
        ' to context menu  before form shows it

    ElseIf (e.Button = MouseButtons.Right) Then

        ' Handle right mouse button click
        :
    End If
End Sub
```

Figure 5-15   *OnMouseDown* event handler to process mouse clicks.

Menu Handling

A form's main menu is just another control that you place on the form using Visual Studio.

The main menu is an important piece of any user interface. It is the primary means through which new users discover your application's functionality, and is the primary contact point throughout the lifetime of the beginner and intermediate users who make up 90 percent or more of your user population. It's important to design your menu well. The main menu on a Windows form is a control that you select from the control toolbox, just like any other type of control. You place menu items on the menu using the editor, typing in their text and setting their properties, as shown in Figure 5-16. You can also do this programmatically at run time, as I'll demonstrate later. The form property *Menu* specifies which menu (your application can contain more than one) is shown as the form's main menu, so you can replace it at run time.

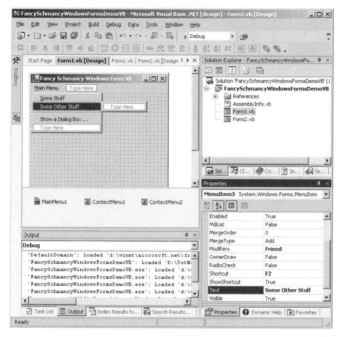

Figure 5-16   Adding a menu and menu items to a form.

Each menu item is its own distinct object with its own properties. Think of it as its own separate child control within its parent—the main menu—which itself is a child of the form. The properties of a menu item include such old friends as *Text*, *Enabled*, and *Checked*. A menu item also contains a property named *Shortcut*, which allows you to designate a key combination that invokes the action of the menu item, such as Ctrl+X for Cut. A menu item fires the *Click* event when the user selects the item. You add a handler for this event to your form and put code in it, just as you would for any other event from any other control.

Each menu item is a separate child control of the main menu.

A context menu is a small popup menu that an application shows when the user clicks the right mouse button. It generally contains items that provide actions appropriate to the location on which the user clicked. A context menu is another type of control you can add to your form from the toolbox, adding menu items to it and setting their properties. A form automatically shows its context menu when the user clicks the right mouse button. The form's *ContextMenu* property designates which of the (potentially many) context menus within the application the form should show. Because context menus can

The form automatically shows a context menu when the user clicks the right mouse button.

vary greatly from one location to another, you will often find yourself changing this property, changing the items within the context menu, or both. The sample program demonstrates both in the listing shown in Figure 5-17. When my form receives the *OnMouseDown* notification, it checks to see if the right mouse button was pressed. It then figures out if the click was on the right or left half of the window, and sets the *ContextMenu* property accordingly. It then figures out if the click was on the upper or lower half of the window, and modifies the last item of the context menu accordingly. These modifications take place before the form automatically shows the context menu.

```
ElseIf (e.Button = MouseButtons.Right) Then

    ' Figure out if we're on left or right side of screen.
    ' Set form's context menu accordingly

    If (e.X < ClientSize.Width / 2) Then
        Me.ContextMenu = ContextMenu1
    Else
        Me.ContextMenu = ContextMenu2
    End If

    ' Check for upper or lower half of window.
    ' Modify last item of selected context menu accordingly

    If (e.Y < ClientSize.Height / 2) Then
        Me.ContextMenu.MenuItems(3).Text = "Upper"

    Else
        Me.ContextMenu.MenuItems(3).Text = "Lower"

    End If

End If
```

Figure 5-17   Code modifying context menu before form automatically shows it.

Keyboard Handling

The operating system calls the *OnKeyDown* method of the window that has input focus when the user depresses a key, and calls the *OnKeyUp* method when the user releases it. The operating system passes an object of type *KeyEventArgs* to tell you which key the user has pressed, and whether any of the modifier keys such as Ctrl, Shift, or Alt was pressed as well. The key code covers all the keys on the standard Windows keyboard, thereby allowing you to differentiate between, say, the cursor movement keys on the numeric keypad and those on the inverted T to its left if you so desire. If the key translates to an ASCII character, you will also receive an *OnKeyPress* notification, containing a different set of arguments. The sample program processes the *OnKeyDown* notification and places descriptive information into the status bar. The code is shown in Figure 5-18:

The operating system calls your form's *OnKey-Down* method when the user presses a key and your form has the input focus.

```
' User pressed a key

Protected Overrides Sub OnKeyDown(ByVal e As _
    System.Windows.Forms.KeyEventArgs)

    ' Place information in status bar describing pressed key
    ' and state of modifier keys.

    StatusBar1.Text = ("Received OnKeyDown, key = " + e.KeyCode.ToString _
                    + " modifiers = " + e.Modifiers.ToString)
End Sub
```

Figure 5-18   Code handling *OnKeyDown* notification.

Dialog Boxes

The main form will often want to pop up dialog boxes to interact with the user. Dialog boxes are themselves forms, which you create in the designer and populate with controls as you would for any other form. To make buttons provide the OK and Cancel functionality that the user expects of a dialog

You use forms as dialog boxes, popping them up via the method *Form.ShowDialog*.

box, set the button property *DialogResult* to the appropriate value. To pop a dialog box up on the screen, the parent form creates an instance of the dialog form and calls the method *ShowDialog*. The return value of this method indicates the button that the user clicked to end the session. If the user clicks OK, the parent reads the information from the controls on the dialog form. The code is shown in Figure 5-19:

```
Private Sub MenuItem12_Click(ByVal sender As System.Object, _
    ByVal e As System.EventArgs) Handles MenuItem12.Click

    ' Create new dialog box form

    Dim dlg As New Form2()

    ' Pop up dialog box on screen

    If (dlg.ShowDialog() = DialogResult.OK) Then

        ' If user clicks OK, read value that he entered
        ' and show to him

        MessageBox.Show("User clicked OK, textBox contains: " + _
                    dlg.TextBox1.Text)

    Else

        ' If user clicks Cancel, report that
        ' fact to user.

        MessageBox.Show("User clicked Cancel")

    End If
End Sub
```

Figure 5-19   Code that displays a dialog box to the user and reports its results.

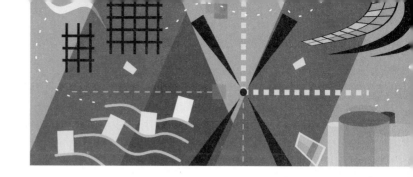

6

Data Access in .NET

An' home again, the Rio run: it's no child's play to go
Steamin' to bell for fourteen days o' snow an' floe an' blow—
The bergs like kelpies overside that girn an' turn an' shift
Whaur, grindin' like the Mills o' God, goes by the big South drift.
(Hail, snow an' ice that praise the lord: I've met them at their work,
An' wished we had anither route or they anither kirk.)

—Rudyard Kipling, writing on the perils of
data access, "McAndrews Hymn," 1894.

Problem Background

Unlike single desktop programs, which usually deal with documents on a user's local hard disk, essentially all distributed programs access remote data stores in some way. Remote data access is the main engine driving the phenomenal growth of the Internet—the incredible potential of easy access to data from anyone who wants to make it available. Sometimes the owner of that data charges money for the data itself. Pornographers were the first who made this business model really sing, as few users would fork over the bucks for any other type of content. Other businesses, such as the *Wall Street Journal* (porn for a different audience, some say) and the *Oxford English Dictionary*, are enjoying limited success with this model today, and mainstream music companies may eventually figure it out if they ever get their heads screwed on right. More often today, the owner of the data makes money by

All Internet applications access remote data stores.

using the Internet's easy access to that data to lower the friction of existing business processes, such as removing human employees from airline reservation systems or overnight package delivery tracking. Accessing remote data over the Internet is primarily why you have a PC today.

Data stores live in many different programs in many different locations.

Once you realize that the goals of most Internet applications differ radically from those of desktop programs, you won't be surprised to learn that we encounter different design problems when we write Internet apps. (Are you starting to see a pattern in this book?) First, the data that we want to see and perhaps change resides in many different locations and many different types of containers. I purposely selected the term *data stores* in this chapter's opening sentence instead of the more narrow *databases*. Certainly an enormous amount of data resides in large relational database programs such as Microsoft SQL Server or Oracle9*i*, but the data that an Internet app uses can and often does reside in many other locations. Some of these sources will be familiar to you, and only the notion of easy remote access will be new. For example, the financial data for my current house remodeling project lives in Microsoft Excel spreadsheets and Microsoft Money files on my hard disk. I'd like my architect and contractor to be able to read these files and update them with their latest cost overruns, and I'd like my banker to be able to read them and recoil in shock before handing over the money to cover the costs. Other data sources are new, and you might not have thought of them as data sources just a year ago. For example, the April 30, 2001, *Wall Street Journal* carried a story about a software product that reports the status of all the remote substations of an electric power utility company using the Web as a transport and display mechanism (oooh, baby, that feels SO good).

We want our many sources of data to look the same to a client program.

Naturally, the greater the number of different data sources, the more difficult becomes the task of writing client applications that access these different sources. We can't take the time to learn different programming models for every conceivable data store: one for SQL Server, a different one for Oracle, yet another for Excel—and heaven knows what programmatic interface those electric power guys are exposing to clients. This problem is especially bad for small-scale data providers because they don't have the clout to make clients learn their proprietary language, as some would argue that Microsoft and Oracle do. We need to have one basic programming model for accessing all types of data no matter where the data lives, otherwise we'll spend all our development budget dealing with different data access schemes and not have any resources left for writing any code that does useful work with the data once we've fetched it.

Our data access strategy needs to work well in the loosely coupled world of the Internet.

Internet data access programming is also difficult because of the heterogeneous and nondeterministic nature of the Internet environment. When a desktop PC accesses a database file on its own hard disk—say, in an application for a small dry-cleaning business looking for a missing garment—the developer can depend on that access being fast because it uses the PC's internal bus. On the Internet, a similar request might have to travel over congested transmission lines and wait for the attention of overloaded servers. The request is slower and the speed varies from one access of data to another. A developer needs to write code to account for these various conditions. In addition, a data source and its client are coupled much more loosely over the Internet than they would be if they resided on the same PC. For example, it's relatively easy to write code that opens a database connection and keeps it open for the duration of the work session of the human user. While this might be reasonable on a single PC, it doesn't work well over the Internet because the server probably has (desperately hopes it has) many concurrent users and the server will buckle under the load of keeping open many simultaneous connections, even if most of them aren't doing anything. We want to be able to access data in a way that can deal with slow and varying response times and doesn't tie up server resources for long periods.

XML (eXtensible Markup Language) is quickly emerging as the lingua franca of the Internet. That Latin term is about 200 years old, and it literally means "French language," but figuratively it means "the language everyone speaks." Today, we'd probably call XML the English of the Internet. I like to call XML the tofu of the Internet because it doesn't have any flavor of its own—it takes on the flavor of whatever you cook it with—or occasionally the WD-40 of the Internet, because it drastically lowers the friction of crossing boundaries. XML makes an excellent wire format for transporting data from one computer system to another because it's widely supported and free of implementation dependencies. Our data access strategy needs to go into and out of XML easily.

We need our data access strategy to work well with XML.

Finally, we need to maintain backward compatibility with existing code and data. The installed base of data access code is enormous, written and tested at great expense, and we can't afford to jettison it. Any new architecture that doesn't provide a bridge from the current state of affairs, whatever it is, doesn't have much chance in the market, no matter how cool it is on its own.

We need our new data access strategy to keep working with what's been working.

Solution Architecture

Microsoft's first attempt at solving the problem of universal data access from a single programming model was OLE DB, released around 1995. That's so long ago in geek years that COM was still called OLE (a MINFU; see Chapter 4), and the author of the *Microsoft Systems Journal* article about the technology provided a CompuServe number (70313,1455) as a contact address. In OLE DB, every data provider implemented a standard set of interfaces for

OLE DB provided a single programmatic interface for all providers of data.

allowing external access that required no knowledge by clients of the data provider's internal implementation. This process is illustrated in Figure 6-1.

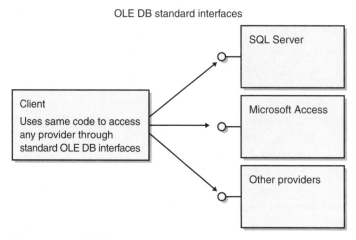

OLE DB standard interfaces

Figure 6-1   OLE DB abstracts away the differences between different data providers.

ADO made OLE DB easy for programmers to use but worked well only in a Microsoft-only environment.

It was a good idea and a good first try, but OLE DB[1] was hard for clients to program against, particularly in Microsoft Visual Basic. Microsoft next released ActiveX Data Objects (this was during the brief period when all things COM were called ActiveX, another MINFU), which Visual Basic programmers seized with cries of delight because it was so much easier (well, relatively) for them to program. ADO's front end provided an easier interface for clients to program against, and its back end spoke OLE DB to the provider, as shown in Figure 6-2. ADO worked fairly well on a Microsoft-only intranet and on the middle tier of a three-tier system accessed by Web clients. But ADO doesn't scale well to the open Internet. It uses DCOM to cross machine boundaries, which means that it can't easily work with non-Microsoft systems and has trouble getting through firewalls at Microsoft-only systems. ADO supported a limited amount of disconnected operation, but it was designed for and worked best in the connected case. It was a good solu-

---

1. You can see that as long ago as seven years, Microsoft foresaw the exhaustion of even the 456,976 unique FLAPs (Four-Letter Acronym Packages, FLAP itself is a FLAP, see Chapter 4) and started experimenting with alternatives. They've dusted off the FLEAP (Five Letter Extended Acronym Package, FLEAP itself is a FLEAP), which has a long and honorable history of military uses. Dwight David Eisenhower, for example, commanded SHAEF, the Supreme Headquarters Allied Expeditionary Force in the Second World War. While the use of FLEAPs hasn't crossed into the civilian sector, probably because there hasn't been any real need for them, 11,881,376 unique FLEAPs exist, so that ought to hold us for a while. If users balk at another increase in word length, the alternative would be to combine FLAPs, for example, CLOS, the Common LISP Object System. I call these FIAFs, which stands for FLAP Inside Another FLAP. And naturally, FIAF itself is a FIAF.

tion for the problem it aimed at, but programmers' needs have changed in the modern Internet world.

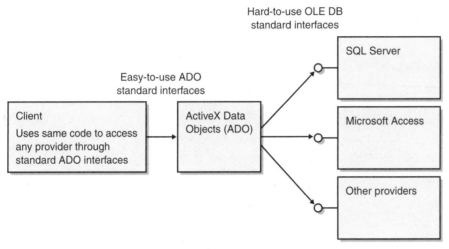

Figure 6-2   ADO object using OLE DB.

Microsoft .NET introduces ADO.NET, Microsoft's architecture for transferring the ideas of universal data access and easy programming from the COM-based world of ADO into the .NET world. ADO.NET is conceptually similar to ADO in the sense that it is a data abstraction layer that smooths over differences between data providers and includes prefabricated objects and functions for easy access to data.

.NET provides data access via ADO.NET.

A data provider that wants to make its data available to .NET clients via ADO.NET implements a standard set of .NET objects that connect the data provider to interested clients. These objects are *Connection*, *DataAdapter*, *Command*, and *DataReader*. A full description of these objects and their functionality requires examples, so I discuss them in the next section of this chapter. The developer of a data source can write his own implementation of these objects that is optimized for that particular data source, in the same manner as each data source today provides its own implementation of the OLE DB objects. Microsoft has provided an implementation of these objects for SQL Server, and these classes are part of the .NET common language runtime. In addition, the common language runtime provides an implementation of these objects that works with any OLE DB provider, so any current data provider that speaks OLE DB speaks ADO.NET automatically as well, as shown in Figure 6-3. Other data providers can choose whether to write their own native implementation of these objects or whether to write an OLE DB interface and use the compatibility layer.

The .NET common language runtime provides objects that access SQL Server and also any OLE DB provider.

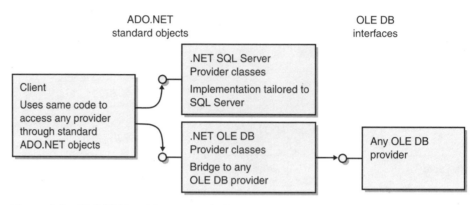

Figure 6-3   ADO.NET architecture and objects.

The server provides an
ADO.NET *DataSet* object
containing the result of a
query.

ADO.NET provides its actual data in the form of a *DataSet* object, as shown in Figure 6-4. *DataSet* is a .NET class that represents a collection of data that results from one or more queries. It contains internal tables and provides methods that allow access to the tables' rows and columns. It also contains a schema describing its internal structure. A *DataSet* object can be untyped (the default), in which case a client asks for items by specifying their names in the form of coded strings. Alternatively, you can create a typed *DataSet* object that contains member variables tied to each individual field, which is easier to write good code for. Either type of *DataSet* object is compatible with .NET's XML serialization capability described in Chapter 7. This means that it knows how to convert itself into and out of XML so that it can be transmitted across process or machine boundaries.

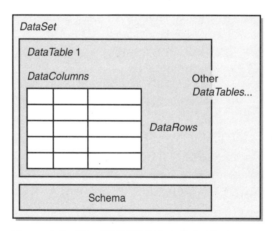

Figure 6-4   The ADO.NET *DataSet* object.

One of the main operations that programmers might want to do with a *DataSet* object when they get one is to display its contents to the user. Both Windows Forms (see Chapter 5) and Web Forms (see Chapter 3) contain controls that know how to take a *DataSet* object and render its contents for display to humans.

If they need it for backwards compatibility, .NET programs can still use original ADO via the COM compatibility feature discussed in Chapter 2.

This chapter provides the briefest glimpse into the features in ADO.NET. Like Windows Forms, in fact, and like every chapter of this book, ADO.NET needs a book of its own. Microsoft Press will publish *Microsoft ADO.NET (Core Reference)*, by David Sceppa, in May 2002.

Windows Forms and Web Forms contain controls for displaying DataSet objects.

Simplest Example

As always, I started my exploration of ADO.NET with the simplest example I could think of that demonstrated anything useful. You can find this sample program on this book's Web site, *www.introducingmicrosoft.net*. The application is an ASP.NET page that performs a canned database query when you request the page. It uses *DataConnection* and *DataAdapter* objects to request all the entries in the *Authors* table in the *pubs* database in the Duwamish Books sample program distributed with the .NET Framework SDK. The query produces an ADO.NET *DataSet* object, which I display to the user in a Web Forms DataGrid control on the Web page. The page itself is shown in Figure 6-5 and the sample code in Figure 6-6.

An ADO.NET example starts here.

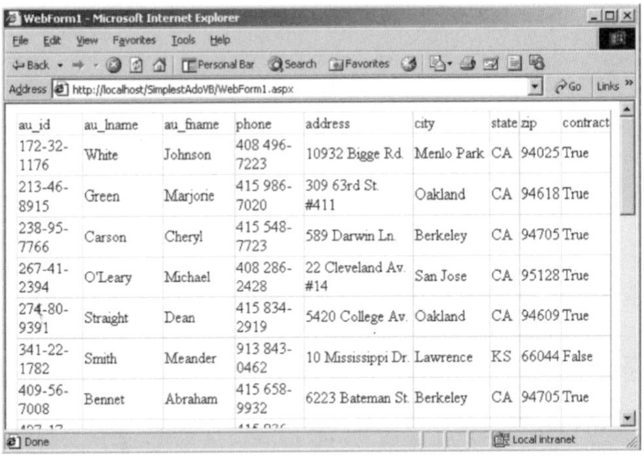

Figure 6-5   Web page from the simplest ADO.NET sample.

```
Private Sub Page_Load(ByVal sender As System.Object, _
                      ByVal e As System.EventArgs) _
                      Handles MyBase.Load

  ' Create Connection object containing connection string

  Dim Connection As New _
      SqlConnection("server=(local);uid=sa;pwd='';database=pubs")

  ' Create DataAdapter object containing query string

  Dim Adapter As New _
      SqlDataAdapter("select * from Authors", Connection)

  ' Create new empty DataSet object

  Dim DS = New DataSet()

  ' Fill DataSet object with results of query

  Adapter.Fill(DS, "Authors")

  ' Place data set into DataGrid control for user to look at

  DataGrid1().DataSource = DS.Tables("Authors").DefaultView

  ' Tell DataGrid control to display its contents

  DataGrid1().DataBind()

  ' Clean up database connection

  Connection.Close()

End Sub
```

Figure 6-6 The *Page_Load* event handler of the simplest ADO.NET sample.

When the user requests the page in her browser, the request comes to Internet Information Services (IIS) and ASP.NET, which fires the *Page_Load* event on the page as part of the rendering process. All the interesting code in this example lives in the handler for this event.

The first thing we have to do is create the *Connection* object. This object represents the opening in the database program through which requests flow in and data flows out, roughly analogous to the Ethernet jack on your office wall. ADO.NET provides two different common language runtime classes that we can use for our database connection. The class *System.Data.SqlClient.Sql-Connection*, which I use in this example, is optimized to work only with Microsoft SQL Server. ADO.NET also provides the class *System.Data.OleDb.OleDbConnection*, which is a generic *Connection* object that works with any OLE DB data provider, including SQL Server. Except for the names of the object classes and some slight differences in the connection string, the generic *Connection* object works the same from a client perspective as the dedicated SQL Server interface. Obviously, writing two different sets of data access objects was more work for Microsoft, but Microsoft probably figured that doing so was worth the effort to make SQL Server work better than generic databases, and they were probably right. I use the SQL-specific classes in this book.

In the constructor of the *SqlConnection* object, we pass it the connection string that we use to connect to the database, containing such items as the data provider's name and location, the database inside the provider to use, and the user ID and password that we use to connect to it. The values in this string are the same as they were in standard, pre-.NET ADO.

Having created the *Connection* object, we now need to create the *Data-Adapter* object, which mediates between the *Connection* object and the client application. Think of the *DataAdapter* object as the Ethernet card in your PC. Programs talk to the network card (the *DataAdapter* object), which in turn talks to the jack on the wall (the *Connection* object). Your client program issues commands to the *DataAdapter* object, which transmits them to the database through the *Connection* object and then accepts the results from the *Connection* object and returns them to your client program. In the *Data-Adapter* class constructor, we pass it the command that we want it to execute in the database—in this case selecting all the entries from a table of authors—and the *Connection* object for it to use in making that query. ADO.NET provides two *DataAdapter* classes, which are *System.Data.OleDb.OleDbData-Adapter* and *System.Data.SqlClient.SqlDataAdapter*. As was the case with *Connection* objects, the former is a generic class that works with any OLE DB–compliant data source, and the latter is optimized to work with SQL Server.

You first create an ADO.NET *Connection* object representing the connection to your database.

You next create a *Data-Adapter* object, which uses the *Connection* object to make calls into the database.

You create an empty *DataSet* object and use the *DataAdapter* object to fill it with data.

Now that we have our *DataAdapter* object, we want to use it to query the database and fetch some data for us to make money with. ADO.NET provides the class *System.Data.DataSet* as the fundamental holder for all types of data. A *DataSet* object contains its own internal tables that will contain the results of the queries that we will make on the data provider through the *DataAdapter* object and the *Connection* object. We start by creating an object of this class, which is empty when we first create it. We fill the *DataSet* object with data by calling the *DataAdapter* object's *Fill* method, passing the *DataSet* object itself and the name of the table inside the *DataSet* object that we want the data to live in. If, as in this case, the table doesn't currently exist in the *DataSet* object, it will be created as a result of this call. The table name need not match the table in the underlying database, as the name is used only within the *DataSet* object by client programs.

Once I have the data set, I use a DataGrid control to easily display it to the user.

Once I have my *DataSet* object filled, I want to display its contents to the user. I do this by placing it into a DataGrid control, a Web Forms control developed expressly for this purpose. The control lives on an .asmx page, and it knows how to eat a *DataSet* object and render its contents into HTML for display to the user. I tell it which *DataSet* object to eat by setting its *Data-Source* property to the *DataSet* object I just got from my query. I then tell the control "make it so" by calling its *DataBind* method. That call produces the HTML output that the user sees.

It's a good idea to explicitly close the database connection.

Finally, when I am finished with the database connection, it's a good idea to explicitly close it by using the *Connection* object's *Close* method. If I simply let the *Connection* object go out of scope, the object wouldn't be finalized and the underlying database connection that it wraps wouldn't be freed until the next garbage collection, whenever that is. Database connections are scarce resources, and I'd like to recover them as soon as possible. Therefore I call the *Close* method to tell the *Connection* object that I am finished with the database connection so that it should reclaim those resources. Enforcing this determinism in a garbage-collected memory management environment is obviously slightly harder to code, and therefore slightly easier to mess up, than was the automatic reference counting scheme used in Visual Basic 6.0, which would have released the *Connection* object immediately. However, garbage collection makes it impossible for you to permanently leak away resources, which reference counting allowed in certain cases. See my discussion of garbage collection in Chapter 2 for more details about the benefits of foolproofness vs. easy determinism.

This example required very little code.

This simple example required very little code, but it illustrates important concepts of ADO.NET and also demonstrates that it doesn't take a lot of programming to get a lot of stuff done.

More Complex Example: Disconnected Operation

The previous example is very simple, therefore it only scratches the surface. It doesn't show your own code reading data from a *DataSet* object; it doesn't show marshaling data across machine boundaries with XML; and it doesn't show disconnected operations, such as making changes to data and posting them back. So I've written a different sample, whose operation is shown in Figure 6-7, to demonstrate these features. Instead of using a browser to display data, I wrote a rich client using Windows Forms (see Chapter 5). The client uses an XML Web service (see Chapter 4) to fetch a data set from the server machine. The client allows a user to edit the results of the query and post the changes back to the underlying database through the XML Web service.

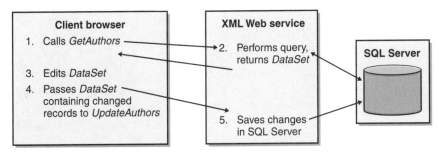

Figure 6-7 Operation of the DataSet sample program.

On the server, I've written a simple XML Web service that exposes the methods *GetAuthors* and *UpdateAuthors*. The first method's code is shown in Figure 6-8, and it's really quite simple.

A sample showing disconnected operations starts here.

```
<WebMethod()> Public Function GetAuthors() As System.Data.DataSet

    ' Create Connection object

    Dim Connection As SqlConnection
    Connection = New _
        SqlConnection("server=(local);uid=sa;pwd='';database=pubs")

    ' Create DataAdapter object

    Dim Adapter As SqlDataAdapter
    Adapter = New _
        SqlDataAdapter("select * from Authors", Connection)

    ' Create empty DataSet object
```

Figure 6-8 The *GetAuthors* method.

Figure 6-8 *(continued)*

```
        Dim DS As Data.DataSet
        DS = New Data.DataSet()

        ' Fill DataSet object with data

        Adapter.Fill(DS, "Authors")

        ' Return DataSet object to caller

        Return DS

    End Function
```

The XML Web service method simply returns a *DataSet* object, which causes it to be transmitted in XML.

When the client calls *GetAuthors*, the method creates a *Connection* object and a *DataAdapter* object and uses these to create a *DataSet* object, as shown in the previous example. I could easily have added additional parameters for the client to pass to the XML Web service that the service could use in performing the query—say, authors whose first name is "John"—but I didn't want to complicate the example. The difference between this example and the previous one is that, instead of displaying the data set on a Web page for a human user, the XML Web service returns the *DataSet* object to the client program that calls it. This causes the *DataSet* object to be serialized into XML and transmitted over the wire to the client. You can see the *DataSet* object layout in XML by using the XML Web service's built-in test capability, as shown in Figure 6-9.

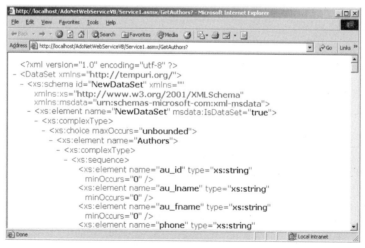

Figure 6-9   The XML layout for the *DataSet* object.

You can run the XML Web service through the sample client app. When the user clicks the Fill button, the app fetches the data set containing all the authors from the XML Web service, as shown in Figure 6-10. The code is shown in Figure 6-11.

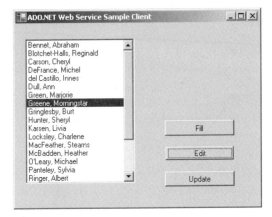

Figure 6-10   Our sample client application.

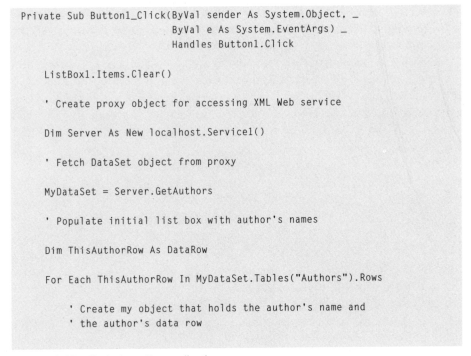

```
Private Sub Button1_Click(ByVal sender As System.Object, _
                    ByVal e As System.EventArgs) _
                    Handles Button1.Click

    ListBox1.Items.Clear()

    ' Create proxy object for accessing XML Web service

    Dim Server As New localhost.Service1()

    ' Fetch DataSet object from proxy

    MyDataSet = Server.GetAuthors

    ' Populate initial list box with author's names

    Dim ThisAuthorRow As DataRow

    For Each ThisAuthorRow In MyDataSet.Tables("Authors").Rows

        ' Create my object that holds the author's name and
        ' the author's data row
```

Figure 6-11   Code from the application.

Figure 6-11 *(continued)*

```
        Dim ThisGuy As New MyOwnListItem(ThisAuthorRow("au_lname") + _
            ", " + ThisAuthorRow("au_fname"), ThisAuthorRow)
        ListBox1.Items.Add(ThisGuy)
    Next

End Sub
```

The client automatically rehydrates the XML into a *DataSet* object.

The client creates an object of the XML Web service class and calls the *GetAuthors* method, which returns the *DataSet* object as I've just described. When the client assigns this return value to a variable, it takes the XML stream sent by the server and rehydrates it into a functioning *DataSet* object. The *DataSet* object has been transmitted using XML and HTTP, which clearly illustrates the fact that it can be sent to any type of client, even a non-Microsoft system.

The *DataSet* object contains .NET properties representing tables and rows.

Once I've gotten the *DataSet* object from server to client, I want to access it on the client side. I fetch the table in the *DataSet* object that I know contains the records of authors by using the *DataSet* object's *Tables* collection, passing the name of the table that I want to access, in this case *Authors*. This call returns an object of class *System.Data.DataTable*. This table contains the author records that I want, each represented by an object called *System.Data.DataRow*. I step through each record sequentially by accessing the collection called *Rows* in the *DataTable* object.

You access an individual column through its name in a *DataRow* object.

I'd like to get each author's first name and last name, assemble them into a string, and display the string in the *ListBox* control. Getting the data from the *DataSet* object is easy. Each *DataRow* object contains a collection of columns that represent the fields in the database that actually contain individual values. I access a column by using its name, in this case *au_lname* and *au_fname*, as shown at the end of the code listing in Figure 6-11.

ListBox controls now require a .NET object because the *ItemData* property has been removed.

Since I want to enable the user to edit the *DataRow* later, I need to associate a *DataRow* with its line in the *ListBox* control. In Visual Basic 6.0, I'd have used the *ListBox* control's *ItemData* property to hold an integer key identifying the row in a separate collection I'd have to somehow manage. But I can't do that in .NET because the *ItemData* property has been removed. Instead, the *ListBox* control can hold a .NET object of any class, but it won't hold two separate items (the string and the key) as it did before. The *ListBox* control displays the string returned by the object's *ToString* method (described in Chapter 2). So to make this app work the way I wanted, I needed to roll my own class that contained all the information I wanted for the *ListBox* control to hold. You'll find that information in the class *MyOwn-ListItem*. It holds a *DataRow* object and a string, both of which it accepts in its constructor. The code is shown in Figure 6-12. It sounds complicated, but it really isn't. It saves me having to manage my own collection of *ListBox* items, which is a net gain even if you use it in only one place. I create an object of this class, passing it the full name string I want to display in the *ListBox* control and the *DataRow* object with which I want the name associated.

```
Public Class MyOwnListItem

    Public m_FullName As String
    Public m_DataRow As Data.DataRow

    ' Class constructor that accepts a name for display and a DataRow
    ' to hold

    Public Sub New(ByVal FullName As String, _
                   ByVal MyDataRow As Data.DataRow)
        m_FullName = FullName
        m_DataRow = MyDataRow
    End Sub

    ' Override System.Object.ToString. The displaying ListBox control
    ' will call this method to get the string to display

    Public Overrides Function ToString() As String
        Return m_FullName
    End Function

End Class
```

Figure 6-12   Code from my own class *MyOwnListItem*.

Now I want to edit an individual entry. When the user selects an entry from the *ListBox* and clicks Edit, I pop up a dialog box showing the status of that author's contract, as shown in Figure 6-13. You can see the code in Figure 6-14.

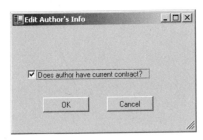

Figure 6-13   The Edit Author's Info dialog box.

```
Private Sub Button2_Click(ByVal sender As System.Object, _
                          ByVal e As System.EventArgs) _
                          Handles Button2.Click

    ' Get selected author's data row from ListBox control

    Dim SelectedListItem As MyOwnListItem
    SelectedListItem = ListBox1.Items(ListBox1.SelectedIndex)

    Dim AuthorsDataRow As Data.DataRow
    AuthorsDataRow = SelectedListItem.m_DataRow

    ' Get state of author's contract from data row

    Dim contract As Boolean
    contract = AuthorsDataRow("contract")

    ' Set control in editing form according to current state
    ' of author's contract

    Dim EditForm As New Form2()
    EditForm.CheckBox1.Checked = contract

    ' Set editing form's text and show to user.
    ' If user clicked OK, then change value in data row
    ' and enable Update button

    If (EditForm.ShowDialog() = DialogResult.OK) Then
        AuthorsDataRow("contract") = EditForm.CheckBox1.Checked
        Button3.Enabled = True
    End If

End Sub
```

Figure 6-14   Code allowing editing of author info.

You read and write columns in the *DataRow* object as if they were simple variables.

I first fetch the *DataRow* object representing the user's selection from the *ListBox*. (See how much easier it is than a separate collection?) I look at the *DataRow* object's *contract* column and set the dialog box's *CheckBox* control to the column's value. If the user clicks OK, I fetch the state of the *CheckBox* control from the dialog box and set the value in the *DataRow* object's *contract* column. You can see that I'm simply treating the *contract* column like a standard variable.

You can easily select only the changed rows to be sent back to the server for updating.

When the user clicks Update, I need to send whatever changes he's made back to the server to update the server's master database tables. I could send the entire data set back to the server and let the server figure out which rows have changed, but this would be a waste of network bandwidth. It would be better to send only the changed rows. I can easily do this by using the method *DataSet.GetChanges*, which returns another *DataSet* object containing only the rows in the original data set to which changes have been made. I send this *DataSet* object back to the XML Web service using the service's *UpdateAuthors* method. You can see the code for *UpdateAuthors* in Figure 6-15.

```
<WebMethod()> Public Function UpdateAuthors( _
    ByVal ChangedItemsDS As System.Data.DataSet) As Integer

  ' Create new Connection object

  Dim Connection As SqlConnection
  Connection = New _
      SqlConnection("server=(local);uid=sa;pwd='';database=pubs")

  ' Create DataAdapter object

  Dim Adapter As SqlDataAdapter
  Adapter = New SqlDataAdapter()

  ' Create and set properties of Command object

  Dim MyUpdateCommand As New _
      Data.SqlClient.SqlCommand( _
      "UPDATE Authors SET contract = @contract WHERE au_id = @au_id", _
      Connection)
  Adapter.UpdateCommand = MyUpdateCommand
  Adapter.UpdateCommand.Parameters.Add("@contract", SqlDbType.Bit, _
                                 1, "contract")
  Adapter.UpdateCommand.Parameters.Add("@au_id", SqlDbType.VarChar, _
                                 11, "au_id")

  ' Send update command to database via DataAdapter object,
  ' specifying the changed records' DataSet object.
  ' The Update method returns an integer, which we return to
  ' the client

  Return Adapter.Update(ChangedItemsDS, "Authors")

End Function
```

Figure 6-15 Updating author information.

On the server side, my XML Web service catches the incoming *DataSet* object containing changes that the client has made. It creates a *Connection* object and a *DataAdapter* object as before. In this case, we are going to be updating data that's already in the database, so we also need a *Command*

The *DataAdapter* object uses a *Command* object to make changes to the underlying database.

object, which represents a command that you use to tell the database to do something. The common language runtime provides two classes of *Command* object, *System.Data.OleDb.OleDbCommand*, which is the generic *Command* object available to any OLE DB provider, and *System.Data.SqlClient.SqlCommand*, which is the version specific to SQL Server. You create one of these objects as shown, passing in its constructor the SQL string that you want executed. You then plug the *Command* object into the *DataAdapter* object by assigning it to the *DataAdapter* object's *UpdateCommand* property. This assignment tells the *DataAdapter* object which SQL command to run when data is updated. You'll see that I also have to add parameter objects to tell the command which variables map to which columns. (The *DataAdapter* object also contains *InsertCommand* and *DeleteCommand* properties, which accept a similar *Command* object used during inserts and deletes, respectively, but I don't use these properties in this example.) Finally, I call the *DataAdapter* object's *Update* method, telling it to take the update command and run it against the database, using the *DataSet* object that I received from the client. This call returns the number of rows updated, which I return to the client.

Design of databases used by ADO.NET needs to take into account its loosely coupled nature.

The loosely coupled nature of ADO.NET *DataSet* objects requires careful thought in database design. Since you don't know how long a client is going to keep a *DataSet* object, you can't afford to keep locks on all your data to prevent conflicts; you'd tie the system into knots very quickly. Instead, you can design your database to use some form of optimistic concurrency. If I had done that, my sample XML Web service would contain code that would check before saving updates to see whether the data it is saving had been changed by someone else in the interim—for example, by checking a timestamp column. If the data had been changed, the unsaved, edited values might be bad, so the XML Web service would throw an error back to the client, and the client would somehow inform the user of this and make the user do it again. We call this type of concurrency *optimistic* because we're hoping that this somewhat painful process won't happen very often. This approach works well in systems that experience low contention rates. For higher contention systems, such as buying tickets online to the latest Harry Belafonte concert (he's still got his stuff, by the way, even at age 75), you might use compensating transactions—remove a specific pair of tickets from the theater database when the user first asks what's available and then perform the opposite operation to put the tickets back in the pool if the user doesn't buy them within ten minutes.

Visual Studio Support and Typed *DataSet* Objects

In the two previous examples, I've written my own code for creating the various objects that I've needed for my data operations, such as the *Connection* and the *Adapter*. I've also had to write code for setting their properties, such as the connection string parameters in the *Connection* object and the query string parameters in the *Adapter* object. As any developer who's struggled with connection strings knows, this can become painful. I don't usually have to write code that creates buttons on a form or sets their properties; instead, Visual Studio provides an editor that generates that code for me and saves me lots of time. I'd really like some of that support for writing my database operation code, and Visual Studio gives it to me.

Visual Studio provides good editor support for writing data applications.

Besides the *Connection* and *Adapter* objects, I'd also like some help with *DataSet*s. Working with a *DataSet* object as shown in the previous example is useful, but it's still somewhat unwieldy because you have to plug in strings to specify the names of tables and columns. Some programming cases require this flexibility, such as a generic data browsing tool that allows a human user to type in any sort of query that occurs to him. But the majority of data access programs perform the same operations on the same data sources over and over and over again—think of the concert ticket application, for example. In cases like these, it doesn't make sense to require the programmer to pass a string name to identify a table or column. The programmer has to look up the name in a manual so that she knows which one to use and then make sure she types it in correctly every time—that she hasn't transposed a key and typed "Auhtors," for example. Mistakes like this are easy to make because raw *DataSet*s don't have development-time support to make sure that you type in the correct string. They are also difficult to debug because your eye isn't good at picking out close misspellings. It may not sound like a terrible problem, but if we could prevent it, we'd save some programmer time, some testing time, and probably some service calls. If you don't want those savings, send yours to me, OK?

Working with standard *DataSet* objects could use some development time support.

What we'd really like is a *DataSet* object that's tailored to the particular data that we expect to receive from a specific operation. It would have table and column names already wired into it as hard-coded variables. It would allow IntelliSense to show these names during programming so that we wouldn't have to reach for the paper manual. We wouldn't have to worry about misspellings because the compiler would catch us if we somehow ignored IntelliSense and got a name wrong. And we'd like good development tool support for generating them.

We want a dedicated *DataSet* class tailored to the results of a specific data operation.

It turns out that all of our wishes have been granted by .NET and Visual Studio. Now that we've seen the nuts and bolts of ADO.NET, I'll show you the tools that make it easier. I've written a sample program that demonstrates it.

Visual Studio .NET supports developers writing data applications by providing its Server Explorer, shown in Figure 6-16. Server Explorer shows the various elements on a server for which it can generate .NET wrapper class objects, such as message queues and performance counters. The most interesting part of Server Explorer for our purposes is that it allows us to see the contents of our local SQL Server installation down to the table level. (It will actually go down to the individual column level, but I'm not using that for this example.)

A database programming example demonstrating intelligent tool support starts here.

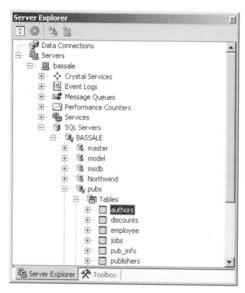

Figure 6-16   Server Explorer within the Visual Studio .NET environment.

Server Explorer in Visual Studio will automatically generate the correct Sql-Connection and SqlData-Adapter objects for accessing a database.

When I click on a table (in this case, *authors*) and drag it onto my design surface, Visual Studio generates *SqlConnection* and *SqlDataAdapter* objects and sets their parameters to the proper values for accessing the selected table. For example, the *SqlDataAdapter* is set to use the created connection, and has appropriate SQL commands added, as shown in Figure 6-17. As with all objects generated by Visual Studio, the code for creating them is placed in the *InitializeComponent* method of the container, in this case my XML Web service. I haven't gained any run-time performance advantage by setting up my connection and adapter objects this way. In fact, I've probably lost a little because Visual Studio generates the Insert and Delete commands that this example doesn't use. But it saves a whole lot of developer time and prevents errors, which means it's usually a good trade-off. And I could manually remove the unneeded pieces if I really cared.

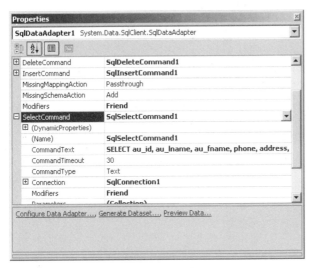

Figure 6-17 *SQLDataAdapter* object properties.

Now that I have my connection and adapter set up nicely, it's time to do something about my *DataSet*. ADO.NET provides the *typed DataSet* class. This is a custom class, derived from *System.Data.DataSet*, that provides named member variables for each specific table, row, and column. If we know at programming time which tables and columns a data set will contain, we can use utility programs to generate a typed *DataSet* class. This feature might not sound like a big deal, and I didn't think it would matter much until I tried it, but now I'm hooked. As long as you know during program development which data queries you are going to want to make, and you usually will, you won't want to program any other way. I've rewritten the authors client example from the previous section to use a typed *DataSet* object. This approach was easy to generate and made my programming somewhat easier to accomplish and somewhat harder to get wrong. The cost is a small amount of extra code, which you don't have to write, in your application. Any time you can trade off larger code size for faster and better programming, you don't have an economic choice.

You generate a typed *DataSet* by selecting Generate Dataset from the Data menu of Visual Studio's main menu. (You can also generate it with the

ADO.NET supports typed *DataSet* classes.

You generate a typed *DataSet* class using Visual Studio's wizards.

command-line utility XSD.exe, which requires an XML schema that describes your data set.) Visual Studio pops up the dialog box shown in Figure 6-18, asking for the name of the new class and the table that you want it to match. You make your selections and Visual Studio generates the code for the new class. In Class View, shown in Figure 6-19, you can see that the new class contains strongly typed classes to represent the table (*authorsDataTable*) and the row within the table (*authorsRow*).

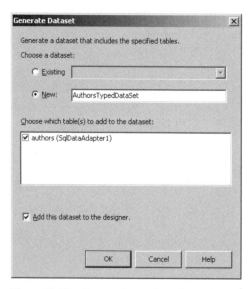

Figure 6-18   Generating a *DataSet* in Visual Studio .NET.

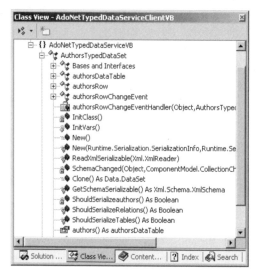

Figure 6-19   Class View showing strongly typed classes.

I rewrote my XML Web service to take advantage of the new objects that it contains. Figure 6-20 shows the code of my XML Web service method. It's much simpler because the connection, adapter, and typed data set have already been created. In my *GetAuthors* method, I simply tell the adapter to fill the data set and then return it. In my *UpdateAuthors* method, I simply tell the adapter to update the database with the new information. Again, I'm not saving any CPU cycles here; the objects are still being created exactly as if I had written the code myself, but I had to write much less code. When either method returns, ASP.NET automatically calls *Dispose* on the XML Web service object, which automatically disposes of all its components, including the connection and adapter.

Writing the database access code is much easier with the objects that Visual Studio has created.

```
<WebMethod()> Public Function GetAuthors() As AuthorsTypedDataSet

    ' Connection, adapter, and dataset objects have been
    ' added by designer instead of with our own code.

    ' Fill DataSet object with data

    Me.SqlDataAdapter1.Fill(Me.AuthorsTypedDataSet1)

    ' Return DataSet object to caller

    Return Me.AuthorsTypedDataSet1

End Function

<WebMethod()> Public Function UpdateAuthors(ByVal ChangedItemsDS _
    As System.Data.DataSet) As Integer

    ' Connection, adapter, and dataset objects have been
    ' added by designer instead of with our own code.

    ' Call Update method on adapter, which makes updates in records

    Return Me.SqlDataAdapter1.Update(ChangedItemsDS)

End Function
```

Figure 6-20   XML Web service sample code for getting and updating author information.

Writing the client code is much easier with the typed data set.

The client code, shown in Figure 6-21, is very similar to the previous example. You can see that instead of saying *MyDataSet.Tables("Authors").Rows*, I say *MyDataSet.authors*. To fetch an individual value, I say *ThisAuthorRow.au_lname* instead of *ThisAuthor-Row("au_lname")*. These differences may not sound like much, but they remove a common source of errors (misspelling the string) and save programmer time by allowing IntelliSense support, as shown in Figure 6-22. If you still don't think it sounds useful, try using it for an hour and then give it up. You'll change your mind very quickly. The rest of the sample gets similarly easier. If you know your query set at development time, you do not have an economic choice.

```
Dim MyDataSet As localhost.AuthorsTypedDataSet

Private Sub Button1_Click(ByVal sender As System.Object, ByVal e As _
    System.EventArgs) Handles Button1.Click

    ListBox1.Items.Clear()

    ' Create proxy object for accessing Web Service

    Dim Server As New localhost.Service1()

    ' Fetch DataSet object from proxy

    MyDataSet = Server.GetAuthors

    ' Populate initial list box with author's names

    Dim ThisAuthorRow As localhost.AuthorsTypedDataSet.authorsRow

    For Each ThisAuthorRow In MyDataSet.authors

    ' Create my object that holds the authors name and
    ' the author's data row

    Dim ThisGuy As New MyOwnListItem(ThisAuthorRow.au_lname + _
        ", " + ThisAuthorRow.au_fname, ThisAuthorRow)
        ListBox1.Items.Add(ThisGuy)
    Next
End Sub
```

Figure 6-21   Client code for typed XML Web service sample.

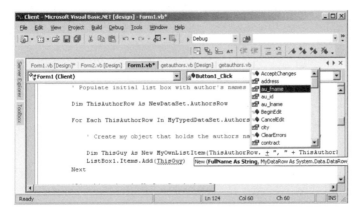

Figure 6-22   IntelliSense support in Visual Studio.

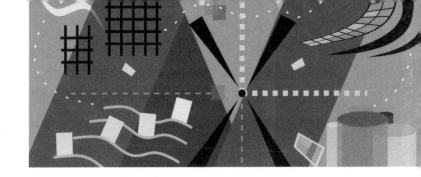

7

Handling XML

That minds me of our Viscount loon—Sir Kenneth's kin—the chap
Wi' russia leather tennis-shoon an' spar-decked yachtin'-cap.
I showed him round last week, o'er all—an' at the last says he:
"Mister McAndrews, don't you think steam spoils romance at sea?"
Damned ijjit! I'd been doon that morn to see what ailed the throws,
Manholin', on my back—the cranks three inches off my nose.

> —Rudyard Kipling, writing on the impossibility of explaining
> technical wizardry to managers, "McAndrew's Hymn," 1894.

Problem Background

XML is now the universally accepted wire format for transmitting data among distributed systems. For example, we saw in Chapter 4 how XML Web services carry the data in cross-machine function calls, and in Chapter 6 how a data set serializes itself into XML for easy transmission from server to client and back. The modern computing world has many other uses for XML, so help with handling XML documents and streams is one of the most important functions that an operating system can provide to an application programmer.

XML pervades the modern computing environment, so we need operating system help with it.

The most common use of XML we encounter is the XML-based industry standard vocabulary for communicating among separate parties in a particular industry or within a company. For example, the insurance industry uses a vocabulary called ACORD XML (*www.acord.org*), and the health care industry uses a vocabulary called Health Level 7, or HL7 (*www.hl7.org*). The process of using an XML vocabulary to communicate is shown in Figure 7-1. For example, let's say a client (a doctor's office, an insurance agent) sends an

Even though we have XML Web services, we still need to read and write XML documents.

XML document containing a command (admit a patient) or a request (quote this proposed policy) and all the data required to support that operation (the patient's name, history, and diagnosis; the location and description of the insured premises and the type of coverage desired) to a recipient (a hospital, an insurance company's head office). The recipient reads the information from the XML document, performs its business logic, and generates a response document to return to the sender (patient admitted to this bed of that unit, your insurance will cost so much—and look at these cool add-ons you can foist on the poor schmoe to raise your commission). While situations of this type may seem tailor-made for XML Web services, distributed systems often don't want to use HTTP as their underlying transport mechanism, preferring asynchronous store-and-forward channels such as MSMQ or even e-mail. We need an easy way to read the contents of incoming XML documents and to generate outgoing documents.

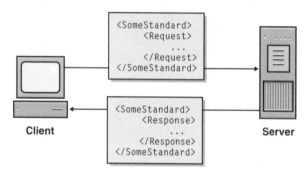

Figure 7-1   XML document used as command or request and response between different systems.

Generic XML parsers are hard to write code for, so we'd like a way to transform XML documents into .NET classes.

Most operating systems come with an XML parser, a utility object that performs the lowest-level tasks of handling XML documents. The parser reads an XML document, checks to see that it is properly constructed, and then exposes some sort of generic interface to allow client programs to read and write it. Application programmers don't have to worry about the lowest-level tasks such as counting angle brackets or matching tag names, which makes life easier than it would be without a parser. But the parsers are by their very nature generic, so they don't fit any particular task very well. Application programmers constantly need to deal with the medium-level implementation details of an XML document—for example, is this particular piece of data represented by an XML element or an attribute? Programmers spend most of their time writing code similar to that shown in Figure 7-2, identifying individual pieces of data with long, complex strings, which are damnably hard to get right. It looks easy, but try it for an hour and you'll see that it isn't. You have to type in the exact string that you want every time, and your program dies if you get just one letter incorrectly capitalized. There's no notion of data typing; the parser returns all values as strings and you have to convert them by hand to whatever you think they ought to be. IntelliSense doesn't work in parsers, so you have to keep flipping back and forth to the documentation. We need a way of accessing XML documents other than from within a generic parser that makes them easier to write and harder to get wrong. We'd really like our XML documents to magically become .NET classes so that we can bring the power of the .NET Framework to bear on them.

```
Password = DocOut.selectSingleNode _
    ("/TXLife/UserAuthRequest/UserPswd/Pswd").Text
```

Figure 7-2   Code used to access an XML element in a generic parser.

While the problem we most frequently encounter is having to repetitively deal with the same type of document, we still need the capabilities of a generic parser. Designers of, say, an XML editor utility have to deal with arbitrary XML documents whose structure they don't know about at design time. The existing Microsoft XML parser uses COM as its interface to client applications. Our .NET applications could use that parser via the COM compatibility layer described in Chapter 2. However, our programs would then require the powerful and double-edged code security permission of accessing unmanaged code, which administrators do not like to grant. So in addition to easy access to repetitive documents, we also need generic parsing capability in our managed .NET world.

We still need generic parsing capability in .NET

Solution Architecture

The solution to the problem of requiring generic parsing capability, as for every compatibility problem in computing, is to add a layer of abstraction. (The solution to every performance problem in computing is to remove a layer of abstraction, but I digress.) Since the operation of reading and writing XML documents is highly repetitive, it makes sense to provide prefabricated functionality that performs the repetitive operations and frees programmers to think about their business logic.

The .NET Framework provides this capability through a class called *System.Xml.Serialization.XmlSerializer*. An object of this class knows how to take any .NET object, read its public properties and member variables, and write them into an XML document. This process is known as *serialization*, and I like to think of it as dehydrating an object and storing the resulting powder. The same serializer can then take the XML document at a later time,

.NET abstracts away the details of XML documents by making them .NET objects.

read its contents, and re-create an object of the same class having the same values as the original object. This process is known as *deserialization*, and I think of it as adding water to rehydrate the object. Figure 7-3 shows a conceptual diagram of the process. The first example in this chapter illustrates this technique.

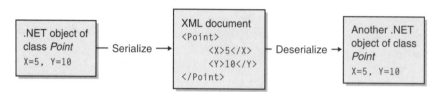

Figure 7-3   Diagram of .NET XML serialization process.

We can control serialization output so as to match other people's XML layout if necessary.

It often happens that the structure of the XML documents that our programs need to deal with is not under our control. Rather than accepting the default output of .NET serialization, we need to control that output to make our dehydrated object layout conform to an XML schema that someone else wrote, perhaps someone who wasn't using .NET or anything else from Microsoft and never intends to. The XML serialization features of .NET let us control the structure of the documents that our objects produce when serialized, thereby allowing us to produce any type of XML document that we require. The second example in this chapter illustrates this technique.

An SDK tool makes the control process easy.

We need the control over our XML serialization to be fast and easy, and .NET provides us with this capability as well. Instead of having to manually write our .NET classes to match an XML schema, we can use a tool to generate them for us. The third example in this chapter illustrates this technique.

.NET comes with a full-fledged generic XML parser.

Finally, .NET provides us with a full-featured generic XML parser for those times when we have to operate at a low level of abstraction. The fourth example in this chapter demonstrates this.

Simplest Example: Basic Serialization

A simple example starts here.

As I always do when learning a new piece of software, I wrote the simplest example I could think of to demonstrate XML serialization, as shown in Figure 7-4. The program contains a class named *Point*, having two member variables named *X* and *Y*, as shown in Figure 7-5. The user enters two integers, the *x* and *y* coordinates of a point. The program then creates a *Point* object containing these values and serializes the object into an XML document. The user can also open an XML document containing a serialized *Point* object, and the program will deserialize the *Point* object and display its values.

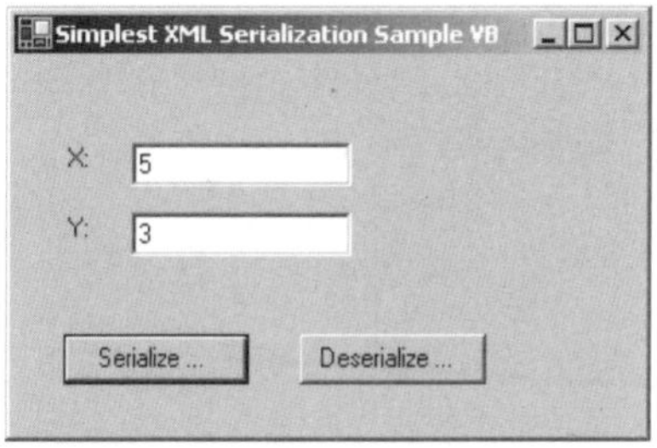

Figure 7-4   Simplest serialization sample program.

```
Public Class Point

    Public X As Integer
    Public Y As Integer

End Class
```

Figure 7-5   *Point* class for simplest serialization example.

The code for serializing a *Point* object into an XML document is shown in Figure 7-6. When the user clicks Serialize, the program pops up a dialog box asking for the name of the file to write the document into and creates an empty file with the name that the user enters. Next the program creates a new object of the *Point* class and sets its member variables *X* and *Y* to the values that the user entered. We then create the serializer object, of class *System.Xml.Serialization.XmlSerializer*, passing in its constructor the type of object that we want it to serialize, in this case a *Point*. Finally, we tell the serializer object to serialize its data into the file by calling its *Serialize* method. The resulting XML document is shown in Figure 7-7. It doesn't get much easier than this, does it?

```
Private Sub Button1_Click(ByVal sender As System.Object, _
                     ByVal e As System.EventArgs) _
                     Handles Button1.Click
    ' Pop up dialog box asking user for file name to
    ' serialize Point object into.

    Dim dlg As New System.Windows.Forms.SaveFileDialog()

    If (dlg.ShowDialog = DialogResult.OK) Then

        ' Create XML document named by the user
```

Figure 7-6   Code for serializing a point.

Figure 7-6 *(continued)*

```
        Dim xmlstream As New _
            System.IO.FileStream(dlg.FileName, _
            System.IO.FileMode.CreateNew, _
            System.IO.FileAccess.ReadWrite)


        ' Make a new object of class Point containing X
        ' and Y values specified by user.

        Dim here As New Point()
        here.X = TextBox1.Text
        here.Y = TextBox2.Text

        ' Make a new serializer for the Point class

        Dim serializer As New _
            Xml.Serialization.XmlSerializer(GetType(Point))

        ' Write (serialize) the Point into the XML document

        serializer.Serialize(xmlstream, here)

        ' Close the file

        xmlstream.Close()

    End If

End Sub
```

```
<Point>
    <X>5</X>
    <Y>3</Y>
</Point>
```

Figure 7-7   XML document produced by serialization.

When I want to deserialize the object, the process is quite similar and it uses the same serializer class. The code is shown in Figure 7-8. The sample program pops up a dialog box allowing the user to select the file containing her serialized point and opens that file for reading. Next we create an object of the same class that did the original serialization, passing it the type of the object we want it to read, again a *Point*. The function *Deserialize* reads the XML document, creates the object of the specified class, sets its public data fields to the values specified in the XML document, and returns it to the caller. The sample program reads the values of the new object and puts them into text boxes for you to look at. Again, this is about as easy as anything ever gets in this business.

```
Private Sub Button2_Click(ByVal sender As System.Object, _
                          ByVal e As System.EventArgs) _
                          Handles Button2.Click

    ' Pop up dialog box asking user which XML
    ' file contains the serialized Point object

    Dim dlg As New System.Windows.Forms.OpenFileDialog()

    If (dlg.ShowDialog = DialogResult.OK) Then

        ' Open the XML document selected by the user

        Dim xmlstream As New _
            System.IO.FileStream(dlg.FileName, _
            System.IO.FileMode.Open, _
            System.IO.FileAccess.ReadWrite)

        ' Make a serializer for the Point class

        Dim serializer As New _
            Xml.Serialization.XmlSerializer(GetType(Point))

        ' Read (deserialize) the document into the Point object

        Dim here As Point
        here = serializer.Deserialize(xmlstream)

        ' Place desired items into text boxes

        TextBox1.Text = here.X
        TextBox2.Text = here.Y

        ' Close the file

        xmlstream.Close()

    End If

End Sub
```

Figure 7-8   Deserializing the XML document into a .NET object.

Creating serializers is somewhat slow, so you probably want to reuse them as often as possible.

When you run the sample, you'll see that the serialization process takes a few seconds. If you explore further, you'll find that creating the serializer takes most of this time and actually serializing the object takes very little. When you create the serializer, it reads through the metadata of the class that you have passed it to find the names and types of the objects and variables it must write to or read from an XML document. This process uses the .NET Reflection API and is somewhat complex, hence the time it takes. You can imagine that because creating a serializer takes a noticeable amount of time for a tiny, stupid object like *Point*, creating a serializer for a larger object will take much more time, and in fact it does. Fortunately, you can reuse the serializer for other operations on the same type of object; you don't need a separate one for each instance. This means that when your program starts up, you will probably want to precreate all the serializers you will require and keep them around throughout your program's execution. ASP.NET applications may find this a good use of the *Application* object. I didn't use this technique in the sample because I wanted each operation's code listing to stand alone, and you can see the performance price that I paid for it.

More Complex Example: Controlling Serialization

You can control the XML document produced by the serialization process

If all we want to do is send objects from one .NET program to another, we don't need any capability beyond what this first example just did. But more often, especially when talking to other platforms, you don't control the XML document layout that other parties are expecting. The XML documents produced by your .NET objects need to conform to someone else's XML schema—often created by a fractious industry standards body—that won't be the default .NET layout. What we'd really like is to somehow control the XML document produced by the .NET serialization process so that we can make it match whatever external standards exist.

You control serialization by decorating class variables with .NET programming attributes

The .NET XML serializer allows us to do this quite easily by using .NET programming attributes. The previous example demonstrated the serializer's default behavior, which involves storing each public member variable's value in a separate XML element. But suppose the person sending me the XML document had placed these items in XML attributes instead. How could I get them out if the serializer expects elements? The answer turns out to be simple. I would modify my *Point* class as shown in Figure 7-9, decorating each member variable with the .NET programming attribute *System.Xml.Serialization.XmlAttribute*. (This attribute name is the abbreviated form of *XMLAttributeAttribute*, as explained in Chapter 2. The names are interchangeable.) When I create the serializer, it reads the .NET programming attributes from the metadata of the type that I pass it. When it sees this attribute on a member variable, the serializer knows that I want it to place the variable into an XML attribute rather than an XML element. The class shown in Figure 7-9 serializes to the document shown in Figure 7-10.

```
Public Class AttributePoint

    <System.Xml.Serialization.XmlAttributeAttribute()> Public X As Integer
    <System.Xml.Serialization.XmlAttributeAttribute()> Public Y As Integer

End Class
```

Figure 7-9   *Point* class that serializes to attributes.

```
<AttributePoint X="15" Y="20" />
```

Figure 7-10   XML representation of serialized class in attributes.

You'll find that *XmlAttribute* and its companion *XmlElement* contain a number of variables allowing you even greater control over the XML produced by serializing your objects. You can, for example, make the element or attribute name in your XML document different from the name of the variable to which it corresponds in your .NET class. This allows your .NET variables to have names that aren't legal in XML, such as names beginning with numbers. You can also add namespaces to your elements and attributes, or serialize to and from data types different from those in your .NET class. I won't go into these operations in this book, and in fact your life will be significantly easier if you don't waste your time with any of these shenanigans, instead allowing your .NET code to match your XML as closely as possible. But they're there if you need them.

> Advanced programmers can get even more control over the serialization process.

How about the case of serializing an object that contains other objects? As long as the contained objects are declared in the class, the serializer handles this case automatically. In fact, you've already seen an example of it and probably didn't realize it. Integers, such as *X* and *Y* in the first example, are objects in the .NET hierarchy—value types, but objects nonetheless. As we can see, they serialized perfectly with no effort on our part. The serializer would also have worked properly had they been complex types of objects, perhaps themselves containing other objects, as long as the serializer knows what they are when you create it.

> The serializer automatically handles the case of objects containing other objects.

What about the case where an object can contain objects of varying types? I've written a sample program that demonstrates this, shown in Figure 7-11.

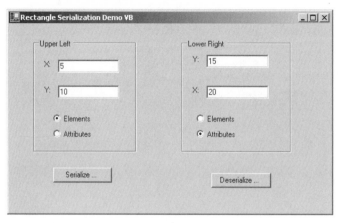

Figure 7-11   Sample program showing serialization of rectangle with different types of points.

You can configure a class to obtain serialization information at run time.

Suppose I have a class that represents a rectangle, which I define by specifying the upper-left and lower-right points. Each of these can be of either class *AttributePoint* (shown previously in Figure 7-9), or *ElementPoint* (a point that serializes to elements, the default behavior shown in the first example). The default settings of the sample program produce a document containing one of each type of point. But the choice of using *ElementPoints* or *AttributePoints* is made at run time based on user input. Unlike the first example, the serializer couldn't possibly know at the time I created it which type of point the rectangle would hold. How can I configure my *Rectangle* class so that the serializer will properly handle whichever type it contains?

You can also have a variable that can contain one of several types, as long as you specify which types at compile time.

It turns out that this isn't hard either. Again, I make use of .NET programming attributes to instruct the serializer how to handle either case. As you can see in Figure 7-12, each of the points is represented by the type *Object*, which means that it can hold any .NET object. How does the serializer know what to serialize it as? You might think that it could know automatically, using the Reflection API at serialization time to determine what type of object it actually has and what the members of that class are. Unfortunately, the serializer doesn't work that way. The designers thought that reading the reflection metadata at the moment of serialization would cost too much in terms of performance every time you read or wrote, so they insisted that the serializer know at the time it's created all of the different classes to which the objects that it serializes might belong. The serializer can then perform the expensive operation of reading the object's metadata and preparing its own internal data structures for serialization only once. You usually give the serializer the list of all the types it might encounter by decorating the variable with a .NET programming attribute of type *System.Xml.Serialization.XmlElement* for each class the object might be, in this case *ElementPoint* and *AttributePoint*. The sample program will properly handle either type, as you can see from the results shown in Figure 7-13.

```
Public Class Rectangle

   <System.Xml.Serialization.XmlElement(GetType(ElementPoint)), _
    System.Xml.Serialization.XmlElement(GetType(AttributePoint))> _
   Public UpperLeft As Object

   Public LowerRight As Object

End Class
```

Figure 7-12   Rectangle class that can hold either element points or attribute points.

```
<Rectangle xmlns:xsi="http://www.w3.org/2001/XMLSchema-instance">
  <ElementPoint>
    <X>5</X>
    <Y>10</Y>
  </ElementPoint>
  <LowerRight xsi:type="AttributePoint" X="15" Y="20" />
</Rectangle>
```

Figure 7-13   XML document produced by serializing rectangle.

But wait! Why have I decorated only one of the points (*UpperLeft*) and not the other if the choice applies to both? Each instance of the serializer maintains an internal list of all the types it expects to see. When the serializer sees the decorations on the first variable, it adds the types to its list of possible types. Placing the same decorations on the second variable would simply add them to the serializer's internal list again. In fact, you'll get a run-time error if you attempt to decorate them both. Each attribute defining a type that you want the serializer to recognize must appear exactly once within each class, even if more than one variable of this type can appear. In fact, if I decorated one point with an attribute specifying the *AttributePoint* class and the other with the attribute specifying the *ElementPoint* class, either object could and would serialize as either class. That's not what you would think as you read the code; it's a clear and blatant violation of the Principle of Least Astonishment. Other .NET programming attributes don't work this way, and neither

You must include each potential type declaration exactly once—astonishing, but true.

do existing variable modifiers such as *private* or *const*. I understand that internally the serializer needs to see it only once, but I think that code would be easier to write, understand, and debug if the serializer simply ignored additional inclusions instead of throwing up.

You can override the compile-time behavior at run time with code.

But what if I don't know all the possible types at compile time? You usually do because you usually work from an XML document schema, as I'll describe in the next section. But if for some reason you don't, you can override the design-time programming attributes (or lack thereof) at run time. You create an object of class *System.Xml.Serialization.XmlAttributeOverrides*, containing the *XmlElement* and *XmlAttribute* declarations that your run-time operations have convinced you that you want. You pass this object to the constructor of the serializer object, which will tell the serializer to override the design time decorations. I don't show this operation because it's more work and you should probably avoid it; but if you can't live without it, it's there.

You can also use programming attributes to accept XML elements and attributes that don't correspond to your .NET class.

What if I don't know or don't want to take the trouble to find out all the potential types of elements I might see, even at run time? This is a common scenario, as most large XML schemas contain a provision for accepting user-defined fields. If you read someone's XML document because you cared about the standard fields, but you didn't know about the user-defined fields that the sender had placed in the document, your serialization process would choke. You can tell the serializer to accept any type of unrecognized input by decorating a variable with the *XmlAnyElement* or *XmlAnyAttribute* programming attributes. These cause any unrecognized elements or attributes to be placed in an array of objects of type *System.Xml.XmlElement* or *System.Xml.XmlAttribute* respectively. You can then work your way through these objects to see what you've actually been given, or just ignore them. If you don't decorate a variable of this type, an unrecognized field in the XML document will cause the serialization process to fail. Unless you are forbidden to accept a document containing an unwanted XML element or attribute, you might want to form the habit of putting in these attributes as sort of an overflow mailbox, just in case.

XML Schemas and Serialization

We need automatic generation of .NET classes

So far we've seen that the .NET XML serializer knows how to move .NET objects into and out of XML documents, and that we can control this process by using .NET programming attributes at design time or by using code at run time. We're still missing one piece, however. The XML documents that we deal with can be quite large and quite complex—hundreds of different element types in a document are common, and thousands are not unheard of. Writing a .NET class that properly wraps every XML element or attribute that anyone might send us or that we might send to anyone is essentially impossible. It would take far too long and cost far too much to get any useful program done, and you'd never get it fully debugged. To take full advantage of this serialization capability and make some money, we need a way of automatically generating the wrapper classes from some definition of the XML documents we expect to encounter.

Fortunately .NET provides us with an easy way to do this, provided we have a schema describing the XML documents that we will be dealing with. The schema of an XML document is the description, written in XML itself, of everything that a valid XML document in a particular problem domain vocabulary might contain. A schema will specify the names of the XML elements and attributes, their occurrence frequencies and optionalities, and their data types. A schema is conceptually similar to the collection of header files that a program compiler uses to ensure that all the variables in a program are properly named and of the right types. A schema is often produced and distributed by the standards agency that governs a particular industry, as discussed earlier.

> An XML schema describes the contents that an XML document can legally contain.

The .NET Framework SDK provides a command line utility program called XSD.exe that generates XML schemas from .NET classes and .NET classes from XML schemas. In the former case, the utility reads a .NET assembly and produces an XML schema describing the XML documents that the assembly's objects would produce if serialized. When I ran XSD against the EXE produced in this chapter's first example, using the command line option to tell it to produce a schema only for the *Point* class, it produced the schema shown in Figure 7-14. If you thought anyone else cared, you would publish this schema so that anyone who wanted to send you a *Point* object serialized in XML would know how to construct their XML document. If you had decorated the classes with attributes to control their serialization, the schema would have been different. Try it on the *ElementPoint*, *AttributePoint*, and *Rectangle* classes from the second example and see what you get.

> A command-line utility can generate an XML schema from a .NET assembly.

```xml
<?xml version="1.0" encoding="utf-8"?>
<xs:schema elementFormDefault="qualified" xmlns:xs="http://www.w3.org/2001/
XMLSchema">
  <xs:element name="Point" nillable="true" type="Point" />
  <xs:complexType name="Point">
    <xs:sequence>
      <xs:element minOccurs="1" maxOccurs="1" name="X" type="xs:int" />
      <xs:element minOccurs="1" maxOccurs="1" name="Y" type="xs:int" />
    </xs:sequence>
  </xs:complexType>
</xs:schema>
```

Figure 7-14   Schema of *Point* class from first example produced by XSD.exe.

A schema sample program starts here.

More useful to us is the ability of the XSD tool to read an XML schema and produce a .NET class that properly wraps a document of the type described. Suppose an industry-wide consortium of Microsoft and non-Microsoft users (i.e., me) have agreed on the XML definition of a polygon and published a schema that describes it. An XML document that conforms to this schema is shown in Figure 7-15. The schema itself is somewhat verbose, even at this level of simplicity, so I won't show it here in the text, but you can examine it in the downloadable sample code.

```
<Polygon >
  <Vertices>
    <Point>
       <X>1</X>
       <Y>1</Y>
    </Point>
    <Point>
       <X>3</X>
       <Y>3</Y>
    </Point>
  </Vertices>
</Polygon>
```

Figure 7-15 Industry-standard XML document describing polygon.

We now want to write a .NET program that will properly read and write documents that conform to this schema. The sample program is shown in Figure 7-16. After I generate a standard Windows Forms project (see Chapter 5), I need to generate my wrapper class. I do this by running XSD from the command line, passing it my XML schema and specifying my choice of output language. The tool then spits out the wrapper class shown in Figure 7-17, which I add to my Visual Studio project. That's all I have to do. I now use the wrapper class just as I did the classes that I wrote by hand in the first two examples, except that this one took me much less time to write. The code that uses the wrapper class objects is very similar to that in the first two examples, so I won't show it here. If you've ever written an application that uses a generic XML parser, you'll realize that .NET serialization combined with automatic wrapper-class generation saves as much time as writing COM programs in Visual Basic instead of C (not C++, just plain C).

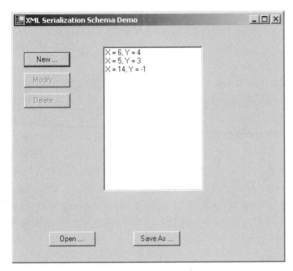

Figure 7-16 Sample program serializing polygon.

```
Public Class Point
    Public X As Integer
    Public Y As Integer
End Class

Public Class Polygon
    Public Vertices() As Point
End Class
```

Figure 7-17 *Polygon* XML document wrapper class produced by XSD.exe.

I need to mention a couple of application notes here. First, to make my sample app look better, I've overridden the method *ToString* in the *Polygon* class in my generated file. This produces the lines showing the point values, such as "X= 5, Y=3" strings in the list box. Modifying the wrapper class is perfectly legal since no other tools have to look at it after you generate it, and you'll probably wind up doing this a fair amount. But if you regenerate your wrapper class, you'll lose all of your changes, so make sure you save a copy.

Any alterations you make to the wrapper class are lost when you regenerate it.

I also encountered a funky Visual Basic-against-the-world problem. In C# and Java, arrays are zero-based, so if you declare an array of five integers, you get five elements numbered 0 through 4. In Visual Basic, arrays were originally one-based, so if you declared an array of five integers, you got elements 1 through 5. Starting with Visual Basic 6 arrays contain an extra element, so if you declare an array of five integers, you'll actually get six, 0 through 5. The Visual Studio .NET team tried to change Visual Basic .NET arrays to be zero-based so as to match the rest of the world, as the first edition

Be careful of zero-based versus one-based arrays in Visual Basic.

of this book reported. They had to rescind that decision under heavy fire from the Visual Basic user community, who threatened to simply add 1 to their existing array declarations rather than change their code. So if you just do the standard Visual Basic thing and have your program count 1 through 5, the element collections in your XML documents will begin with an extra element that's empty. Some schemas don't allow empty elements, and it will look like hell in any event. Visual Basic programmers will have to carefully write their code to handle this off-by-one problem, as I did in this sample. And C# programmers, who imagine themselves to be wearing halos, will have to teach their tech support departments how to diagnose this problem and explain it to callers who program in Visual Basic. As the French say, *Plus ça change, plus c'est la même chose.* ("The more things change, the more they stay the same.") Does your dual Pentium-2000 PC with 1 gigabyte of RAM process words any faster than your 1-megabyte 286-12 did? Mine neither.

Generic Parsing

We still need generic parsing capability.

Handling repetitive documents with wrapper classes solves our most common XML problems in .NET. However, certain classes of applications—for example, XML programming tools such as XSD.exe or the serializer—require us to pick apart an XML document at run time, where we can never have the slightest idea in advance what we will encounter. Therefore, it is necessary to have a generic parser to which we can feed an unknown XML document and discover the document's contents dynamically at run time.

Microsoft provides a .NET XML parser that supports DOM, the W3C Document Object Model.

The .NET Framework provides two separate implementations of an XML parser. The first provides an implementation of the W3C standard called DOM, the Document Object Model. The DOM parser reads an entire document into memory and holds it in a tree-based structure, representing every part of the document (elements, attributes, text, and so on) as a node on the tree. You can add and delete nodes, read and modify their values, and save the entire document. It's a very convenient way to look at the world provided the file isn't too large, in which case keeping the entire thing in memory at once can be cumbersome.

Here's a sample program demonstrating the .NET version of DOM.

I've written a sample program, shown in Figure 7-18, that opens an XML document using Microsoft's DOM parser and displays it in a tree control. When the user clicks Open, a dialog box pops up and the user selects a file name. The program creates an object of the class *System.Xml.XmlDocument* and calls its *Load* method, thereby reading in the specified file. Each node in the document is represented in the form of an object of class *System.Xml.XmlNode*, containing such properties as *Name*, *Value*, and *ChildNodes*. The *ChildNodes* property is a potentially empty collection of all the nodes in the next level down in the tree. My enumeration function, shown in Figure 7-19, loops through this collection, reading the names and values and types of the nodes and putting them on the tree control for you to look at. It then calls itself recursively on each child node until it reaches the bottom.

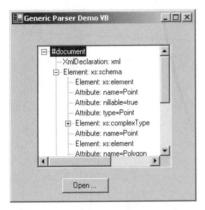

Figure 7-18 Sample program demonstrating DOM parser.

```
Private Sub EnumerateNodes(ByVal ThisNode As Xml.XmlNode, _
                    ByVal TreeNode As System.Windows.Forms.TreeNode)

    ' Step through each child in the collection of the supplied XML
    ' document node
    Dim child As Xml.XmlNode
    For Each child In ThisNode.ChildNodes

        ' Create new node and add it to tree
        Dim NewTreeNode As New Windows.Forms.TreeNode()
        TreeNode.Nodes.Add(NewTreeNode)

        ' If it's a text element, then put its value there
        If child.NodeType = Xml.XmlNodeType.Text Or _
           child.NodeType = Xml.XmlNodeType.Comment Then

            NewTreeNode.Text = child.NodeType.ToString + ": " + _
                            child.Value

        ' Otherwise put its name there
        Else
            NewTreeNode.Text = child.NodeType.ToString + ": " + _
                            child.Name

        End If
```

Figure 7-19 Enumeration code using DOM parser.

Figure 7-19 *(continued)*

```
      ' Enumeration of attributes omitted for space

      ' If the child node itself has children, then enumerate
      ' them as well
      If (child.HasChildNodes) Then
          Call EnumerateNodes(child, NewTreeNode)
      End If

    Next child
End Sub
```

.NET also supports parsing options that don't require keeping an entire document in memory.

The main drawback to DOM is that it requires you to hold the entire XML document in memory, which can be a problem if the document is large. Sometimes you are reading a large document, only a small portion of which you care about or are converting into something different anyway. In this case, you might rather use the second implementation of an XML parser, the class *System.Xml.XmlTextReader* or its validating relative, *System.Xml.XmlValidatingReader*. These objects provide forward-only read-only non-cached access to an XML document. You can also perform output using their counterpart, *System.Xml.XmlTextWriter*. This might be a good choice if you have a collection of non-XML data, say, from a database search, that you want to convert into XML. Rather than make a copy in DOM, you'd use this class to do direct output. All of these classes hold only a small portion of the XML document in memory at any one time, reading from or writing to disk on demand. These are lower levels of abstraction and are thus much less used. But again, as with so many things in this chapter, these options are there when you need them.

8

Events and Delegates

A bonus on the coal I save? Ou ay, the Scots are close,
But when I grudge the strength Ye gave I'll grudge their food to 'those.'
(There's bricks that I might recommend—an' clink the fire-bars cruel.
No! Welsh—Wangarti [coal] at the worst—an' damn all patent fuel!)
  —Rudyard Kipling, writing on the false economy of failing to supply
  enough RAM in a programmer's machine, "McAndrew's Hymn," 1894.

Problem Background

We've spent a great deal of time in this book looking at the situation in which Object A creates Object B and calls methods or accesses properties on it. For example, we've seen how a form can create a button and set properties for its text and colors. So far we haven't examined the reverse situation, where Object B makes calls back to its creator, Object A, to notify it that something interesting has happened, for example, the button notifying the form when the user clicks on it. We've used callbacks and seen them work, but we haven't looked at the mechanism that .NET provides to make callbacks happen. Now it's time to dive in.

> We need to handle the situation of an object making a call back to its creator.

The need for callbacks is not new, and Windows has implemented them through many different architectures over the years. For example, original Windows controls such as buttons were child windows of their containers, the dialog box or form on which they appeared. They notified their containers of events such as clicks by sending Windows messages to them. This approach made it difficult to pass parameters of more than a few bytes, and it worked only if the objects were actual windows, not just any object. Still,

> We need our callback mechanism to be standardized across all languages and implementations.

this callback implementation was useful, and in fact many objects that weren't windows would create windows simply to be able to receive these notifications. Some Windows API functions, such as those for asynchronous file reading and writing, required the caller to pass as a parameter the address of a callback function that would be used to notify the caller of process completion. This approach worked pretty well for code written in C, but it didn't work well in C++ because C++ couldn't call a method on an individual object, and, naturally, Visual Basic programmers couldn't use this approach at all. COM components used COM interfaces to provide callbacks, but again, differences in implementations between various development platforms led to far more expensive testing and special casing than COM's architects ever envisioned. You never quite knew when you had it right, especially across multiple languages, which was ostensibly the whole point of COM. Enough! We need a generic, standardized way for one object to make calls back to another.

We need our callback mechanism to contain metadata for the use of intelligent development and runtime environments.

Because no standard for implementation of callbacks existed, it should come as no surprise that no standard for design-time or run-time discovery of callback capabilities existed either. Windows controls provided no information whatsoever, and Win32 API functions contained just a little information in their header files. You had to program these things with a paper manual in one hand. COM objects provided this information in type libraries, with all their drawbacks—they were often absent and rarely standardized. As our .NET components contain standard metadata describing themselves to interested parties, so must our .NET callback mechanism support self-description to clients and development environments.

We need our callback mechanism to fit into the .NET runtime environment.

The .NET Framework is an entirely new programming environment. While many of its concepts (inheritance, garbage collection, exception handling) are not new, the extension of these concepts to all applications through commonality of implementation is. We need our callback mechanism to fit into this framework. For example, we need it to be able to call methods of individual objects instead of being limited to raw functions, as the Win32 file I/O functions are. We need it to be built into the framework as a fullfledged member, not just bolted onto the side as an afterthought, as COM connection points are.

Solution Architecture

The .NET Framework standardizes the callback process by using the same commonality of implementation that permeates its other parts. An object—the listener—that wants to receive a callback from another object—the sender—provides the sender with a delegate. A delegate is a .NET object, of class *System.Delegate* or its derivatives, that wraps the address (pointer, to you C++ geeks) of a function, which I call the *target function*, that is implemented in the listener. The delegate contains methods that the sender can use to invoke the target function, either synchronously or asynchronously. Don't worry if it sounds like a lot of work, the system does most of it for you. The target function can be either a class static function or, more commonly, a method on an individual object. When the sender wants to call back into the listener, it uses the delegate's invocation method to call the target function. The process is shown in Figure 8-1.

An object makes a call back into another object by means of a delegate, the .NET version of a function pointer.

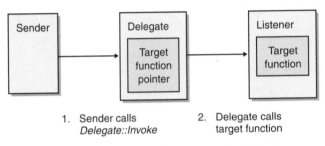

1. Sender calls *Delegate::Invoke*

2. Delegate calls target function

Figure 8-1 Calling a function by means of a delegate.

To support run-time and design-time discovery of its capabilities, each sender object contains .NET metadata describing the types of delegates that it is capable of accepting for use in callbacks. This metadata can take the form of definition statements, such as *Delegate Function DelegateName(...)*, in the sender class. This information allows intelligent development environments to provide various types of user interface support, such as IntelliSense and wizards, that make it much easier for programmers to use delegates.

A .NET object contains metadata specifying the types of delegates it is capable of using.

Delegates can be used to signal events. An event is a named occurrence on the sender that the sender thinks a listener might want to know about or react to. A sender that is capable of signaling an event to a listener declares this capability by using a keyword in its source code language specifying the name of the event and the delegate that a listener must supply in order to receive the information associated with the event. A listener that wants to receive notification of an event and take action based on that event imple-

Delegates are used to signal events, such as button clicks.

ments the required delegate and provides it to the sender, specifying the name of the event to which the delegate should be connected. When the event takes place, the sender uses the delegate's invocation function to call the target function on the listener, thereby notifying the listener of the event. This process is shown in Figure 8-2. I discuss events, first simply and then in more complexity, in the first two examples in this chapter.

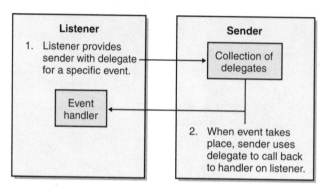

Figure 8-2   Connecting an event delegate.

Delegates are also useful as generic callback objects.

Although events are by far the most common use of delegates, you know there's no way programmers would leave such a useful and generic mechanism alone. Delegates are employed as generic .NET function pointers even when not part of a named event. For example, a client can use a delegate's asynchronous invocation capability to call any function asynchronously. I discuss the generic use of delegates in the third example in this chapter.

Simplest Example

A simple event and delegate example begins here.

As I've done throughout this book, I wrote the simplest program I could imagine to demonstrate the use of delegates and events. The code itself is quite easy to write, but the hoops through which the .NET Framework jumps to make it all happen are quite complex. We can now examine and understand the event system without any business logic getting in the way.

I wrote a simple .NET class library containing an object that is capable of signaling an event to its client. Unlike most parts of .NET, the syntax differs significantly between Visual Basic .NET and C#, so I'll show both languages in this text. Figure 8-3 shows the Visual Basic .NET code, and Figure 8-4 shows the C# code for my object.

```
Public Class Class1EventVB
    Inherits System.ComponentModel.Component

    ' Declare an event that this component can fire to its container.

    Public Event SomethingHappened(ByVal WhenItHappened As DateTime)

    ' This is a method that the client can call to cause the server
    ' to fire the event back to it.

    Public Sub CauseComponentToFireEvent()

        ' Use the keyword RaiseEvent to signal the event mechanism
        ' to call the handler functions in each listener, if any.

        RaiseEvent SomethingHappened(Now)

    End Sub

End Class
```

Figure 8-3   Visual Basic .NET code for the simplest event component.

```
public class Class1EventCS : System.ComponentModel.Component
{

    // Declare the delegate, which is a function signature
    // that a listener must implement.

    public delegate void SomethingHappenedEventHandler (
        DateTime WhenItHappened) ;

    // Declare an event, which is something our component can
    // notify its container of, specifying the declared delegate
    // that a listener must implement to hear about it.

    public event SomethingHappenedEventHandler SomethingHappened ;
```

Figure 8-4   C# code for simplest event.

Figure 8-4   *(continued)*

```
// This is a method that the client can call to cause the server
// to fire the event back to it.

public void CauseComponentToFireEvent()
{

    // Invoke the event directly by means of its name.
    // This causes the event mechanism to call the
    // handler functions in each listener, if any.

    SomethingHappened (DateTime.Now) ;
}
}
```

Declaring an event is
extremely simple.

First you'll see that both objects inherit from the system base class *System.ComponentModel.Component*. This inheritance is *not* required for sourcing events. I've added it to this example because, as you'll see a little later when we start implementing the listener, by deriving from this class I can load the component into the Visual Studio .NET designer and use the wizards to add handlers for the events to my sample client program. You could omit this inheritance and your events would still work fine; they'd just be a little harder for clients to program against. In Visual Basic .NET, I use the keyword *Event* to declare an event, specifying its name, in this case *SomethingHappened*. I also provide a list of parameters that I want the event to pass to its recipient, in this case a single *DateTime* object specifying the time at which the event took place. In C# syntax, I use the keyword *delegate*. This keyword declares a delegate with the name *SomethingHappenedEventHandler* that wraps a target function having the specified parameter list. In the next line, I use the keyword *event* to say that the event named *SomethingHappened* requires a delegate of the type *SomethingHappenedEventHandler*. I can, and often will, have many events with different names that require the same type of delegate. All events from Windows Forms controls, for example, use the same generic delegate class *System.EventHandler*. In my Visual Basic .NET example, the compiler implied the delegate declaration from the *Event* statement, although Visual Basic .NET also supports syntax similar to C# syntax if you want to use the same type of delegate for many different events. But in either language, I have to write only one or two lines of code to create an event that listeners can connect to and that my component can signal. Now let's look at the prefabricated event support that .NET has built into the component.

I used ILDASM (the intermediate language disassembler; see Chapter 2) to produce the disassembly of my Visual Basic component, shown in Figure 8-5. Despite the different source code syntax, the ILDASM of the Visual Basic and C# components are nearly identical, so I'll show only one.

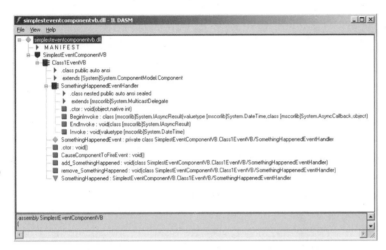

Figure 8-5   Disassembly view of the class that fires the event.

Looking at the bottom line of the window shown in Figure 8-5, we see a downward-pointing triangle (colored green when you look at it on your PC). This line contains metadata that says that this component fires an event named *SomethingHappened*. Scanning along the same line, we see a reference to an object of class *SomethingHappenedEventHandler*. This object is the delegate that a listener must provide to this sender if the listener wants to receive notifications of this event. Any client, such as a development environment that provides wizard support for writing event handlers, that wants to see the events that this class signals and the handlers those events require can find that information here.

OK, what is this mysterious delegate called *SomethingHappened-EventHandler*? Looking again at Figure 8-5, we can see the delegate nested inside our component class, and we can see that it is listed as extending (inheriting, or deriving from) *System.MulticastDelegate*, which in turn derives from *System.Delegate*. A *MulticastDelegate* object can hold more than one target function pointer, thereby allowing a sender to signal an event to multiple listeners with a single function call. The private variable marked with a diamond, called *SomethingHappenedEvent*, is an instance of the *SomethingHappenedEventHandler* class. *SomethingHappenedEvent* is the actual object that our sending object will use to signal the event. Since *SomethingHappened-Event* is private, a listener can't talk to it directly. Instead, we can see public

> The compiler also generates a delegate class to hold the event listeners' callback functions.

methods on our main object called *add_SomethingHappened* and *remove_SomethingHappened*. A listener will call these methods to connect to the event. You won't actually write these functions in your class; your language compiler will add them for you while you write more abstract statements, as we will see later in this chapter. The compiler did something similar when you wrote code that accessed an object property, exposed by means of hidden set and get methods, which you can see with ILDASM if you ever care to look for them.

I place the component on my project using the toolbox.

Now that we've seen the simple syntax we need to write an object that generates an event, and the much larger amount of internal support that .NET generates for us as a result, we next wonder what kind of code the developer of a listener needs to write to be a recipient of an event notification. In this case I've written the event-sending components as deriving from the system base class *System.ComponentModel.Component*, as we saw in Figures 8-3 and 8-4. This means that I can load the components into Visual Studio .NET and use its designers and wizards to make writing a listener easier. First I generate a Windows Forms application (see Chapter 5) to provide a user interface for my sample listener program. Then I add the sending component (SimplestEventComponent*xx*.dll) to my toolbox by right-clicking in the Components section of the toolbox, selecting Customize Toolbox, selecting the .NET Framework Components tab, and browsing to locate that component. The component will appear in the toolbox (as Class1Event*xx*). When I drag it onto my client form, it will appear in the design window below the form, as shown in Figure 8-6, because it doesn't have its own user interface.

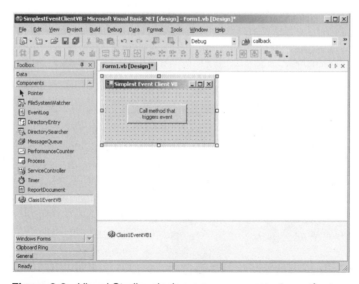

Figure 8-6   Visual Studio, placing a new component on a form.

The Visual Basic .NET code for the listening form class is shown in Figure 8-7. You'll find when you look at the Windows Forms Designer–generated code that Visual Studio .NET has added a member variable for our component declared with the keyword *WithEvents*. This keyword tells the compiler that the component is a potential sender of events of the specified type to interested listeners.

```
Public Class Form1
    Inherits System.Windows.Forms.Form

    ⋮

    Friend WithEvents Class1EventVB1 As _
        SimplestEventComponentVB.Class1EventVB

    ⋮


    ' Call the method on the sample object that fires
    ' an event for us to handle.

    Private Sub Button1_Click(ByVal sender As System.Object, _
        ByVal e As System.EventArgs) Handles Button2.Click
        Class1EventVB1.CauseComponentToFireEvent()
    End Sub

    ' This handler function gets invoked when the
    ' "SomethingHappened" event comes in.

    Private Sub Class1EventVB1_SomethingHappened(ByVal WhenItHappened _
        As Date) Handles Class1EventVB1.SomethingHappened
        MessageBox.Show("Event SomethingHappened received, fired at " + _
                        WhenItHappened.ToString)
    End Sub
End Class
```

Figure 8-7   Visual Basic .NET code for handling events.

When I drop down the Class Name list box in the Visual Basic Code Editor, I'll see this variable. When I select it, I can drop down the Method Name list box and see my sample event *SomethingHappened*. Visual Basic .NET knew to populate the Method Name list box with the methods and events associated with my chosen component name by reading the component's metadata, which I showed you in the viewer in Figure 8-5. When I select this event, Visual Studio .NET adds the event handler function to the form (listener) class. The event handler implements the signature required to receive the event notification from the sending object. The modifier *Handles Class1EventVB1.SomethingHappened* tells the Visual Basic compiler to generate the code that creates a delegate with this function as its target and that

Visual Basic provides an easy way to add an event handler function to a form.

calls *add_SomethingHappened* on the sending object to connect this delegate to the object's delegate that represents the event.

Adding an event handler in C# is again different, but still simple.

C# provides a slightly different way of connecting a handler to an event. To create this project in C#, I generate the Windows Forms project and add the component to the project just as I did in Visual Basic. Events don't appear in a drop-down list, as they do in Visual Basic. Instead, when I select the component on the designer window below the form and view its properties, the Properties window contains a little lightning bolt icon. When I click that, I'll see a list of events in the Properties window, as shown in Figure 8-8. I type in the name of a handler function (*HandleSomethingHappened*), and C# adds it to the code with the proper signature, as shown in Figure 8-9. You don't see the *Handles* notation as you did with Visual Basic. Instead, the event hookup code is performed in the *InitializeComponent* method where the rest of the properties are set. It uses the syntax I'll discuss in the next example, where I'll show you how to write it yourself in dynamic hookup cases that the wizard can't handle.

Figure 8-8 C# Properties window showing events fired by the sample component.

```
// This handler function gets invoked when the
// "SomethingHappened" event comes in.

private void HandleSomethingHappened(System.DateTime WhenItHappened)
{
    MessageBox.Show ("Event SomethingHappened received, fired at " +
                WhenItHappened.ToString()) ;
}
```

Figure 8-9 C# event handler code added by the wizard.

My sample object contains only one way for the component to signal an event to its registered listeners—through a method named *CauseComponent-ToFireEvent*, as shown previously in Figures 8-3 and 8-4. When the client calls this method, the control fires the event. In Visual Basic, an event is fired through the keyword *RaiseEvent*.   In C#, we simply call the event. Internally, in both cases firing the event calls the *Invoke* method on the component's *SomethingHappenedEvent* object (the private delegate discussed earlier). This call causes the delegate to look through its list of listener delegates and call the target functions on every one. In this example, we have only one target function—the event handler on our form.   In C#, signaling an event that has no listeners causes an exception, so you'll have to add your own exception handler (see Chapter 2) if you think this case will ever occur. In Visual Basic, the *RaiseEvent* keyword contains its own internal exception handler for this case, so you don't have to write it. (It feels like there ought to be a tree-falling-in-the-forest joke here, but I can't quite figure out what it is.)

A component fires an event with RaiseEvent in Visual Basic or by calling its name in C#.

More Complex Example

Suppose we want to do more complex things than in the previous example, such as add or remove event handlers dynamically as our code executes rather than statically through a designer? And what about the case in which an event has more than one handler function, or a single handler function has more than one event?   All of these scenarios are possible and, in fact, quite easy to implement, using the generic event mechanism that we saw in the previous example. I've written a sample program that demonstrates each of these cases. The program, shown in Figure 8-10, uses the component from the previous example for one demonstration and standard Windows Forms controls for the others.

A more complex events and delegates sample starts here.

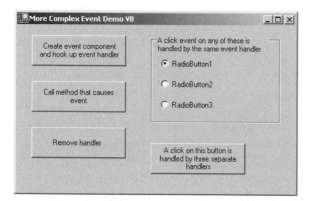

Figure 8-10   Sample program demonstrating dynamic hookup of event handlers.

Suppose I create an object dynamically while a program is running rather than statically in a designer. How could I hook up handler functions to the events fired by that object? It turns out to be quite simple. As before, I need a handler function that matches the proper signature, but in this case the handler doesn't use the *Handles* keyword shown in the previous static example. Instead, in Visual Basic .NET, I use the run-time keyword *AddHandler*, as shown in Figure 8-11, to connect my handler function to the specified event on the object.

```vb
Private Sub Button1_Click(ByVal sender As System.Object, _
    ByVal e As System.EventArgs) Handles Button1.Click

    ' Create new component that fires events.

    EventFiringComponent = New ClassLibrary1.Class1EventVB()

    ' Add a handler function that gets called
    ' when the event is received

    AddHandler EventFiringComponent.SomethingHappened, _
            AddressOf Me.HandleSomethingHappenedEvent

End Sub


Private Sub Button3_Click(ByVal sender As System.Object, _
    ByVal e As System.EventArgs) Handles Button3.Click

    ' Remove the handler for the event

    RemoveHandler EventFiringComponent.SomethingHappened, _
            AddressOf Me.HandleSomethingHappenedEvent

End Sub

' Event received from component. Signal user with message box

Private Sub HandleSomethingHappenedEvent(ByVal WhenItHappened As DateTime)
    MessageBox.Show("SomethingHappened event received, time = " + _
            WhenItHappened)
End Sub
```

Figure 8-11   Visual Basic code for adding and removing an event handler.

The *AddressOf* keyword tells Visual Basic to find the address of the handler function. This is exactly what the *Handles* keyword told Visual Basic to do in the previous static case, but now we're writing the explicit code for it. Visual Basic actually creates a delegate of the proper type, places the handler function into the delegate, and adds the new delegate to the handler list in the object's delegate. You can see this more clearly in the C# example, shown in Figure 8-12.

```
private void button1_Click(object sender, System.EventArgs e)
{
    // Create new component that fires events.

    EventFiringComponent =
        new SimplestEventComponentVB.Class1EventCS ();

    // Add a handler function that gets called
    // when the event is received

    EventFiringComponent.SomethingHappened +=
        new SimplestEventComponentVB.Class1EventVB.
        SomethingHappenedEventHandler (
            this.HandleSomethingHappenedEvent) ;

}


private void button3_Click(object sender, System.EventArgs e)
{
    // Remove event handler

    EventFiringComponent.SomethingHappened -=
        new SimplestEventComponentVB.Class1EventVB.
        SomethingHappenedEventHandler (
            this.HandleSomethingHappenedEvent) ;
}

// Event received from component. Signal user with message box

private void HandleSomethingHappenedEvent(DateTime WhenItHappened)
{
    MessageBox.Show("SomethingHappened event received, time = " +
        WhenItHappened) ;
}
```

Figure 8-12 C# code for adding and removing an event handler.

I create a new *SomethingHappenedEventHandler* delegate, passing it the address of the handler function (*this.HandleSomethingHappenedEvent*) in its constructor. This handler function becomes the target function of the new

Adding and removing event handlers dynamically is easy.

delegate. I then use the += operator to add this new delegate to the handler list in the object's delegate. When the component signals the event, it calls the *Invoke* method on its own delegate, which looks at its list of handler delegates and uses the delegates' *Invoke* methods to call their target functions. Removing an event handler involves the same operation in reverse, using *RemoveHandler* in Visual Basic and the - = operator in C#.

This manual hookup of events lets me do some useful things. For example, it's quite easy to make one handler function handle any number of events. I might want to have the same function handle the selection of a menu item by a user, the click of a toolbar button, and a keyboard shortcut, all signaling the same command choice. This would let all of my code for handling a single user choice live in one place, regardless of the various locations of the logic that triggers it. To demonstrate this, I've written the code in Figure 8-13, which uses the same handler function to respond to clicks on any of three radio buttons. In the initialization of my form, I manually add a handler to each radio button, specifying the same handler function for each. If you follow this design pattern for your own events, you probably want to have them pass a parameter to the handler that allows it to distinguish between various senders.

```
Public Sub New()
    MyBase.New()

    'This call is required by the Windows Form Designer.
    InitializeComponent()

    ' Add a handler for each separate radio button
    ' routing the Click event to the same handler function

    AddHandler RadioButton1.Click, _
        AddressOf Me.HandleClickOnAnyRadioButton
    AddHandler RadioButton2.Click, _
        AddressOf Me.HandleClickOnAnyRadioButton
    AddHandler RadioButton3.Click, _
        AddressOf Me.HandleClickOnAnyRadioButton

    ' Add three separate handler functions to the click
    ' event of a single button
```

Figure 8-13   Adding a handler for various events.

```
AddHandler Button4.Click, AddressOf FirstHandlerOfClick
AddHandler Button4.Click, AddressOf SecondHandlerOfClick
AddHandler Button4.Click, AddressOf ThirdHandlerOfClick

End Sub
```

Radio buttons use the *System.EventHandler* delegate for their event handlers, as do all Windows Forms controls. The first parameter of this delegate is the object that is sending the event. My handler code looks at this parameter to tell me which control the user has clicked on.

You can connect one handler function to multiple events.

You can also repeat the hookup operation (discussed previously) multiple times to hook up more than one handler function to a single event. The code in Figure 8-13 shows my sample program hooking up three separate handler functions to the *Click* event from a single button. This lets you perform more than one action in response to an event, without each handler needing to know about the others.

You can also connect multiple handler functions to a single event.

Delegates

We've seen how events make use of delegates internally. The event mechanism that I've described covers most situations, but occasionally we'll need to do something different. For example, we might not want our use of callbacks exposed in the public event list, preferring it to be private for those in the know. Or we might want to perform some business logic when a listener connects a handler to our delegate, perhaps checking to see whether the listener's developer license for our component is current, in which case we'd need to replace the automatic event hookup discussed previously. In such cases, we'll want to use delegates at a lower level of abstraction, closer to their core. I've written a sample program, shown in Figure 8-14, that demonstrates this process by using delegates to illustrate the asynchronous operation of function calls.

A low-level delegate example begins here, demonstrating asynchronous operation.

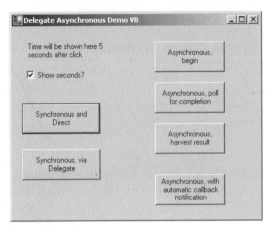

Figure 8-14 Sample program using delegates for asynchronous operation.

When a standard Windows Forms program makes a function call, it waits for the call to return before going on to the next line of code. This functionality at first makes it relatively easy to write consistent programs—do this, then do that with the result of this, then do something else with the result of that, and so on until you're finished or you get sick of it. But while your application is waiting for the function to return, it isn't servicing its internal hidden message loop that handles user interface events such as mouse clicks and keystrokes. Your application's user interface is frozen for the length of the function call. Most function calls are short enough that it doesn't matter, but you can't leave the user frozen for more than a couple of seconds or she'll get really annoyed. If your function call takes longer than this, say in recalculating a spreadsheet, you have to write code that will hand the function off to some sort of background processing, continue to service the user interface while the background operation takes place, and harvest the results at some later time. You could write multithreaded code, as described in the next chapter, but this approach can become complicated and is often overkill for a simple user interface application. We'd like a simple, easy to use, hard to break way of performing function calls asynchronously.

We need a way of calling object methods asynchronously.

Objects that expose methods that take a long time to finish processing often provide assistance by splitting their functionality. They'll expose a method named *BeginSomething* that starts an operation in the background and returns quickly. They'll also expose a corresponding *EndSomething* method to harvest the result, with some other method to check whether the result is ready. But for various reasons, not every object is written that way. Maybe an object is slow only in certain situations such as encountering large data sets, or maybe the developer has a superfast machine and doesn't realize that many of his less fortunate customers are still running the creaky, ancient machines they bought nine months ago. We'd like our clients to be able to invoke any object method asynchronously, regardless of whether the object's developer has taken the time to write code that handles this case.

Delegates allow us to do this. Remember, a .NET delegate is an object that wraps a pointer to another object method, the target function. The delegate contains logic for invoking the target function. One of these pieces of invocation logic is a standardized way of performing a call to the target function asynchronously. The client starts the operation by calling a method on the delegate called *BeginInvoke*. This call hands off the function call to a different thread of execution (selected from a pool that the system creates for just such a purpose, as discussed in the next chapter) and returns quickly, so your user interface thread is free to perform its other tasks. The background thread calls the target function and waits for the result, which it returns to the delegate. At some later time, the client calls the delegate's *EndInvoke* method to harvest the result of the asynchronous function call. The process is shown in Figure 8-15.

> .NET delegates support asynchronous operation of any function call.

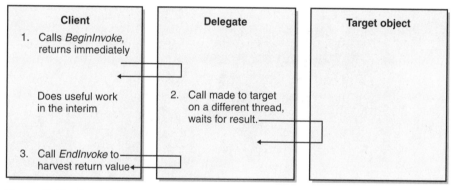

Figure 8-15   Asynchronous operation.

The sample client program creates an object (*OrdinaryObject*) and calls its *GetTime* method. I've written the method to wait for 5 seconds before returning the time. Rather than hang the user interface while waiting for the method to complete (try it and see; you'll be surprised how annoying even this silly example can be), I want to make this call asynchronously, which means that I need a delegate that wraps the target method. The code for creating the delegate is shown in Figure 8-16. First I declare my delegate type, which is conceptually similar to deriving a new class from *System.Delegate* except that you must use the features built into your compiler to do it rather than the usual inheritance notation. I declare a delegate with the signature of the target function I want it to wrap. I then create an object of the class that I want to use the delegate to call. The object doesn't need to know anything about delegates and asynchronous operation, and you can see from the source code that this one doesn't. Finally I create an instance of my new delegate class, passing it the target function pointer in its constructor. The delegate is now wrapping the target function on this particular object instance. I can now call the target function synchronously through the delegate, using the *Invoke* method in Visual Basic .NET or the target method name (in this case *GetTime*) in C#.

```
Public Class Form1
    Inherits System.Windows.Forms.Form

    ' Using the compiler's keyword, declare a delegate class with the
    ' signature of the target function I want it to call.

    Delegate Function GetTimeDelegate(ByVal ShowSeconds As Boolean) _
        As String

    ' Create an ordinary object that doesn't know anything about delegates
    ' or asynchronous operation

    Dim OrdinaryObject As New AsyncFuncCallComponentVB.Class1()

    ' Create a new instance of the delegate class, wrapping the target
    ' function I want to use the delegate to invoke.

    Dim DelegateInstance As New GetTimeDelegate( _
        AddressOf OrdinaryObject.GetTime)

    < handler functions omitted, see next figure>

End Class
```

Figure 8-16   Declaring and creating the delegate for asynchronous operation.

A delegate contains the methods *BeginInvoke* and *EndInvoke* to support asynchronous operation.

A delegate contains methods named *BeginInvoke* and *EndInvoke* to perform function calls asynchronously. You won't see these methods in the documentation of the *Delegate* class, as they are not members of the underlying class but are instead generated by the compiler. The reason for this is that *BeginInvoke* accepts all the parameters of the target function, in addition to several of its own, which means that the parameter list will be different from one delegate to another. This is a good way of handling delegates, and it works about the way you think it should, but I still think this functionality could have been better documented. You'll see the *BeginInvoke* and *EndInvoke* methods in Visual Basic IntelliSense but not in C# (sigh), even though they exist in both languages. In case you haven't figured it out by now,

BeginInvoke starts the asynchronous function call and returns quickly, while *EndInvoke* harvests the results at completion.

In order to invoke my method asynchronously, I first need to decide how I want to find out when the operation completes. The two choices are polling or a callback function. I'll discuss the former case first, using the code shown in Figure 8-17.

```
Dim result As System.IAsyncResult

' User clicked button to begin asynchronous function call.
' Call BeginInvoke and store IAsyncResult that we get
' in return

Private Sub Button3_Click(ByVal sender As System.Object, _
    ByVal e As System.EventArgs) Handles Button3.Click
        result = DelegateInstance.BeginInvoke(CheckBox1.Checked, _
            Nothing, Nothing)
End Sub

' User clicked button to check for completion of asynchronous call.
' Check the IsCompleted property and report value.

Private Sub Button4_Click(ByVal sender As System.Object, _
    ByVal e As System.EventArgs) Handles Button4.Click
        MessageBox.Show(result.IsCompleted.ToString)
End Sub

' User clicked button to harvest result of asynchronous call.
' Call EndInvoke, passing IAsyncResult, to get return value
' of called function.

Private Sub Button5_Click(ByVal sender As System.Object, _
    ByVal e As System.EventArgs) Handles Button5.Click
        Label1.Text = DelegateInstance.EndInvoke(result)
End Sub
```

Figure 8-17 Functions for an asynchronous call with a polled completion signal.

When I call *BeginInvoke*, it starts the asynchronous function call as discussed previously and returns an object of type *IAsyncResult*. This call represents my connection to the asynchronous operation, sort of like the order number you get when you buy books from Amazon.com. To find out whether the operation is complete, I read the *IsCompleted* property from this object. The value of *IsCompleted* will be *false* until the operation is done, at which time the value becomes *true*. When I'm ready to use the result, I call *EndInvoke*, passing *IAsyncResult*, and it returns the return value of the target function. If I call *EndInvoke* before the target function has returned and the operation is complete, *EndInvoke* will block until the operation completes.

There are several ways to wait for the operation to complete.

Like most programmers, I don't care for polling. You waste a lot of time saying, "Are you done yet?" and the polled object wastes a lot more saying, "No, I'm not. Quit wasting all my CPU cycles and maybe I'll get something done, OK?" We'd rather be notified of the completion by some sort of callback. Since this chapter is about delegates, it shouldn't surprise you too much to learn that we do this callback notification by passing a delegate. The code for this case is shown in Figure 8-18.

```
' User clicked button to begin invocation of asynchronous
' function call, passing callback delegate to receive the
' signal of completion.

Private Sub Button6_Click(ByVal sender As System.Object, _
    ByVal e As System.EventArgs) Handles Button6.Click
    DelegateInstance.BeginInvoke(CheckBox1.Checked, _
        AddressOf MyOwnCallback, Nothing)
End Sub

' Callback function that receives notification of asynchronous
' completion. Harvest result by calling EndInvoke.

Public Sub MyOwnCallback(ByVal ar As IAsyncResult)
    Label1.Text = DelegateInstance.EndInvoke(ar)
End Sub
```

Figure 8-18   A handler function for an asynchronous method invocation with a callback completion signal.

Or I can make it call me back by using another delegate.

When we call *BeginInvoke* on the delegate wrapping our object's target function, we pass as its second parameter (in this example, but the position will vary because *BeginInvoke* wraps target functions with different numbers of parameters) another delegate, this one of type *System.AsyncCallback*. This delegate wraps a target function that we have written to receive the notification of the function completion. When the operation completes, the .NET Framework uses the delegate to call my target function. It passes me an *IAsyncResult* object, which I use to call *EndInvoke* and retrieve the return value.

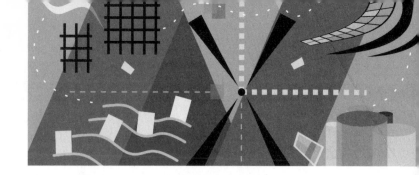

9

Threads

Ye mind that word? Clear as our gongs—again, an' once again,
When rippin' down through coral—trash ran out our moorin' chain;
An' by Thy Grace I had the Light to see my duty plain.
Light on the engine-room-no more-bright as our carbons burn.
I've lost it since a thousand times, but never past return.

—Rudyard Kipling, writing on dedication
to a profession, "McAndrew's Hymn," 1894.

Preliminary Note

Don't panic! More programmers, especially of the Visual Basic persuasion, have run for the hills over the issue of threading than anything else I know of. Threading to them was just this mysterious thing that screwed them up because Visual Basic didn't do it. That's all in the past now, as threading is a full-fledged part of the .NET common language runtime, available to programmers of any language. Even if you're not currently planning on writing multithreaded code yourself, the Windows environment in which your code runs uses threads extensively, and the success of your project will depend in no small measure on how well you manage to live with them. I'm writing this chapter as an introduction to threading for programmers who haven't worked with it before. The goal is to crack the topic open easily so you can get your first taste of what's

---

(continued)

Preliminary Note   *(continued)*

inside. This chapter won't make you a complete thread guru, but it will allow you to read the Microsoft documentation and other books, actually understand what they are talking about, and participate intelligently in design discussions on the topic. If it seems overwhelming at first, I'll say to you what I used to say to my students when I taught rock climbing years ago: "When you start getting into trouble, don't look down, look at me." (To which the usual reply was some variation on "Aieeeeeeeeee [thunk]".)

Problem Background

Computers originally performed only one task at a time.

In the beginning, personal computers did only one thing at a time. You ran your word processor until you were finished, then you closed it and opened your spreadsheet. After working with that for a while, you closed it and treated yourself to a rousing text-based adventure game like Zork. MS-DOS made that possible, and if we sneer at it today, it was a whole lot better than what we had before it, which was nothing. As the next step, 16-bit Windows allowed you to keep several programs open and cut and paste between them if you had enough RAM. You could create a misleading chart in Excel and import it into a pointless Word report that no one ever read. Again you snicker, but it was a big advance at the time. If you've forgotten how much fun you had as a kid on your first tricycle, before you learned about fast cars and the opposite sex and throughput scalability, well, too bad for you.

16-bit Windows featured co-operative multitasking, which had severe limitations.

Users loved keeping several applications open at once, but it made the programmer's job harder. Most PCs even today contain only a single CPU chip to run program code. By definition, while the CPU runs one application's code, it isn't running any of the others', so we need a way to share the CPU among all the programs running at any given time, without the programs needing to know about each other. Sixteen-bit Windows accomplished this through cooperative multitasking. The operating system would give the CPU to a program by sending it a message, usually triggered by a user event such as a keystroke or a mouse click. The program would process the message and keep the CPU until the program finished with that message, at which time it voluntarily yielded the CPU back to Windows by calling a particular function. While one program had the CPU, no other programs could do anything at all, so you had to write your programs for short, "bursty" operations to keep from hanging everything else. That architecture made Windows itself easy to write, and it worked well for simple programs such as Notepad. But it didn't work well when a program needed to run a background operation, such as recalculating a spreadsheet. Users love to tell stories about the bad old days when they had time to brew and drink a cup of coffee (and go to the bathroom, and maybe play a few quick hands of pinochle with paper cards, and finish *War and Peace*) before the recalculation finished, because of the fact that the spreadsheet processing took up the entire CPU and wouldn't let any other programs run. As dedicated Windows users, they naturally wanted to play Solitaire or Minesweeper during the recalculation, even if this delayed its completion somewhat.

That was a rotten user experience, so programmers naturally began working on ways to fix it. The basic approach required you to divide your background processing logic into small chunks. The spreadsheet would do a chunk of recalculation, write some internal state data to remember where it was in the recalculation process, then yield the CPU to any other app that wanted it. When the other apps had finished with the CPU (the user finished moving the card in Solitaire), Windows would give the CPU back to the spreadsheet. The spreadsheet would then read its previously saved state to remember where it had left off, do the next chunk, and yield again. This process would continue until the task was finished. Writing all this chunk-dividing and state-remembering and CPU-yielding code required a great deal of expensive programmer effort that could have been better spent on business logic.

Writing code for background operations, such as spreadsheet recalculations, was difficult.

That's where matters sat with 16-bit Windows. I remember gripe sessions at the local brewpub after teaching my Harvard class on the subject: Every application needs this background processing capability, so why doesn't Microsoft build it into the operating system instead of making us roll our own every time? We wanted some part of the operating system to deal with scheduling the various tasks that wanted the CPU. We wanted to be able to set priorities, so that low-priority tasks, such as a screensaver, would run only when no higher priority tasks, such as a recalculation, had work to do, and the recalculation would automatically get out of the way when a command from the user came in. We wanted to be able to make tasks wait for external events (say, I/O completion) to occur before starting to run so that we wouldn't waste CPU cycles on them before they were ready to go. And we wanted the new architecture to contain its own ready solutions to the new problems it would inevitably generate, such as the conflict that would occur if two tasks wanted to access the same piece of data at the same time.

We want the operating system to handling multitasking for us.

Solution Architecture

Windows NT introduced the concept of a thread, an object in a process that executes code.

Windows NT, released in 1993, introduced the concept of a thread, which has appeared in every 32-bit release of Windows since then. Every application is a separate process, which is a virtual address space. Each process contains at least one thread, which is an object within a process that executes program code, as shown in Figure 9-1. You can think of a process as a garage and a thread as an engine-powered machine within that garage. Every garage has at least one car or else you wouldn't have built it, but many contain other engine-powered machines such as lawn mowers, chain saws, or more cars. A process doesn't run, any more than a garage does; only threads within a process ever run (although many processes contain only one thread, which makes it look like the process is running).

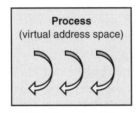

Multiple threads within a
process execute program code

Figure 9-1   Process containing threads.

The operating system transparently swaps the CPU engine between the threads that want to run.

The difference between the garage analogy and computer threading is that each car or lawn mower generally contains its own engine. The engine in a computer is the CPU chip, and most client machines contain only one, or, in extremely geeky cases like mine, two of them. Server machines sometimes have more in order to increase their throughput, perhaps four or eight (the largest I've ever heard of for Windows is 96), but this number is still small compared to the number of threads that want to run at any given time. A CPU chip can run only one thread at a time, while the others have to wait their turn. The Windows operating system cleverly switches the CPU engine between the threads that want it, naturally consuming some engine power itself in the process.

Read this whole paragraph.

Windows maintains a list of all the threads in the entire computer that are ready, willing, and able to run. Every 10 milliseconds or so (an interval known as the *timeslice*), the operating system performs an interrupt and checks to see which thread should have the CPU. Each thread has a priority, and the scheduler picks the highest priority thread in the computer-wide ready list to run. If several threads share the highest priority level, the scheduler alternates them in a round-robin fashion. If the machine contains more than one CPU, each CPU is assigned a thread from the ready list, working from the highest priority downward. The register values of the currently running thread are saved in memory ("swapped out"), and those of the incoming thread placed into the CPU ("swapped in"), which then starts running the incoming thread at the point where it was swapped out the last time. A thread doesn't know when it is swapped in or out. As far as it knows, it's simply executing to completion at a speed over which it has no control. The first example in this chapter illustrates a multithreaded operation running to completion in the background, competing for CPU time with other threads trying to do the same thing.

Not all threads in the system are in the ready state, squabbling with each other over CPU cycles; in fact most of them usually aren't. One of the most useful features of threads is that they can be made to wait, without consuming CPU cycles, for various external events to happen. For example, a Windows Forms application's main thread is generally waiting to receive a message from the operating system announcing that the user has clicked the mouse or pressed a key. A thread in this waiting state is said to be *blocked*. Think of this thread as a car waiting at a stoplight. It's more efficient than that, however, as the thread doesn't have its own engine, so it's not wasting gas sitting there idling. Other threads can use the CPU while the blocked thread waits. When the block clears, the thread goes back into the ready list to compete for CPU time with the rest of the threads.

Threads often block, consuming no CPU cycles, while they wait for external events to happen.

Threading appeared in Windows almost nine years ago, a very long time in this business, but multithreaded programs have historically been excruciatingly difficult to write. Different development environments provided different levels of support for writing multithreaded code. As usual, C++ developers had access to all the threading functions in the Windows API, but (again, as usual) at a low level of abstraction that forced them to spend a lot of time on repetitive boilerplate. Visual J++ version 6 tried to abstract away a lot of the mess in an object-oriented way, but it only partially succeeded at a technical level, and you don't need me to rehash its legal difficulties. Visual Basic 6.0 and earlier versions not only didn't write multithreaded code at all, the COM components that it produced didn't work well in many multithreaded environments such as COM+ because their mandatory thread affinity severely limited their throughput (of which we'll discuss more later).

Threading code has historically been difficult to write because of a lack of development tool support.

The .NET Framework provides a great deal of support for programmers who want to write multithreaded code or code that, while not multithreaded itself, needs to run well in a multithreaded environment. Every process contains a pool of threads, which a programmer can use without needing to create and destroy her own. I discuss the thread pool in the first example in this

The .NET Framework provides great threading support for all languages.

chapter, which is also the simplest example for explaining this whole multi-threaded craziness to beginners. The .NET Framework also contains a set of synchronization objects, which we use to regulate the operations of different threads that try to access the same resources. I discuss the operation of synchronization in this chapter's second example. Finally, the .NET Framework provides support for creating, destroying, prioritizing, and otherwise messing about with threads. I discuss these operations in the third example in this chapter. As with all .NET Framework features, threading support is available to all languages that are fully compliant with the common language runtime.

COM had great difficulty reconciling the threading needs and capabilities of components built by different development tools, but .NET doesn't.

Because different development environments provided different levels of support for threading, a COM client didn't know whether an object it was using was capable of operating successfully with different threads. Reciprocally, a COM object didn't know what threading demands a client might make on it. COM involved a whole "apartment-free-single-multi-neutral" mess that was Microsoft's best effort to allow COM clients and objects with different threading capabilities and requirements to interoperate with each other. Fortunately, you don't need to know about that when you work with your .NET components. Because all development environments have access to all threading capabilities, it isn't needed. You will, however, still find a few mentions of threading apartments in the .NET documentation. These apply only to the relatively rare case of .NET objects interoperating with COM and not to interaction of one .NET object with another.

> **Warning**   More than in any other chapter in this book, I would strongly urge anyone who is new to threading to follow the examples in this one in order.

Simplest Threading Example: Using The Process Thread Pool

A simple threading example (can there be such a thing?) starts here.

I've written the simplest threading example that I could think of so you can get your feet wet without freaking out. In particular, this example will help you understand how your code interacts with a multithreaded environment that you didn't write yourself and that interacts with your code in new and nonintuitive ways. Remember, threads are all around you in Windows. Even though you don't think you've written any threading code, your code lives in a multithreaded environment, which you must understand if you are to successfully coexist with it.

We saw in the previous chapter that a .NET process contains a pool of threads that a programmer can use to make asynchronous method calls. Although that case is quite useful, that's not the only thing you can do with the thread pool. It's available to your applications for any purpose you might like to use it for. Using the thread pool allows you to reap most of the benefits of threading in common situations, without requiring you to write all the nasty code for creating, pooling, and destroying your own threads. It's important to understand that the thread pool manager is a separate piece of logic that sits on top of the basic threading system. You can use the underlying system without going through the pool manager if you don't want the latter's intercession, as I'll demonstrate in the last example in this chapter.

Every process contains a pool of threads that your program can use.

Figure 9-2 shows my simple sample application. The program uses the thread pool to execute tasks in the background and the list view shows you the progress of the various tasks.

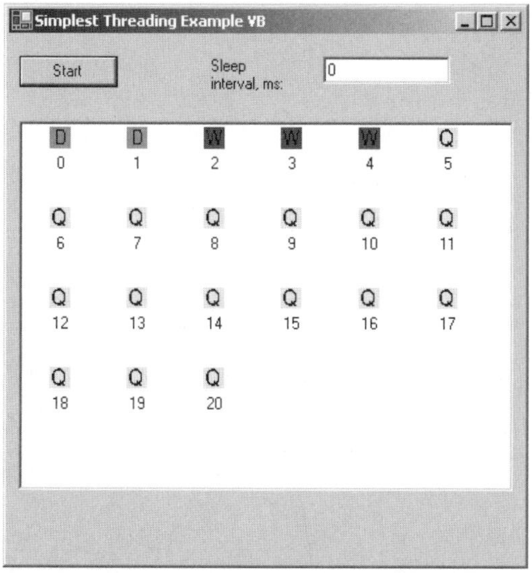

Figure 9-2   Simplest threading sample application.

When the user clicks the Start button, the sample application calls the function *System.Threading.ThreadPool.QueueUserWorkItem*, thereby telling the thread pool manager, "Hey, here's a piece of program logic that I'd like executed in the background on another thread, please." This code is shown in Figure 9-3. I pass this function a delegate (a pointer to a method on an object; see Chapter 8) containing the code that I want the background thread to execute. In this case, it points to a method on my form named *DoSomeWork*, shown in

I put a unit of work into a background pool for processing in a thread pool.

Figure 9-4. You can see that the target function simply wastes time in a tight loop to simulate actually doing something. Just before making the call, I place a yellow Q icon in the list view box to show you that the request has been queued. The thread pool manager puts each delegate in its list of queued work items, from which it will assign the delegate to one of its worker threads for execution. The sample program repeats the request 21 times.

```
Private Sub Button1_Click(ByVal sender As System.Object, _
    ByVal e As System.EventArgs) Handles Button1.Click

    ' Enqueue 21 work items

    Dim i As Integer
    For i = 0 To 20

        ' Set icon to show our enqueued status

        ListView1.Items.Add(i.ToString, 0)

        ' Actually enqueue the work item, passing the delegate of our
        ' callback function. The second variable is a state object that
        ' gets passed to the callback function so that it knows what it's
        ' working on. In this case, it's just its index in the list view
        ' so it knows which icon to set.

        System.Threading.ThreadPool.QueueUserWorkItem( _
            AddressOf DoSomeWork, i)

    Next i
End Sub
```

Figure 9-3   Simplest threading sample application code that queues a work item.

```
Public Sub DoSomeWork(ByVal state As Object)

    ' We've started our processing loop. Set our icon to show
    ' that we're in-process.

    ListView1.Items(CInt(state)).ImageIndex = 1

    ' Perform a time-wasting loop to simulate real work

    Dim i As Integer
    For i = 1 To 1000000000
    Next i
```

Figure 9-4   Simplest threading application target function that does the work.

```
' Set icon to show we're sleeping. Then sleep for the
' number of milliseconds specified by the user

ListView1.Items(CInt(state)).ImageIndex = 2
System.Threading.Thread.Sleep(TextBox1.Text)
' We're finished. Set our icon to show that.

ListView1.Items(CInt(state)).ImageIndex = 3

End Sub
```

It's entirely up to the pool manager how many worker threads to create and have competing for the CPU simultaneously. The developers of this system component put a great deal of thought into making the best use of available CPU cycles. The pool manager uses an internal algorithm to figure out the optimum number of threads to deploy in order to get all of its jobs done in the minimum amount of time. When the pool manager hands off the delegate to one of its worker threads, the thread calls the target function in the delegate, which contains the code that performs the work item. This process is shown in Figure 9-5.

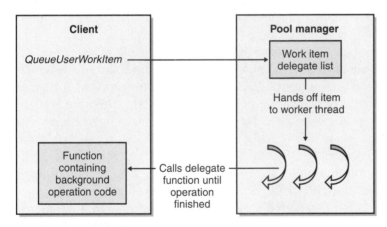

Figure 9-5   Pooled thread executing a delegate.

At the start of the target function (shown previously in Figure 9-4), I change the list view icon to a red W so that you can see when the work item is dequeued and the pool thread starts working on it. At the end of the target function, I change the icon to a green D so that you can see when it's done. Since it's fairly common to use the same delegate function to handle work items on a number of threads, as I've done here, you'll sometimes want to provide the function with information about the data set that you want it to

The user interface of the sample application tracks the process of a task through a thread.

work on in this particular instance. The method *QueueUserWorkItem* accepts as its second parameter an object of any type, which it then passes to the work item target function. To demonstrate passing state information to the target function, I pass the sequence number of each request, which the target places into the list view so that you can see that it got there.

The pool manager decides the number of worker threads to assign to its queued tasks.

The pool manager is quite clever. When I run this sample application on my big server machine, with two 2-GHz processors and 2 GB of RAM, it runs only three worker threads at a time, as you can see in Figure 9-2. The machine correctly figures that since each thread is attempting to run to completion without blocking, then adding more threads than this and swapping between them would only slow down the process. Suppose we have a task that takes 10 seconds to do, and we have five such tasks to complete. If we switch tasks after every second of work, we won't complete the first task until 46 seconds into the process. If, however, we plow straight through the first one, we get the first result after 10 seconds, the second result after 20 seconds, and so on. We still use the same amount of time to accomplish all the tasks (actually a little less because we don't have as much swapping overhead), but we get some results sooner. You will sometimes hear people disparage multithreading as "nothing but smoke and mirrors," meaning that it sometimes doesn't get an individual job done any faster. In the case of a task that proceeds directly to completion, they're right.

If the threads stop to wait for something else, the pool manager spins up more of them to most effectively use CPU time.

But that's not how our computing tasks usually work. If one thread has to wait for something else to happen before it can finish its task—a remote machine to answer a request or a disk I/O operation to complete, for example—we could improve overall throughput by allowing another thread to use the CPU while the first one waits. This is the main advantage of preemptive multithreading: it allows you to make efficient use of CPU cycles that would otherwise be wasted, without writing the scheduling code yourself. The sample program demonstrates this case as well. You will see in the code listing in Figure 9-4 that at the end of the target function I've placed a call to *System.Threading.Thread.Sleep()*. This method tells the operating system to block the calling thread for the specified number of milliseconds. You'll notice a blue S icon appear in the list box to tell the user that the thread is sleeping. The operating system removes a sleeping thread from the ready list and does not assign it any more CPU cycles until the sleep interval expires, at which time the operating system puts the thread back into the ready list to compete for CPU cycles again. There are other ways for a thread to enter this efficient waiting state, and other criteria that you can specify to cause your thread to leave it, as I will discuss later in this chapter. When I enter a reasonable number of milliseconds in this sample program, say, 1000, I find that the pool manager starts more threads, usually six or eight, and assigns them to the task of executing my work items. The pool manager noticed that its two original threads were sleeping and that CPU cycles were going to waste. It figured, again correctly, that it made sense to deploy more threads to use the available CPU cycles on other work items.

This example was easy to write and, I hope, easy for newcomers to understand. You should now be able to see how threads run and how they get swapped in and out. However, don't let the simplicity of this example fool you into thinking that threading is easy. There are at least two major classes of problems that this simple program hasn't dealt with. The first is called thread safety, and refers to the case in which more than one thread tries to access the same resource, say, an item of data, at the same time. Looking at the code in Figure 9-4, we can see that the target function calls methods on the control ListView1 to set the icon representing that work item's state. What happens if two threads try to do this at the same time—is it safe or not? It isn't usually unless we write code to make it so, which I haven't done here. It's a bug waiting to happen, but on the systems on which I've tested it, the timing of the worker threads is different enough that I haven't encountered a conflict. There's no guarantee, however, that the pool manager's strategy or other thread activity in a particular system won't change the thread timing enough to cause a conflict. I left this problem in purposely so you could see how benign-looking code sometimes belies its appearance in multithreaded cases. You must consider thread safety in any multithreaded operation, so I'll discuss this in my next example.

> This example looks cool, but it doesn't cover the problem of two threads accessing the same data.

The second problem that this simple example doesn't cover is control over your threads. The pool manager uses different optimization strategies in different environments. If I run this same example program on my notebook PC, with only 1 CPU running at 800 MHz and with only 512 MB of RAM, the pool manager will immediately assign 12 threads and give each a work item. This thread management doesn't appear optimum for overall throughput, as I explained before. I think the reason that the pool manager changes its strategy is that this less powerful machine is subject to more contention for the fewer available CPU cycles. Since all the threads in the machine are fighting over fewer cycles, the pool manager creates more of its own threads to increase its overall share. That's good game theory from one app's own standpoint, but probably won't work well when several apps all try the same strategy. The pool manager also doesn't employ certain strategies at all, such as changing thread priorities. If you don't like the way the pool manager operates, you'll have to write your own code that creates threads, assigns them to tasks, and destroys them when you are finished with them. I describe this case in the last sample of the chapter.

> This example doesn't cover creating and scheduling your own threads, either.

More Complex Example: Thread Safety

The previous example looks cool. Multiple work items? No problem: hand them off to the thread pool and run them in the background on multiple threads. But, like Jayne Torvill and Christopher Dean ice dancing, doing it smoothly is significantly harder than it looks. The operating system swaps running threads in and out of the CPU without any regard to where a thread is in the course of its work, which can cause problems. Writing good multi-threaded code is primarily about dealing with the interactions of the various threads swapping in and out at times you can't control.

The first problem new thread programmers usually envision is their threads being swapped out in the middle of some time-critical task. Imagining their applications timing out, these programmers feel like a carpenter who's just spread glue on some pieces of wood and needs to assemble them before the glue dries. However, standard applications don't usually need to execute uninterrupted until they reach a specific point. The operating system saves and restores the processor register values as it swaps threads, so each thread picks up right where it left off. If you find your operations timing out too often, you probably have a bottleneck somewhere that more CPU cycles won't fix. In the relatively few cases of dealing with a time-limited process that might time out, the thread priority mechanism discussed in the last section of this chapter usually solves the problem. If that's not true, and you are in fact CPU bound, then threading won't help; if you raise one thread's priority to keep it from timing out, you'll starve another thread and now it will time out instead of the first one. Low-level system and driver designers sometimes need more control than this, and they will probably need to drop out of the managed .NET environment into native unmanaged code to get that control, but this introduction isn't aimed at them. Don't worry about this timing out problem just yet, as you've got a much bigger headache to handle first.

The main problem in multithreaded code arises when one thread modifies data that another thread is using. Think of two children sharing one set of watercolor paints, or two programmers working on the same file. When voluntarily taking turns does in fact work in real life, it works because you don't hand over the resource until you've reached a safe point in your operations with it at which to do so. But we ditched cooperative multitasking almost a decade ago because expecting all programmers to write code that made their applications share nicely just didn't work. In preemptive multithreading, you have no control over when the operating system swaps threads, so you have to worry about someone else making changes that undo pieces of setup that you've carefully performed during your turn—for example, wiping out a custom color you've mixed on the lid of the paint box—before you get a chance to use them instead of after you're done with them.

Consider the code snippet *N = N + 1*. Most programmers can't imagine anything simpler, easier, and safer. And indeed, every thread has its own stack, so if *N* is a stack (automatic) variable or a function parameter, each thread that executes the code has its own copy and we have no problem. But if two threads try to share the same copy of *N*, we're looking at a nasty, hard-to-find bug waiting to happen. The threads will occasionally mix each other up and produce the wrong result. Such a mix-up can occur if *N* is a global variable (or a shared class variable, which is just a politically correct form of global) and two threads access it simultaneously. It can also occur if *N* is an object member variable and two threads access the same object simultaneously.

How could such a simple piece of code as *N = N + 1* possibly screw up? Look at Figure 9-6, which shows the assembler instructions to which the source line compiles: move the contents of the variable's memory location to a processor register, increment the value in the register, and move the result back to the variable's memory location.

Two threads accessing the same shared data will occasionally mix each other up.

```
mov  AX, [N]     ; move variable memory location contents to CPU register
add  AX, 1       ; add 1 to contents of register
mov ·[N], AX     ; move contents of register back to memory location
```

Figure 9-6   Assembler code produced by compiling that source code.

The problem occurs if threads are swapped at the wrong time. Suppose the memory location of the variable *N* contains the value 4. Suppose Thread A executes the first two statements—it moves 4 into the AX register and adds 1 to it to get 5—but further suppose that Thread A reaches this code near the end of its timeslice so that it is swapped out before it can execute the last statement, which would have stored the result. This isn't immediately a problem. The operating system retains the values of Thread A's registers in its own memory along with other administrative information about Thread A, so that doesn't get lost. But now suppose that Thread B is swapped in and starts executing the same code—it fetches 4 from memory (because Thread A hasn't had time to store its result), adds 1, and moves 5 back to memory. At some future time, Thread B exhausts its timeslice and the operating system swaps in Thread A, restoring the value of 5 to register AX. Thread A picks up where it left off and moves 5 into the memory location. The variable *N* now contains an incorrect value of 5, whereas if Thread A had been allowed to complete its operation before Thread B ran, *N* would contain the correct value of 6. We lost one of our increments because thread swapping happened at the wrong moment. This kind of bug is the most difficult, frustrating kind to track down

Threading introduces some very hard to find types of bugs.

that I've ever encountered because, as you can see, it is devilishly hard to reproduce. It happens only when the threads get swapped in and out at exactly the wrong moments. If Thread A had finished its operation before getting swapped out, or hadn't started it, or Thread B executed some other code during its timeslice, we wouldn't have encountered this problem. This is the kind of bug that causes programmers to smash their keyboards and take up goat herding.

We need some way to make sure that no thread messes with operations that other threads have started but haven't finished.

How can we solve this problem? The easiest way, obviously, is not to run threads that access the same data, but this is hard to do because threads are so useful. Much as you might think you'd like to, it's essentially impossible to keep Thread A from being swapped out during its access of the global variable by raising its priority. Changing Thread A's priority wouldn't work definitively because lower-priority threads occasionally get a few CPU cycles (see the last example in this chapter), it could have nasty side effects by preempting system threads performing such tasks as disk buffer maintenance, and maybe Thread A's work isn't the most important piece being done by the whole computer at that time. Swapping isn't the fundamental problem here. We don't greatly care whether Thread A is in or out at any given moment. We need some way to ensure that Thread A's operation produces the correct result no matter when it swaps in or out. We need to ensure that Thread B doesn't mess with any operations that Thread A has started but hasn't yet finished. We need to make any access to shared resources *atomic* with respect to threads.

We make shared access atomic by means of synchronization objects.

We obtain thread safety by using synchronization objects provided by the .NET Framework. I find the term "synchronization" somewhat misleading, as it means making things happen at the same time, but we're using the objects to make things happen one after the other, *not* at the same time. I think serialization would be a better name, but since the documentation uses synchronization throughout, I'll stick with it. Don't be surprised if you see these two seemingly opposite terms used synonymously in some books.[1]

I've written a sample program that demonstrates some of the ways that you can use synchronization objects to make your code thread safe. The sample client program is shown in Figure 9-7. For you to understand its functionality more easily, I've written it so that all the synchronization happens inside the objects themselves rather than in the client. Sometimes this is the right location for synchronization code and sometimes it isn't, as I'll come back to discuss once I've shown you how synchronization works.

---

1. The English language abounds in just such contradictions, which I love. For example, a man and a guy are more or less the same thing, but a wise man and a wise guy are opposites.

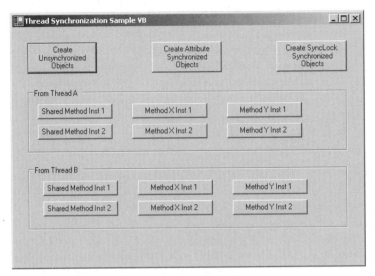

Figure 9-7   Synchronization sample program.

I've written three classes of objects. One is unsynchronized, and the other two each use a different mechanism for synchronization. Each object class contains one shared (static, per-class) method called *SharedMethod*, and two non-shared (instanced, per-object) methods called *MethodX* and *MethodY*. Each of the methods pops up a message box reporting its name and the thread from which it was called. When you click any of the buttons in the top row, the client program creates two instances (named 1 and 2) of the specified object class. The client application has two worker threads, labeled A and B. The associated buttons allow you to call any of the methods on either of the object instances from either of the threads. If you create unsynchronized objects and call a method from Thread A and the same method from Thread B, you'll see two message boxes on the screen and know that there's a potential for conflict. If you try the same exercise with the synchronized classes, you'll see how the second call blocks while waiting for the first to complete.

A synchronization sample program starts here.

Apart from doing nothing, we have three basic design options in synchronization. Our first option is to dump the whole problem onto the common language runtime environment. We can mark an object class with the attribute *System.Runtime.Remoting.Contexts.SynchronizationAttribute* (do not confuse this with *System.EnterpriseServices.SynchronizationAttribute*, which is an unrelated COM+ compatibility feature) and have it inherit from the base class *ContextBoundObject*. The code for such an object is shown in Figure 9-8. When a thread calls any instance (non-shared) method on an object, the common language runtime places a synchronization lock on that object, which is released when the method returns. If another thread calls any

You can synchronize all the methods on an individual object by marking it with an attribute.

method on that particular object, the common language runtime will cause that thread to block until the method returns to the original caller. At that time the second thread's block will clear and the method call will proceed. Try it in the sample program; you may find that easier to understand than parsing my words.

```
<System.Runtime.Remoting.Contexts.SynchronizationAttribute()> _
Public Class UsesSynchronizationAttribute
    Inherits ContextBoundObject

    (methods omitted)

End Class
```

Figure 9-8   Attribute-synchronized component.

This approach doesn't handle shared (static) methods.

The main advantage of this approach is that it's very easy to write; add a couple of declarations and it all just happens. The main drawback is that its synchronization rules are simultaneously too blunt and not blunt enough. It's too blunt in the sense that it maintains one lock on all methods per object instance. If Thread A is calling Method X on one object, Thread B can't call Method Y on the same object (although it can on other objects of the same class). The common language runtime locks every method on the object whether it needs it or not. Acquiring and releasing locks consumes microseconds. If your object has many methods that don't require synchronization, you'll be wasting them here. On the other hand, the synchronization produced by this attribute is not blunt enough because it doesn't serialize access to shared (static) methods. Try it and see: Thread A and Thread B can each call the shared method simultaneously, despite the presence of the synchronization attribute. This synchronization mechanism is a good choice when your object class contains no shared methods or data, and when all instance methods need to be locked—for example, object classes (such as middleware objects that participate in transactions) that expect short lifetimes and maintain no state information between calls.

The keywords *SyncLock* and *End SyncLock* (*lock* in C#) cause the compiler to emit synchronization locking code.

Suppose instead that our class does contain shared methods, or instance methods modifying shared class data. This means that we need to synchronize the methods on a per-class, rather than a per-object, basis. Also suppose that not all of our methods require synchronization, so we'd like to omit it to save CPU cycles in cases where we don't care about it. The .NET Framework provides the class *System.Threading.Monitor* for synchronizing this type of code. You probably won't use this class directly, although you can if you want to. Instead, you'll probably use the support for shared methods that's built into the compiler. Figures 9-9 and 9-10 show an object that uses this approach. The Visual Basic keyword *SyncLock* (*lock* in C#, with curly braces to delineate the code block) tells the compiler to generate code that uses a *Monitor* object to ensure that only one thread at a time can execute the next block of code. The Visual Basic keywords *End SyncLock* mark the end of the synchronized block. These keywords cause the compiler to emit a call to *Monitor.Enter* on entrance to the block and to *Monitor.Exit* on exit from the block. The first thread to enter acquires a lock, which it releases on exit. If another thread attempts to enter while the first thread holds the lock, the second thread will block until the first thread exits and releases the lock. In this sense, the behavior is similar to the attribute synchronization case that I discussed previously.

```
Public Sub MethodX()

    ' Acquire a synchronization lock on this object

    SyncLock Me

        ' Perform work we don't want other threads to do
        ' until we finish

        MessageBox.Show("SyncLock-synchronized component " + _
                        MyInstance.ToString + _
                        " received call to MethodX on thread " + _
                        System.Threading.Thread.CurrentThread.Name)

        ' Release the lock

    End SyncLock

End Sub
```

Figure 9-9   Individual method using *SyncLock* for synchronization in Visual Basic.

```
public void MethodX ()
{
    // Acquire lock on this object

    lock (this)
    {
        // Perform work we don't want another
        // thread to perform until we're finished
```

Figure 9-10   Same functionality in C#.

Figure 9-10 *(continued)*

```
MessageBox.Show("lock-synchronized component " +
                MyInstance.ToString() +
                " received call to MethodX on thread " +
                System.Threading.Thread.CurrentThread.Name) ;

        // lock automatically released when we leave
        // this code block


    }
}
```

SyncLock provides you with a more flexible type of lock.

This synchronization technique is, however, more flexible than the previous one. The parameter that you pass to *SyncLock* is the scope of the lock. If you want a lock on an individual object instance only, you will pass *Me* (or *this* in C#). For methods that access shared data, you can pass the type of the object class, which acquires a lock over all instances of that class. Only one thread per class will be granted this lock at any time. This allows you to modify per-class data without worrying about other threads. Also unlike the attribute synchronized case, this synchronization mechanism works only in the cases where you write the code to call it. If you omit *SyncLock* from a method, your call will proceed no matter which thread it's on, and no matter which other locks might exist on that object or class. This means that you can omit the lock on methods that don't need it, essentially locking the front door but leaving the back door open. While this sounds extremely dangerous, sometimes it makes sense. For example, your class might contain a pure calculation method that does all of its work on the parameters its client passes and doesn't use any mutable internal state. In such a case, locking other methods but leaving this one unlocked would be like locking your house but leaving your garden shed unlocked because you know it doesn't contain anything valuable. On the other hand, it can be easy to forget to put the code in where you need it, resulting in the weird bugs that I discussed earlier.

The .NET Framework provides more sophisticated synchronization objects, which naturally are harder to use.

Finally if neither of these synchronization approaches works for you, you can implement your own synchronization manually. You can use the class *System.Threading.Monitor* directly to get more flexibility. This allows you to do things like attempt to acquire a lock but return immediately (or after a specified interval) with an error if the lock isn't available. The class *System.Threading.Interlocked* provides the methods *Increment*, *Decrement*, *Exchange*, and *CompareExchange* that perform their functions in an atomic, uninterruptible fashion. They use internal system primitives to perform their limited operations more efficiently than acquiring and releasing a lock. For example, if all you want to do is increment a shared variable in a thread-safe manner, you'd simply call the function *System.Threading.Interlocked.Increment* instead of using a *SyncLock* section. The class *System.Threading.ReaderWriterLock* provides an easy way of handling the common case of a single writer with multiple readers. Other classes such as *System.Threading.Mutex*, which I won't discuss because they are too geeky for this introduction, are also available to you. Check out the *System.Threading* namespace to see the whole list. Most regular applications won't want them, but you should know that the operating system provides as much power and flexibility as you feel like writing the code to handle.

Now that we've seen how to synchronize multithreaded code, the question is, who should write the code that does the synchronizing and where should that code live? Should an object make itself safe no matter what the client does, or should a client handle an object class with kid gloves, not knowing whether it's safe or not? Different pundits will preach different approaches, and I won't take sides here, except to say that it is absolutely critical for you to think through these questions carefully and pick the approach that makes you the most money. Decide what level of functionality your clients want to buy and provide that level. Obviously, the safer you make your objects, the less your clients have to worry about threading and the fewer calls to tech support you'll get for those nasty, elusive bugs. On the other hand, if most of your clients are not multithreaded but you put in unnecessary locks to handle the few that are, you'll be burning everyone's microseconds to benefit a few ultra-geeky customers. For example, throughout the .NET Framework, shared class methods generally are thread safe, but individual object methods generally are not. Microsoft thought that was the best tradeoff for the most developers in the most cases, and in a large, general-purpose environment like this they were probably right. Occasionally you might provide both thread-safe and non-thread-safe methods on the same object, one for fast operation in single-threaded cases and one for slower but safe operation in multithreaded cases. What do your customers want? What do they need? Never mind that nonsense, what are they willing to pay for? Know thy customer. For he is not thee.

> It is up to an object vendor to decide how much safety to build into an object versus how much to leave for the client.

Now that I've explained the necessity of synchronization, I need to warn you of several dangerous cases. I've already said that locking and unlocking burns CPU cycles, which you don't want. Worse than that, unnecessary locking can put bottlenecks into your system. If you have a shared class method that you synchronize with a per-class lock, then when one thread is accessing the method, any other thread that wants to use an object of that class has to block and wait for the release. A bottleneck of this type can nullify the value of multiple threads and really knock the stuffing out of your performance. A load test with a good profiler will detect problems of this type.

A second type of synchronization problem you can encounter is dead-locking, or the deadly embrace. If Thread A acquires lock 1 and waits on lock 2, but meanwhile Thread B acquires lock 2 and waits on lock 1, the threads are tied up together and will never become unsnarled. Try very hard to think through your algorithms and use locking only when you need it so that you can avoid problems of this type. If you can't defeat the problem by thinking it through, change your synchronization to time out with an error instead of blocking infinitely.

The last type of evil problem I'll discuss is thread affinity. You usually see this in legacy code, particularly code that deals with the Windows user interface. For historical reasons, certain operating system objects, generally those dealing with window handles, insist on receiving all of their calls on the thread that originally created them. Windows Forms controls are the largest category of objects with this problem. The developers of these types of objects provide methods that can be called from any thread and will switch (marshal) to the original thread and copy the result back. This is hideously inefficient, so don't write objects that require it. I ignored it in my first sample, calling list view methods from other threads even though I shouldn't have. The list box wasn't smart enough to detect and reject the call from a different thread, though don't be surprised if you run into a component someday that is. I wouldn't be surprised if it came back to bite me on some user's machine in some obscure, impossible-to-reproduce situation.

Synchronization also contains some of its own problems.

Still More Complex Example: Managing Your Own Threads

You might want to create your own threads for finer-grained control.

So far in this chapter we've seen how to use threads in a preexisting pool, and we've seen how to synchronize our threads so that they don't step on each other's feet. What we haven't seen yet is how to create, manage, and destroy our own threads when we want to take this responsibility on ourselves. The thread pool will work for most operations most of the time, but sometimes you need customized behavior. You might need to tightly control the number of threads running at any time, which the pool manager doesn't let you do. Or you might need to set the priority of your threads higher or lower than normal, which the pool manager doesn't let you do either. Or if you want your threads to interoperate with COM objects, you might want to control the COM threading apartment that they live in. All pool manager threads live nonnegotiably in the multithreaded apartment (MTA). In short, managing your own threads is one choice in the eternal trade-off of all computing—more work in return for finer-grained control.

The .NET Framework provides us with the capability of exerting this control when we feel it's worth the trouble. I've written a sample program, shown in Figure 9-11, that demonstrates these advanced threading features. It shows a number of balls that bounce around the screen, painting streaks in various colors. I've seen it hypnotize audiences, especially those who had already had a lot to drink. ("You are getting sleepy. You will check the 'Excellent' box on the evaluation form...")

An advanced threading sample program starts here.

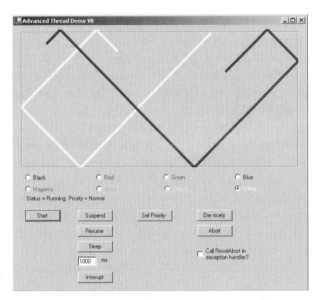

Figure 9-11   Complex threading sample program.

The .NET Framework represents a thread via the object class *System.Threading.Thread*. You will probably want to associate a thread with your own object class, thereby giving the thread data to work on. I'd have derived my own class from the .NET Framework *Thread* class, except the developers have made that impossible by marking the class as uninheritable. I therefore wrote my own class called *BounceThreadHolder*, which contains a *Thread* object as a member variable. You create a new *Thread* in the same way you create any other object in .NET, by using the *new* operator to call its constructor. This object's constructor requires us to pass it a delegate pointing to the code function that we want the thread to run, just as we did for the work item in the pooled thread case. In this sample program, I pass the member function of my *BounceThreadHolder* class that draws bouncing balls on the screen.

You create a new System.Threading.Thread just like any other .NET object.

A thread can exist in a variety of states.

Every thread exists in one of a number of states reflecting its current operating status. You can read a thread's state via the read-only property *Thread.ThreadState*. You change the state through the various methods that affect a thread's operation. Every thread is created in the *Unstarted* state, which allows you to set up its processing environment (the member variables, data sets, and so on that you want it to use) before it goes charging off to do its work. Calling the method *Thread.Start* places it into the *Running* state, which puts it into the operating system's ready list and lets it compete for CPU cycles. Calling the method *Thread.Suspend* places it into the *Suspended* state, in which it receives no CPU cycles until a call to its *Thread.Resume* method puts it back into the *Running* state.

A thread that is sleeping or waiting can be interrupted.

A thread that calls *Thread.Sleep*, as I showed in this chapter's first example, or blocks while waiting for a synchronization lock, as I discussed in this chapter's second example, enters the *WaitSleepJoin* state. This state is similar to the *Suspended* state in that the thread receives no CPU cycles, but it is different in that it receives an automatic wake-up call when the sleep interval expires or the lock is released. A thread that is sleeping or waiting can also be released from its state via the method *Thread.Interrupt*. This causes the sleep interval to expire or the block to clear immediately. Since this is an abnormal termination of the sleep or wait, and the waiting thread may well not own the lock for which it was waiting, the system then throws an exception of type *System.Threading.ThreadInterruptedException* onto the thread's stack. If you want to recover from the interruption and keep on processing, you'll have to write code to handle this exception, figure out what caused it, and clean up as best you can.

Every thread has a priority level.

Each thread has its own priority level, one of five choices: *Highest*, *AboveNormal*, *Normal*, *BelowNormal*, and *Lowest*. The underlying operating system contains a number of other values, but these are not exposed in the .NET-managed threading environment. You'll have to go under the hood to get your hands on these, which you really don't want to do. Every thread is created with *Normal* priority. You can read or change the priority via the property *Thread.Priority*.

Threads compete for CPU cycles according to their priorities.

The thread that has the highest priority that's ready, willing, and able to run gets the CPU. If you set one thread to highest priority, you'll find that it slows down all the other threads, even the sample program's user interface. You'll also notice, however, that the highest priority thread doesn't get absolutely all the CPU cycles. Every few seconds, you'll see another bouncing ball move just a little, indicating that its thread has gotten a timeslice. Every once in a while the operating system gives a lower priority thread a temporary priority boost so that it can have at least a few CPU cycles. This is done to prevent a runaway high priority thread from completely starving all the threads in your entire application so badly that you can't stop it. The more your thread wants to run without blocking, the lower you want its priority to be. For example, it's common to set the user interface thread's priority higher than background recalculation threads. The UI thread spends most of its time blocked, waiting for user input, in which case it doesn't consume CPU cycles. But when it does receive a message, its higher priority lets it knock background operations out of the way quickly, providing better responsiveness to the user. When the program has finished responding to the user's command, the UI thread blocks again, waiting in readiness for the next user command and allowing the background threads to run again. Remember, thread priorities are relative only to each other. You can't get your work done faster by setting every thread to the highest priority, as one of my former bosses often tried to do (and, knowing this guy, probably still does).

A thread terminates when its delegate function returns. The sample program does this when you click the Die Nicely button. The user interface sets a flag in the *BounceThreadHolder* object, which the thread function checks on each pass through its drawing loop, returning when it finds it set to *true*. From outside a thread function, you can kill a thread via the method *Abort*. This throws an exception of type *System.Threading.ThreadAbortException* up the thread's stack. Unlike most exceptions, simply catching it in a try-catch block will not stop it from terminating the thread. You have to explicitly call the method *Thread.ResetAbort* from within the exception handler to keep it from terminating. Once a thread is terminated, it can't be restarted.

A thread terminates when its delegate function returns, or it's aborted by an external method.

It is often important to clean up after threads in an orderly manner. I've just told you how to get rid of a thread. The method *Thread.Join* blocks the thread *from* which you call it until the thread object *on* which you call it terminates. As you can see in Figure 9-12, in the sample program my form calls *Thead.Join* on each of the bouncing ball threads in the form's *Dispose* method. If I don't do this, my form disappears while the bouncing threads continue to run, causing them to throw exceptions as they try to draw on a nonexistent window. The exception dialog boxes look terrible to a user. Calling *Join* on an unstarted thread causes an exception, so you can see me checking the thread's state before I call it.

The method *Thread.Join* blocks the calling thread until the target thread terminates.

```
Protected Overloads Overrides Sub Dispose(ByVal disposing As Boolean)
    If disposing Then

        ' Shut down all threads nicely. Use Thread.Join to make
        ' sure they have shut down before proceeding further.
        ' Can't call it on an unstarted thread.

        Dim i As Integer
        For i = 0 To 7
            ThreadHolder(i).DieNicely = True

            If (ThreadHolder(i).Thread.ThreadState <> _
                Threading.ThreadState.Unstarted) Then
                ThreadHolder(i).Thread.Join()
            End If
        Next

        <other disposal code omitted>

    End If
    MyBase.Dispose(disposing)
End Sub
```

Figure 9-12   Code providing orderly shutdown of multithreaded app.

10

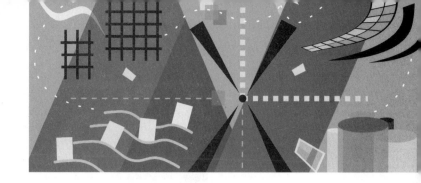

Windows Forms Controls

Inventions? Ye must stay in port to mak' a patent pay.
My Deeferential Valve-Gear taught me how that business lay,
I blame no chaps wi' clearer head for aught they make or sell.
I found that I could not invent an' look to these—as well.
So, wrestled wi' Apollyon—Nah!—fretted like a bairn—
But burned the workin'-plans last run wi' all I hoped to earn.
Ye know how hard an Idol dies, an' what that meant to me—
E'en tak' it for a sacrifice acceptable to Thee....

> —Rudyard Kipling, writing on the inevitability of a three-tier
> component marketplace, "McAndrew's Hymn," 1894.

Problem Background

The concept of a control, a reusable piece of software functionality that provides a visible item used in a human interface, has been fantastically successful for Microsoft and its customers. Providing application programmers with controls such as buttons for invoking commands and text boxes for entering strings was a radical idea when it debuted in Windows 1 in 1985. Programmers didn't have to write the code to accomplish the tasks of these user interface widgets, so development was faster. Since all programmers shared the same buttons and text boxes, these controls looked and worked the same from one application to another, so the user experience got easier and richer. And since controls were used in many places by many application programmers, the people who wrote the controls had the unit volume they needed to recover a large investment in writing rich and powerful controls.

> Controls, reusable pieces of user interface functionality, have been fantastically successful.

Controls have been implemented many different ways in Windows.

That was over 15 years ago, an eternity in this business. It shouldn't surprise anyone that while the concept has remained constant the implementation of controls in the Windows environment has gone through at least three radical changes. Original Windows controls were implemented as child windows that communicated with their containers by means of Windows messages. This worked well as a proof of concept but was unwieldy to program. A decade ago Microsoft released Visual Basic, featuring a new control implementation called VBX controls. These controls featured methods (verbs you could invoke on a control), properties (adjectives describing a control's appearance or behavior, such as its background color), and events (notifications by a control to its container that something interesting has happened). They lived on Visual Basic forms and were much easier to program than the original child windows, which caused Visual Basic to become deservedly quite popular. This in turn led third parties to write and sell many VBX controls, offering almost any sort of functionality you could think of (although I don't think I'd want to be a patient in a hospital that used the 16-bit electrocardiogram control for ICU patient monitoring). However, when Windows switched from 16 bits to 32 bits, the VBX implementation couldn't port without major headaches, so Microsoft switched to OCX controls (later renamed ActiveX controls, for no reason I've ever understood). These controls looked and felt to programmers more or less the same way that VBX controls had, using methods, properties, and events, but internally they worked by means of COM. Again, third parties jumped on the bandwagon, writing all kinds of great ActiveX controls, as you can see from flipping through the pages of industry journals such as *MSDN Magazine* or *Visual Basic Programming Journal*. And now that COM, for a variety of good reasons, is giving way to Microsoft .NET, it only makes sense that controls will be implemented in .NET because we can't live without them.

ActiveX controls required extensive development tool support, which led to differences in functionality.

ActiveX controls were difficult to write because the operating system didn't supply any infrastructure for them; you had to write every bit of it yourself. I wrote one in raw C++ once, just for the sheer pain of it, and I'd rather have a root canal without anesthesia than do it again. No company could afford to write an industrial-strength implementation of an ActiveX control, even if they did have the skill set, and the volume of infrastructural code that a control required meant that there was no way to get it all correct. So no one wrote or used ActiveX controls until various tools emerged that prefabricated the common portions of their infrastructure, such as the MFC *COleControl* class or the Active Template library *CComControl*. But even with these tools, all the base control implementations differed in subtle and hard-to-fix kinds of ways. Controls built with the Visual Basic Control Creation Edition had their own set of quirks, those built with MFC another set, and those built with

ATL and Visual J++ still others. The prefabricated infrastructures made controls relatively easy to write but difficult to make completely compatible everywhere, which is the entire point of a control. Furthermore, because COM didn't support inheritance, controls had no commonality of implementation. This meant that there was no good way for a purchaser of an existing ActiveX control to extend or modify its functionality.

Solution Architecture

As I've discussed extensively throughout this book, the .NET common language runtime is a standardized set of the base functionality for every type of Windows program or component. Every source code language compiles to the same intermediate language (MSIL), which is then compiled into object code by a just-in-time compiler. This means that every programmer's implementation uses the same language at run time, regardless of the source language in which it was originally written. Developers reuse code from the system libraries by means of the object-oriented programming technique known as inheritance. When we inherit software functionality we write a new object class called a derived class and tell the compiler that it inherits from another class known as the base class. The compiler will then include all the base class's functionality in our derived class by reference.

> Remember how .NET allows our applications to inherit prefabricated functionality from system base classes?

Developers who write Windows Forms controls (hereafter simply "controls" for the duration of this chapter) will find that they inherit a control's base functionality from a .NET common language runtime base class. The choice of base class is the first design decision to make in developing a control. It determines the functionality that you inherit and thus the amount that you need to write yourself. The three basic choices are:

> Developers of Windows Forms controls will inherit all their base functionality from one of several common language runtime base classes.

- **Inherit from the common language runtime base class *System.Windows.Forms.Control.***   This is the simplest and most basic option. Your control inherits a set of default properties and methods that many controls need, such as foreground and background colors, along with the ability to add your own custom colors. Your control inherits a set of default events, such as *Click*, also with the ability to add your own custom ones. It inherits the ability to be hosted by a form and to live in the toolbox for the use of designers. You don't inherit any type of code for rendering the control's appearance, but you do inherit a convenient place to put your own. Developers who are used to writing ActiveX controls will find this the most familiar approach, particularly if they use MFC or ATL.

- **Inherit from an existing control, say *System.Windows.Forms .TextBox*, which itself derives from *System.Windows.Forms .Control*.** You choose this option if you basically like the functionality of an existing control but want to modify it or extend it in some way. For example, you might use this option to write a text box control that accepts only numbers. Developers who remember (dating myself here) subclassing a Windows control (replacing the window response function so as to filter and modify incoming Windows messages before passing them to the control's original response function, or occasionally swallowing them) will find this approach familiar. You couldn't really do this with an ActiveX control because COM did not support inheritance, but with .NET it's now quite easy. You inherit all the methods, properties, and events of the existing control, as well as its painting behavior. You write only the code for the behavior that differs from the existing control. You can also do this for nonsystem controls as long as the developer has made the control's methods overridable, as discussed later in this chapter.

- **Inherit from the common language runtime base class *System.Windows.Forms.UserControl*, which itself derives from *System.Windows.Forms.Control*.** Your control will essentially be a miniature form containing other controls, thereby allowing you to write more complex pieces of prefabricated functionality. For example, you can produce a control that contains text boxes for a user ID and password, labels identifying each text box, buttons for the user to signal when she has finished entering her data, and validation code to ensure that each control contains legal data. You could then reuse this control among a number of different applications that require a user to log in. Each login screen would share the same user interface look and feel and you wouldn't have to write the code every time. The internal "constituent" controls paint themselves, and you can also write additional custom painting code if you want to. If your new control can be expressed even partially in terms of other existing controls, this is probably the choice for you.

I discuss each of these options in the remainder of this chapter and provide sample programs that demonstrate their functionality. You will find all the sample code, in both Visual Basic and C#, on this book's Web site, http://www.introducingmicrosoft.net.

> **Note**   In the first edition of this book, I wrote about a way for ActiveX containers to host .NET Windows Forms controls. That functionality existed when I wrote about it, but it was removed from the final release and I have heard of no plans to add it back in.

Simplest Control Example

As I always do when learning or demonstrating (funny how those two are often the same thing) a new piece of software, I wrote the simplest example I could think of. To learn Windows Forms controls, I decided to write a blinking label control. You can see a client program containing this control in Figure 10-1. While a book figure can't show it, you'll find if you download and run the client containing this control that the label switches color from black to the form's background color (hence seeming to disappear) and back again every second. The label control fires an event to its container every time it changes color. I've programmed the container to emit a beep every time the control changes color.

A simple Windows Forms control example starts here.

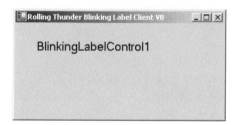

Figure 10-1   Client program showing blinking label control.

To start my control development project, I wanted to create a new project containing a class that derives from *System.Windows.Forms.Control*. The designers of Visual Studio seem to think that you won't want to do this very often, or perhaps they want to discourage you from doing this, as there is no way of accomplishing it directly. You must first create a project with a Class Library type to generate the necessary files for building a .NET DLL assembly. Then right-click the project and pick Add New Item from the context menu, at which time you will see the dialog box shown in Figure 10-2. Select the Custom Control icon. You can now delete the original project source code files if you want to. Alternatively, you can simply change the base class on the original generated class to *System.Windows.Forms.Control*. In this case, you will have to manually add the handler for the base class's *OnPaint* event, described later in the section.

My sample control class derives from System.Windows.Forms.Control.

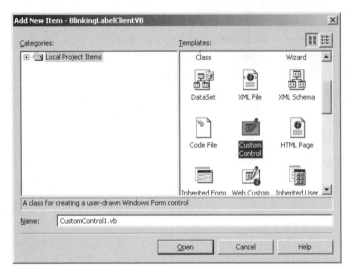

Figure 10-2 Dialog box for adding a custom control.

You add methods and properties to a control as you would to any other .NET object.

Next I wanted to add the custom properties that I want my control to offer to the world. In this case, I added a property called *BlinkInterval*, which specifies the time interval in seconds after which my control changes color. I add this to my control's source code file in the same manner as I would for any other property in any other .NET component. Visual Basic users type it in, whereas C# users have a Wizard to help. The code for this property is shown in Figure 10-3.

```
' Control properties. This is the interval at which the blinking label
' changes its color from on to off or back again, in seconds.

Private m_BlinkInterval As Integer = 1

Public Property BlinkInterval() As Integer
    Get
        Return m_BlinkInterval
    End Get

    ' Property has changed. Remember its new value, and set the
    ' control's timer to use it.

    Set(ByVal Value As Integer)
        m_BlinkInterval = Value
        myTimer.Interval = m_BlinkInterval * 1000
    End Set
End Property
```

Figure 10-3 Code for custom property in a Visual Basic control.

I added another property called *BlinkOffColor*, which is the color that the control user wants the control to display during its time off cycle. I also added to the control's constructor my own code to start a timer and set its expiration to the *BlinkInterval* property set by the user. It doesn't demonstrate anything useful about controls, but so readers don't think I'm using the Dark Side of the Force, I show this code in Figure 10-4.

```
Public Sub New()
    MyBase.New()

    ' Hook up handler function for timer, and set timer variables

    AddHandler myTimer.Elapsed, AddressOf OnTimerExpired
    myTimer.AutoReset = True
    myTimer.Interval = 1000
    myTimer.Enabled = True

    ' Create brushes used for drawing label text

    m_BlinkOnBrush = New System.Drawing.SolidBrush(Me.ForeColor)
    m_BlinkOffBrush = New System.Drawing.SolidBrush(Me.BackColor)
End Sub

    ' Handler for our control's internal timer.

Private Sub OnTimerExpired(ByVal Source As Object, ByVal e As _
    System.Timers.ElapsedEventArgs)

    ' Toggle the flag the tells the painting code whether to use the
    ' BlinkOnColor or the BlinkOffColor

    If (m_UseBlinkOnColor = True) Then
        m_UseBlinkOnColor = False
    Else
        m_UseBlinkOnColor = True
    End If

    ' Invalidate the control to force a repaint.

    Me.Invalidate()

    ' Fire the blink event to the control's container, in case it cares.

    RaiseEvent BlinkStateChanged(m_UseBlinkOnColor)

End Sub
```

Figure 10-4   Code showing a control starting and using an internal timer.

A control must render its own appearance in response to the *OnPaint* notification.

A custom control is responsible for rendering its own appearance. Since every control is different, Microsoft couldn't provide any sort of meaningful default drawing code. You need to override the base class's *OnPaint* method, which corresponds to the Windows *WM_PAINT* message handler. (Remember Windows messages?) Your control receives this notification when the operating system's window manager detects that a portion of your control has been invalidated (marked as needing repainting) by the movement of other windows on the screen or by program control from within your application, as shown in the timer function in Figure 10-4. The control's base class contains a default implementation of the *OnPaint* method, which performs certain internal housekeeping but draws nothing on the screen. You must write your own code to make the control look the way you want it to. If you generate a custom control for the project an override of the *OnPaint* method gets added automatically to your code. If you change the base class of a UserControl project you'll have to add it yourself. The *OnPaint* method contains no code when you first add it, so if you simply build an empty control and add that control to a form, you won't see anything there and you'll think it's broken. It isn't, you just haven't added any drawing code yet.

You set a control's appearance by making calls on the *Graphics* object that the system passes to your *OnPaint* handler.

The *OnPaint* handler for my blinking label control is shown in Figure 10-5. The event handler receives a single parameter, an object of class *System.Windows.Forms.PaintEventArgs*. This object contains two properties that interest us here, both of which are read-only. The first, a rectangle named *ClipRectangle*, specifies the coordinates, relative to the control itself, that require painting. Large controls, or those with slow drawing algorithms, can check this rectangle so they don't bother trying to repaint portions of the control that don't need it. Our simple control here ignores it. Of more interest is the property named *Graphics*, which is an object of class *System.Drawing.Graphics*. This object contains methods that allow your program to access the GDI+ code of .NET, which produces output on the screen. A full examination of GDI+ requires a chapter in itself, probably a whole book, so I won't go into it in any detail here. In this case, I use the object's *DrawString* method to paint my label's text string onto the control surface. The variables *m_BlinkOnBrush* and *m_BlinkOffBrush* represent two brushes that I've created elsewhere in the program. The former contains the color that the designer has set in the control's properties to use when the control is in the "on" portion of its blink cycle; the latter contains the color that the designer wants when it is in the "off" portion.

```
Private m_BlinkOnBrush As System.Drawing.SolidBrush
Private m_BlinkOffBrush As System.Drawing.SolidBrush
Private m_UseBlinkOnColor As Boolean = True

' This function gets called when the control needs painting

Protected Overrides Sub OnPaint(ByVal pe As _
    System.Windows.Forms.PaintEventArgs)

    MyBase.OnPaint(pe)

    Dim BrushToUse As System.Drawing.Brush

    ' Choose the brush to use for the text color. If the blink cycle is
    ' currently on, or if we're in design mode (in which case we never
    ' want to blink), select the first brush. Otherwise select the second.

    If (m_UseBlinkOnColor = True Or Me.DesignMode = True) Then
        BrushToUse = m_BlinkOnBrush
    Else
        BrushToUse = m_BlinkOffBrush
    End If

    ' Draw the control's current Text property

    pe.Graphics.DrawString (Me.Text, Me.Font, BrushToUse, 0, 0)

End Sub
```

Figure 10-5   Paint event handler code of a Visual Basic control.

When we derived our control from the base class we inherited all the methods and properties of that base class. A list of all these is beyond the scope of this chapter; suffice it to say that there are a lot of them. I've used several of them in this control. Looking at the *OnPaint* handler method, every variable you see with the prefix *Me* is a member of the base class. You don't have to type the *Me* first; your code will work just fine if you omit it. (In C#, you would use *this* rather than *Me*, and you could likewise omit it.) But I show it in this example so that you can see at a glance which of the properties that I'm using belong to the base class. I'm using the base class property called *Text* for my label's text instead of creating a new property. The base class also contains a property called *Font*, which I use in the same manner. It also contains a property called *DesignMode*, which tells me if my control is being used in a designer, such as Visual Studio, as opposed to an actual client app. In the former case, I turn off the blinking by always painting with the

My control uses inherited base class properties such as *Text* and *Font*.

same brush because it would drive you crazy looking at it while programming. In another part of my control I use the base class property *ForeColor* to create the brush used as the color of the text during the "on" part of the blink cycle.

A control can easily fire events to its container.

I want my control to fire events to its container. This is how the control notifies the container that something interesting has happened to it. The .NET Framework contains a built-in eventing system (described in Chapter 8) that any component can use. A component assembly contains metadata identifying the events that it knows how to fire. The client of that component, in this case the form containing the controls, reads the list of possible events and adds handler functions for the ones that it wants to hear about. The control's base class already contains many events, such as *Click*, which I don't use in this sample. But I wanted to add at least one custom event so you can see how the mechanism works. Adding an event to my control is quite easy. In Visual Basic, I simply declare the fact that my control fires an event and what the parameters of the event are, as shown in Figure 10-6. It's slightly different in C#, where I need one line declaring what the handler function for the event should look like and a second line saying, "OK, here's an event that uses that handler," as shown in Figure 10-7.

```
' Declare an event that this control will fire to its container. This
' event is called Blink, and is fired when the internal timer expires
' and the blinking label changes color. The single parameter tells the
' event recipient whether the color is changing to BlinkOn (true) or to
' BlinkOff (false).

    Public Event BlinkStateChanged(ByVal UseBlinkOnColor As Boolean)
```

Figure 10-6   Declaring an event in a Visual Basic control.

```
// Declare an event that this control will fire to its container. This
// event is called Blink, and is fired when the internal timer expires
// and the blinking label changes color. The single parameter tells the
// event recipient whether the color is changing to BlinkOn (true) or to
// BlinkOff (false).

    public delegate void BlinkStateChangedHandler (bool UseBlinkColor) ;
    public event  BlinkStateChangedHandler BlinkStateChanged ;
```

Figure 10-7   Declaring an event in a C# control.

You'll have to agree that both of these declarations are simple. In order to fire the event to any interested listeners, Visual Basic requires the use of the keyword *RaiseEvent*, as shown here:

```
' Fire the blink event to the control's container, in case it cares.
```

```
RaiseEvent BlinkStateChanged(m_UseBlinkOnColor)
```

C# simply requires you to call the declared event handler function:

```
BlinkStateChanged (m_UseBlinkOnColor) ;
```

That's all I needed to do to write my control. Now I want to use it in a client program. I create a normal solution containing a Windows Application project. With the application's main form open, I want to add my new control to the toolbox so that I can use it on my form. To do that, I right click in the toolbox and select Customize Toolbox from the context menu. This brings up the dialog box that you see in Figure 10-8. Under the .NET Framework Components tab you surf to your new control, select the DLL and check it, and it appears in your toolbox. You can now add the control to a form, set its properties, write code that calls its methods, and write handler code for its events.

The Visual Studio toolbox can host our new control.

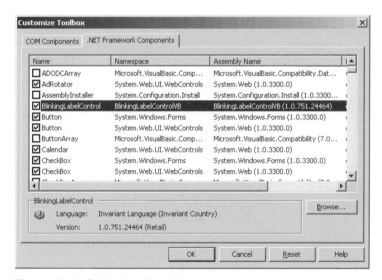

Figure 10-8 Dialog box for adding a new custom control to the toolbox.

More Complex Example: Extending an Existing Control

This example demonstrates changing the behavior of an existing control by inheritance.

Next I wanted to experiment with writing a control that derived from an existing control. I decided to extend the system text box control by writing code that would validate an e-mail address, making sure that it contains an @ sign and a dot. Every time the text in the box changes, I examine it and turn the background color pink when it does not contain what appears to be a valid e-mail address and green when it does. You can see a client program containing this control in Figure 10-9.

Figure 10-9   Sample program showing inherited control.

You override methods of the base class to change its functionality.

Writing this control was almost absurdly easy. The code is shown in Figure 10-10. I generated a solution containing a custom control project as described in the previous section. I then changed its base class to *System.Windows.Forms.TextBox*. Hey, presto, my control suddenly knew how to do everything a text box does. Next I needed to write the code specifying how my control's behavior differs from that of the base class. In this case, I overrode a base class method called *OnTextChanged*. You can see a list of possible functions to override, and add the override handler, by selecting Overrides in the Class Name drop-down list in Visual Studio and then selecting the method in the Method Name list. In C#, you need to open the Class View window to search the class hierarchy down through TextBox and Bases And Interfaces, then right click the appropriate method and select Add and then Override from the context menu.

```
Public Class InheritTextBoxControl1VB
    Inherits System.Windows.Forms.TextBox


    ' Check to see if string in text box appears to be a valid e-mail
    ' address. In this case, that means that it contains at least one
    ' @ sign and at least one period.
```

Figure 10-10   Code of inherited control.

```
     Protected Overrides Sub OnTextChanged(ByVal e As System.EventArgs)

         ' Pass call to base class

         MyBase.OnTextChanged(e)

         ' Perform our checking logic using inherited property Text, and
         ' set value of inherited property BackColor accordingly

         If (Me.Text.IndexOf("@") <> -1 And _
             Me.Text.IndexOf(".") <> -1) Then
             Me.BackColor = System.Drawing.Color.LightGreen
         Else
             Me.BackColor = System.Drawing.Color.LightPink
         End If

     End Sub
End Class
```

In my overriding function, you can see that I first forward the call to my base class by calling *MyBase.OnTextChanged*. (The same holds for C# except that the keyword is *base* rather than *MyBase*.) I do this because I want to add my validation functionality to the control, not replace that functionality. If I wanted to replace what the text box normally does in this case I wouldn't make this call. It is entirely up to me to choose which behavior I want to use, or which behavior I think my customers want to buy, and write my code accordingly. When you are writing override code, it is important to determine what the base class method does in order to decide whether to replace it or piggyback on it, and, in the latter case, whether your code should go before the base class call or after (or some of each). You can't just omit the call, run a quick check to see if the sky falls in, and leave the call out if it doesn't. You have to go look up the method in the documentation, which in the case of *Control.OnTextChanged* reads, "Notes to Inheritors: When overriding *OnTextChanged* in a derived class, be sure to call the base class's *OnTextChanged* method so that registered delegates receive the event." This means that if my control's container was also listening for the *TextChanged* event, which it has every right to do, it wouldn't receive that event if I hadn't forwarded the call to the base class. This would violate the Principle of Least Astonishment, and probably annoy the heck out of my customer.

It is important to remember that the author of the original control has the final say over whether you can or cannot override any particular method. If a method is declared with the keyword *Overridable* in Visual Basic or *virtual* in C#, then a derived class can override it, but if it isn't, then the derived class can't. For example, the base class method *TextBox.Clear* is not declared

> Your derived class sometimes wants to call the base class's overridden method as well as providing its own functionality.

> A control developer can make any method non-overridable, though I wish he wouldn't.

in this manner so you cannot override it. You can see which methods are overridable by selecting the method in the Object Browser and looking at the bottom pane, as shown in Figure 10-11. When you are designing your own controls, you will need to decide which of your custom methods can be overridden and which cannot. I've always leaned toward making everything overridable. Whenever I ask control developers why this or that method of their controls was not overridable, they invariably reply, "Why would you want to do that?" And my answer is, "You can't possibly know everything that every one of your customers might ever want to do. I'm well over 21 years old, I'm paying you, so unless my overriding a method might inadvertently hurt an innocent bystander and expose you to potential liability, you shouldn't be telling me what I can and can't do. Therefore all methods should be overridable."

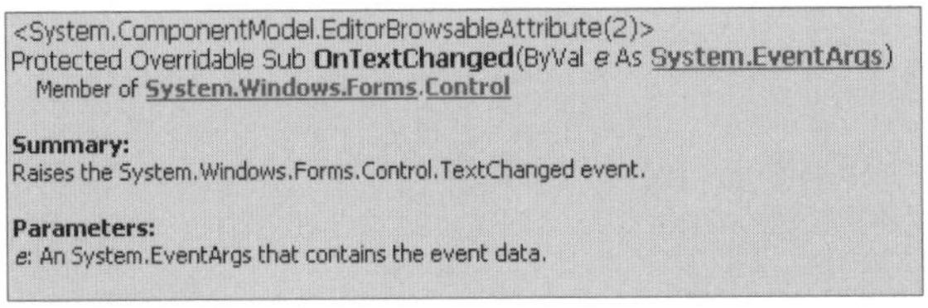

```
<System.ComponentModel.EditorBrowsableAttribute(2)>
Protected Overridable Sub OnTextChanged(ByVal e As System.EventArgs)
   Member of System.Windows.Forms.Control

Summary:
Raises the System.Windows.Forms.Control.TextChanged event.

Parameters:
e: An System.EventArgs that contains the event data.
```

Figure 10-11   Properties pane showing non-overridable method.

Extending an existing control by inheritance is a very cool thing.

Continuing with my overriding function, we see the business logic of checking the control's text, found in the base class property *Text*, and setting the background color, found in the base class property *BackColor*, according to its content. That's all I need to do, and I've written a new control that inherits from an existing control. I couldn't do that before .NET, and I think it's a cool thing to be able to do. You won't have to live with controls that almost work, you can use inheritance to derive new controls that do exactly what you want them to do.

User Control Example: Containing Other Controls

An example of a control containing other controls starts here.

One of the first questions students would ask me when I taught them to write ActiveX controls was whether one control could contain another control. You could do it, but it took a lot of work and was creaky when it ran. This is a useful feature, however, and .NET supports it natively through the class *UserControl*. A *UserControl* is a control that contains its own little form on which you can place other .NET controls, either standard or custom. Since *UserControl* derives from the system base class *Control*, you inherit all the base class functionality that I described in the preceding sections of this chapter.

I wanted to write a simple *UserControl*, which meant that I had to think of a business purpose that could be usefully served by an agglomeration of standard controls. I decided to write a login control that contained text boxes for the user to type in his ID and password, labels for explaining what goes where, OK and Cancel buttons for signaling to the container the user's intentions, and an *ErrorProvider* control for signaling errors. A screen shot of a client program containing this control is shown in Figure 10-12.

The base class *System.Windows .Forms.UserControl* is a control that contains other controls.

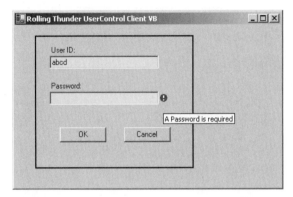

Figure 10-12   Client program showing a *UserControl*.

A *UserControl* object can do anything that you can do in a standard *Control* object, as the former derives from the latter. While the Wizard does not generate an *OnPaint* event for a *UserControl*, you can easily add it yourself and put in it whatever code you want to be executed. In this sample program, I added code to draw a rectangle around the control's border to demonstrate this fact.

A *UserControl* can do anything that a standard control can do.

A *UserControl* exists primarily to hold the controls it contains, which are called *constituent controls*, and to write logic tying their operations together. After I generated my solution and project, I used the standard Visual Studio designer and toolbox to drag controls to my *UserControl*, just as if it was a plain old form. It's easy, it's fast, you're used to it. You then write whatever glue code you want that ties the controls together. In this sample program, I put in a handler for the OK and Cancel buttons' *Click* events. In the former case, I check to make sure that both text boxes contain data. If not, I set the *ErrorProvider* control to signal the user that the text box cannot be empty. If both text boxes contain data, then I fire a custom event (that I added, as shown earlier in this chapter) to notify the container that the user has clicked the OK button. This event passes two parameters containing the user ID and password that the user has entered, as shown in Figure 10-13. In the case of the Cancel button, I fire a second event containing no parameters to notify the container that the user has clicked this button.

A *UserControl* exists primarily to contain its inner constituent controls.

```vb
Public Class UserControlVB
    Inherits System.Windows.Forms.UserControl


   ' User clicked OK.

   Private Sub Button1_Click(ByVal sender As System.Object, ByVal e As _
       System.EventArgs) Handles Button1.Click

       Dim bFieldsValid As Boolean = True

       ' Check to make sure that required fields are filled in.
       ' Set error provider control to signal errors to the user if
       ' they're not.

       If (TextBox1.Text.Length = 0) Then
           ErrorProvider1.SetError(TextBox1, "A UserID is required")
           bFieldsValid = False
       Else
           ErrorProvider1.SetError(TextBox1, "")
       End If

       If (TextBox2.Text.Length = 0) Then
           ErrorProvider1.SetError(TextBox2, "A Password is required")
           bFieldsValid = False
       Else
           ErrorProvider1.SetError(TextBox2, "")
       End If

       ' Fire event to container if the fields are filled in.

       If (bFieldsValid = True) Then
           RaiseEvent OkClicked(TextBox1.Text, TextBox2.Text)
       End If

   End Sub

   ' User clicked Cancel. Fire event to container.

   Private Sub Button2_Click(ByVal sender As System.Object, ByVal e As _
       System.EventArgs) Handles Button2.Click
       RaiseEvent CancelClicked()
   End Sub
   ' Events that this control fires to its container when the user clicks
   ' the OK button or the Cancel button.
```

Figure 10-13   Code of sample user control.

```
       Public Event OkClicked(ByVal UserID As String, _
                              ByVal Password As String)
       Public Event CancelClicked()

  End Class
```

The constituent controls of a *UserControl* are private. Actually, they are declared as *Friend*, which means that any code in the same assembly can access them but code outside the assembly cannot. On the one hand, this is good because it means that you don't have to worry about some application designer messing with constituent properties that your *UserControl* needs for its business logic. On the other hand, this means that if you want the designers that use your *UserControl* to have access to any of the constituents' properties or methods you must write code to expose them through accessor functions or properties on the containing *UserControl*. In the sample that I've written here for you, the *UserControl* contains a property called *BothTextBoxesBackColor*. I've written the code, as shown in Figure 10-14, to set the background color of both constituent text boxes to the value of this property on the containing *UserControl*. Its value defaults to the text box class's own background color, but the designer of the sample client app has set it to a tasteful light yellow.

> The methods and properties of the constituent controls are private to your *UserControl*.

```
  Public Property BothTextBoxesBackColor() As System.Drawing.Color
      Get
          Return m_BothTextBoxesBackColor
      End Get
      Set(ByVal Value As System.Drawing.Color)
          m_BothTextBoxesBackColor = Value
          TextBox1.BackColor = m_BothTextBoxesBackColor
          TextBox2.BackColor = m_BothTextBoxesBackColor
      End Set
  End Property
```

Figure 10-14   Single *UserControl* property controlling background of all constituent text boxes.

The control developer (me) has decided that in this control both text boxes will have the same background color no matter how badly the form designer (also me) wants a different one. If this example were a production control, it might be nice to add a property to the *UserControl* that would allow the container to set the initial strings in the User ID text box. This would allow the application designer to remember the user ID from one session to the next and automatically show it next time, thereby saving a step for the user. I'll leave this as an exercise for you.

11

Web Forms Controls

Then, at the last, we'll get to port an' hoist their baggage clear—
The passengers, wi' gloves an' canes—an' this is what I'll hear:
"Well, thank ye for a pleasant voyage. The tender's comin' now."
While I go testin' follower-bolts an' watch the skipper bow.
They've words for everyone but me—shake hands wi' half the crew,
Except the dour Scots engineer, the man they never knew.

> —Rudyard Kipling, writing on the social ostracism
> of geeks,"McAndrew's Hymn," 1894.

Problem Background

As we saw in the previous chapter on Windows Forms, the concept of a control is a big winner. Having access to prefabricated user interface functionality provides lower design cost, shorter design time, and a more consistent user interface across applications. It is rare to find such a virtuous combination of advantages in a single package. These advantages far outweigh the downside of controls, which is somewhat larger code size and slower execution than something we'd hand tune to a specific task. The modern software industry could never have grown to one tenth its current size without controls, just as modern society could never have grown to anything like its current scale without reinsurance companies (companies that spread the risk of large accounts, such as an airline, among consortia of other insurance companies) and sewage system designers (I sure hope that's self-explanatory).

Controls are fantastically successful in the Windows environment.

Duplicating the success of controls in the heterogeneous Internet environment is more difficult.

What really made controls take off is the extensible architecture that allowed third parties to write whatever controls they thought their customers might want to buy. The pages of most developer magazines are crammed with ads for such controls. However, the limiting factor of Windows-based control architectures, such as Windows Forms controls and its predecessors ActiveX, OCX, and VBX controls, is that they run only in a Windows environment. That made sense five years ago but poses a problem in today's highly heterogeneous Internet world, with new types of platforms appearing almost daily. In order to write applications that support these multitudes, designers fall back on HTML browser applications. Web page designers spend all their time up to their elbows in the bloody guts of HTML, wasting their time programming repetitive actions at a low level of abstraction, sort of like trying to write Microsoft Word for Windows using only ones and zeroes. We need some way of extending the concept of controls to browser-hosted applications.

Solution Architecture

Read this whole paragraph.

To solve this problem, Microsoft designed the Web Forms architecture of ASP.NET. Using Visual Studio .NET, a developer selects components called Web Forms controls[1] from a toolbox and places them on an ASPX page. The developer can set a control's properties and write code tying its behavior to other controls in her choice of Visual Studio language. The process consciously, as the result of careful design, feels very much like writing a Visual Basic forms app, a familiar model to most programmers. When a client requests a page containing the Web Forms control, the ASP.NET processor loads the page and creates the controls on the server (hence the cumbersome name ASP.NET Server Controls), then executes the page's programming logic that the designer wrote, tying the controls together. At the end of the process, each control provides ASP.NET with the HTML describing its current appearance, which gets returned to the client and rendered in the browser. This process is shown in Figure 11-1.

---

1. Technically, the documentation says that these things are called "ASP.NET Server Controls." The controls that you select from a toolbox entitled "Windows Forms" and place on a surface called a Windows Form are officially and logically called "Windows Forms Controls." To provide users with a toolbox entitled "Web Forms", to have the users place the occupants thereof on a surface called a Web Form, and then expect the users to call these things anything except "Web Forms Controls," is to commit the colossal but all-too-common hubris of trying to force a customer into your mindset instead of adjusting your nomenclature to his. Most MINFUs (see why I coined the term?) stem from this type of action. I will use the two-syllable modifier "Web Forms" in front of the noun "control," instead of the seven-syllable "ASP.NET server," for the duration of this chapter. Anyone who doesn't like it can take a poll of first-time readers and ask them which they understand better.

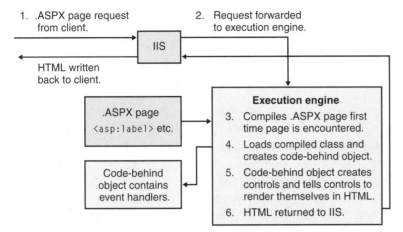

1. .ASPX page request
    from client.

2. Request forwarded
    to execution engine.

IIS

HTML written
back to client.

.ASPX page
<asp:label> etc.

Code-behind
object contains
event handlers.

Execution engine

3. Compiles .ASPX page first
    time page is encountered.

4. Loads compiled class and
    creates code-behind object.

5. Code-behind object creates
    controls and tells controls to
    render themselves in HTML.

6. HTML returned to IIS.

Figure 11-1   ASP.NET Web Forms controls rendering process.

Visual Studio .NET comes with a generic set of Web Forms controls, described in Chapter 3, more or less mirroring the set available in Windows Forms. It contains such old favorites as the label and text box, along with newer, more sophisticated ones such as the DataGrid. But the whole point of controls, the thing that made VBX, then ActiveX, then Windows Forms, and now Web Forms take off, is the ability of third-party software vendors to write their own controls for whatever purposes they think their customers will pay for. This chapter describes the process of writing your own Web Forms controls. Since I've already covered the basic concepts of controlness (methods, properties, events) in the previous chapter, I'll concentrate this one on the differences between Web Forms controls and the Windows Forms controls with which you're already familiar. These differences stem primarily from the fact that Web Forms controls run in the relatively austere browser runtime environment rather than in the rich Windows environment.

> You can write your own Web Forms controls.

The Microsoft .NET Framework contains prefabricated software classes that make writing a Web Forms control relatively easy. While you need to understand HTML in order to produce the control's required output (as a Windows Forms control designer needs to understand the Windows GDI), the infrastructure common to all controls—such features as hooking into the ASP.NET page life cycle, maintaining control state across multiple invocations, and detecting the capabilities of the hosting browser—has already been written for you.

> Inheritance makes writing your own Web Forms control fairly easy.

You write a control in your choice of .NET language, using the prefabricated infrastructure, by inheriting from your choice of several .NET classes. These base classes correspond roughly to similar classes in Windows Forms that I discussed in Chapter 10. But Microsoft has used the same name to mean different things in similar-looking environments so you have to tread carefully and read the fine print. Your choices for developing a Web Forms control are:

■ **A basic Web Forms control can inherit from *System .Web.UI.Control.*** Derive from *System.Web.UI.Control*, the fundamental base class for all Web Forms controls. It participates in all the life cycle events of the ASP.NET page rendering process. The documentation states that this class "does not have any user interface (UI) specific features," despite the fact that it lives in the *System.Web.UI* namespace. I don't agree. It contains a *Render* method (described in the next section), which is used by a control to emit HTML that displays the control's appearance in the browser. It has fewer built-in UI properties than the *System.Web.UI.WebControls.WebControl* class (described next), lacking, for example, *Width*, *Height*, *ForeColor*, *BackColor*, and *Font* properties, but you can still very easily build a UI with it if you so desire. It's of slightly lighter weight than *WebControl* because of these omissions, but not by enough to notice. If you don't care about any of the functionality it omits, it's perfectly fine to use this as your base class.

■ **A Web Forms control with a snazzier user interface will probably derive from *System.Web.UI.WebControls.WebControl.*** Derive from *System.Web.UI.WebControls.WebControl* (which in turn derives from *System.Web.UI.Control*). This is a control with basic user interface properties added. Visual Studio automatically uses this as the base class when you generate a new Web Control Library project. If you are writing a control that provides a user interface, which most controls do, you should probably start here.

■ **A Web Forms control that wants to alter the behavior of another can derive from the first one and override its methods.** Derive from an existing Web Forms control, either one that ships with Visual Studio or one that you bought from a third party, that already does a decent portion of what you want. In this case, you will derive your control from the existing control using the .NET inheritance mechanism. You'll reuse whatever portions of the existing functionality you want, override the pieces you want to change, and add whatever further functionality you want your control to have. In the previous chapter I showed how to do this with a Windows Forms text box control. Doing it for a Web Forms control is the same process, so I won't bother showing it again for reasons of space.

- **A Web Forms control that wants to contain other Web Forms controls uses one of these classes, and you do lots of extra work.** Design a control that contains other controls. This is called a User Control in Windows Forms, but in Web Forms it is called a Composite Control. You can choose any of the three inheritance scenarios that I've already described for your base class. Unfortunately, Web Forms does not contain designer support for adding the child controls, as Windows Forms does. Therefore, you must do the work of creating and positioning the child controls by hand in your code. It's not hard, but the omission stands out by contrast with the other portions of the Web Forms control architecture, so I hope they fix it one day. I've omitted it from this chapter to save space for more interesting items.

- **A Web Forms User Control is a lightweight, not-very-useful way of making HTML pages into controls.** Each of the previous controls that I've discussed is a fully compiled .NET assembly. It works with the Visual Studio toolbox and designers and can live in the GAC so you don't need a separate copy for every client that wants to use it. Web Forms provides one more way of producing a reusable control package, called a User Control. Like the User Control we saw in Windows Forms, a Web Forms User Control is produced in the Visual Studio designer by placing other controls onto a design surface. Unlike the Windows Forms User Control, the Web Forms User Control is an HTML page rather than a compiled assembly and therefore cannot live in the GAC. It cannot live in the Visual Studio toolbox, either, and it does not show its appearance in the Visual Studio designer. For these reasons, I find it much less useful than any other type of Web Forms control I've discussed so far and will not discuss it further. I suspect it exists because of the lack of designer support in Web Forms Composite Controls.

Simplest Web Forms Control Example

A Web Forms control example starts here.

As I always do when learning or teaching a new piece of software, I started with the simplest Web Forms control example I could think of. It's a label control containing a property called *Text*, which is the string displayed by the label, and a property called *ForeColor*, which is the color in which a browser displays the text string. A sample Web page displaying this control is shown in Figure 11-2.

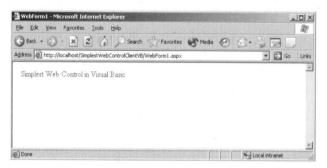

Figure 11-2   Simplest Web Forms control in Visual Basic .NET.

Visual Studio generates a project for a Web Forms control.

I started by generating the project in Visual Studio, selecting Web Control Library from the New Project dialog box, as shown in Figure 11-3. The Wizard generates a project containing a new class, derived from the system-provided base class *System.Web.UI.WebControls.WebControl*. Adding methods and properties to this class is exactly the same as adding them to any other .NET class, so I won't bother showing it in any more detail. In fact, our system-provided base class already contains properties called *Text* and *Fore-Color*, which I use in this example. Told you it was simple, didn't I?

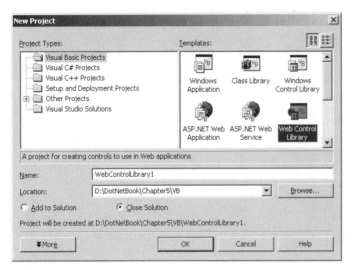

Figure 11-3   The New Project dialog box.

Well, sort of. The key to understanding a custom Web Forms control is the *Render* method. A Web Forms control's *Render* method is conceptually identical to a Windows Forms *OnPaint* method, except the former emits HTML and the latter emits GDI calls. When the ASP.NET page framework assembles your Web Forms page in response to a request from a user, it creates the controls listed on the page, sets their properties and persistent data, executes the page's programming logic, and then calls each of the controls' *Render* methods. The framework is telling your control, "You're alive and in the state you're supposed to be in. Now I need you to tell me what you look like because I have no other way of knowing, and tell me in the form of HTML that I can give back to the client's browser, please." The author of a Web Forms control places code in the *Render* method that emits HTML telling a browser how to display the control's appearance, based on the control's current state and properties and anything else in the world that the control cares about.

If you're going to author a Web Forms control you need to know HTML. The Web Forms environment provides very little abstraction of it. The HTML that makes a browser display text in a specified color is shown in Figure 11-4. In order to produce this HTML, I wrote the code you see in Figure 11-5. (I show the sample code in Visual Basic because that's what my readers have told me they prefer, by a margin of about 5:1. However, for the sake of my C# readers, I've written the downloadable sample code in both Visual Basic and C#.)

> You write code in the control's *Render* method to describe the control's appearance in HTML.

> Your control emits its HTML to the browser by making calls on an *HtmlTextWriter* object it gets passed in the *Render* method.

```
<span style="color:green;">
Here is some text
</span>
```

Figure 11-4   HTML showing text in a specified color.

```
<DefaultProperty("Text"), ToolboxData("<{0}:SimplestWebControlCtrlVB _
runat=server></{0}:SimplestWebControlCtrlVB>")> _
Public Class SimplestWebControlCtrlVB
    Inherits System.Web.UI.WebControls.WebControl

    Protected Overrides Sub Render (ByVal output As _
        System.Web.UI.HtmlTextWriter)

        ' Create a new attribute named "style" in the writer's buffer.
        ' Set its value to be "color:[value of forecolor property]"

        output.AddStyleAttribute("color", _
                            Me.ForeColor.ToKnownColor.ToString)

        ' Create an HTML tag named "span", place the attributes from the
        ' buffer into it, and write it to the output stream.

        output.RenderBeginTag("span")

        ' Write the control's current text property to the output stream.

        output.Write(Text)

        ' Write the close tag for the last open HTML tag, in this case
        ' span, to the output stream.

        output.RenderEndTag()

    End Sub

End Class
```

Figure 11-5   Web Forms control code used to generate the HTML shown
in Figure 11-4.

When the ASP.NET page framework calls your control's *Render* method,
it passes an object of type *System.Web.UI.HtmlTextWriter*. This is conceptually similar to the *Graphics* member of *System.Windows.Forms.PaintEvent-
Args*, which your *OnPaint* method receives in a Windows Forms control.
Both represent the connection to the framework that directs your output to its
proper location. The *HtmlTextWriter* object contains methods, properties, and

constants that allow your control to emit HTML into the output page that will be sent to the client's browser. In the sample code, I first call the method *AddStyleAttribute*, which creates an HTML attribute called *style*, sets its value to the value of the control's inherited *ForeColor* property, and adds it to an internal buffer. Additional values of the *style* attribute can be added to the buffer by additional calls to the *AddStyleAttribute* method, and values of other attributes can be added by calling the *AddAttribute* method, though I didn't need either one in this example. I next call the method *RenderBeginTag*, specifying the name of the HTML tag I want to appear in the text, in this case *span*. This call fetches any attributes (in this case, the style) from the internal buffer, places them into the tag, and writes them to the HTML output stream. These two calls together produce the first line of HTML in Figure 11-4. Next, to write the text of the label, I call the method *HtmlTextWriter.Write*, passing the control's internal text string. This call passes the text string verbatim into the HTML output stream, thereby producing the second line in Figure 11-4. Finally, to close the ** tag, I call *HtmlTextWriter.RenderEndTag*. This causes the writer to look back to the last open tag and emit the closing tag for it, in this case **, thereby producing the last line of HTML in Figure 11-4. (Note: This object contains other methods for performing output, which provide finer control but which are somewhat more complex to use. For the sake of simplicity, I'll stick to these methods for the rest of this chapter.)

Finally I need a client to use this control so I can debug and display it, so to my existing solution I add a new ASP.NET Web Application that contains an ASP.NET page. To add my new Web Forms control to the toolbox, I right click in the toolbox and select Customize Toolbox, which brings up the dialog box shown in Figure 11-6. I select the .NET Framework Components tab, click Browse, surf to my new Web control DLL and select it, click OK, and the control appears in the control list as shown in Figure 11-7. I can then place it on my ASPX page and set its properties. When I build the project and start it in the browser, I see the control as shown previously in Figure 11-2.

Visual Studio can host your Web Forms control in its toolbox.

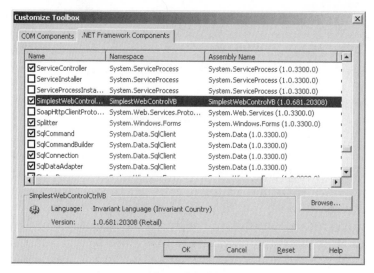

Figure 11-6   Customize Toolbox dialog box.

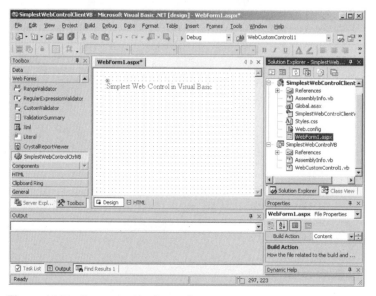

Figure 11-7   Our control in the toolbox.

More Complex Web Forms Example

An example demonstrating events in Web Forms controls starts here.

Now that we've seen the basic functionality of a .NET Web Forms control, let's look at an example that demonstrates how a Web Forms control can fire .NET events to other controls on its page. I find the .NET Framework SDK documentation murky when it comes to Web Forms control events, primarily because its authors use the word "event" to identify the click by the user on the browser that starts the process, and also the postback to the server that it triggers, and also the notifications that the server-side control that receives the postback sends to other controls on the page. I'll attempt to separate these happenings more clearly in this section.

I've written a more complex sample control, shown on an ASPX page in Figure 11-8. It displays a table in the user's browser, each cell of which displays its row and column number. The control exposes properties called *Rows* and *Columns*. Both are integers that are set at design time. When the user clicks any cell in the table, the form gets posted back to the server. Once the page has been assembled and initialized on the server, the table control determines which cell the user has clicked, and fires a .NET Framework event on the server to any other control on the page that cares to listen. In this example, the page contains an event handler that sets the value of a separate label control, displaying the row and column of the cell that the user has clicked.

> The control is a table that highlights the cell selected by the user.

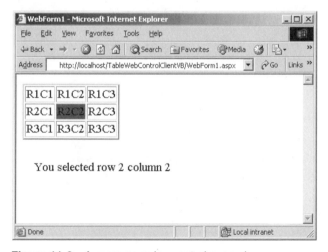

Figure 11-8   A more complex control example.

When I developed this control, I first wrote my *Render* method to simply cough up the HTML to make the browser display a table with the desired number of rows and columns, which was quite easy. I next wanted to add the HTML that would cause the browser to post the form back to the server when

> The *Render* method of this control produces HTML that posts the form back to the server when the user clicks a table cell.

the user clicked a cell in the table. This required a little more fancy footwork, the HTML for which is shown in Figure 11-9. You can see that each *<td>* entry (*t*able *d*ata, creates a single cell) contains an *onClick* attribute that calls a client-side script, passing the ID of the server-side control that I want to handle the postback (in this case, our table control) and a string that contains an arbitrary argument. In this case, the string contains the text of the table cell, which allows the server-side control to identify the cell that the user has clicked, but it can be anything we want. The client-side postback script, which you can see at the bottom of the figure, places these parameters into hidden input controls and performs a postback to the server.

```
<!DOCTYPE HTML PUBLIC "-//W3C//DTD HTML 4.0 Transitional//EN">
<HTML>
  <body MS_POSITIONING="GridLayout">
    <form name="Form1" method="post"
    action="WebForm1.aspx" id="Form1">
<input type="hidden" name="__VIEWSTATE" value="dDwxMDM2ODAwMjQzOzs+" />

<table Border="2">
  <tr>
    <td onClick="__doPostBack('TableWebControlCtrlVB1','R1C1')">R1C1</td>
    <td onClick="__doPostBack('TableWebControlCtrlVB1','R1C2')">R1C2</td>
    <td onClick="__doPostBack('TableWebControlCtrlVB1','R1C3')">R1C3</td>
  </tr><tr>
    <td onClick="__doPostBack('TableWebControlCtrlVB1','R2C1')">R2C1</td>
    <td onClick="__doPostBack('TableWebControlCtrlVB1','R2C2')">R2C2</td>
    <td onClick="__doPostBack('TableWebControlCtrlVB1','R2C3')">R2C3</td>
  </tr><tr>
    <td onClick="__doPostBack('TableWebControlCtrlVB1','R3C1')">R3C1</td>
    <td onClick="__doPostBack('TableWebControlCtrlVB1','R3C2')">R3C2</td>
    <td onClick="__doPostBack('TableWebControlCtrlVB1','R3C3')">R3C3</td>
  </tr>
</table>
<span id="Label2" style="Z-INDEX: 103; LEFT: 20px; POSITION: absolute;
 TOP: 114px">Your selection will be shown here</span>

<input type="hidden" name="__EVENTTARGET" value="" />
<input type="hidden" name="__EVENTARGUMENT" value="" />
<script language="javascript">
<!--
```

Figure 11-9   HTML generating table control.

```
    function __doPostBack(eventTarget, eventArgument) {
        var theform = document.Form1;
        theform.__EVENTTARGET.value = eventTarget;
        theform.__EVENTARGUMENT.value = eventArgument;
        theform.submit();
    }
// -->
</script>
</form>
</body>
</HTML>
```

I'll discuss the server-side handling of this postback shortly, but first let's see how I produced this HTML. It looks ugly, and you'll be happy to learn that you don't have to write it yourself. Remember, your control lives on an ASP.NET page, and therefore has access to all the methods of this page through its base class member variable named *Page*. The method *Page.Get-PostBackEventReference* causes the framework to generate the HTML script on the page, and to return the HTML string that calls it. I then add this string to the attributes of the *<td>* element, which is no problem using the *HtmlTextWriter* methods shown previously. You can see the *Render* method's code in Figure 11-10. (Ignore for now the portions of the code dealing with view state; I'll explain these in the next section.) What happens if the browser doesn't have the capability of running JavaScript? I discuss that later in the section on client-side scripting. Right now, assume that it does, or rather, explicitly declare that we are only handling the case where it does.

```
Protected Overrides Sub Render(ByVal output As _
                            System.Web.UI.HtmlTextWriter)

    ' Fetch selected row and column from control's view state

    Dim SelectedRow, SelectedColumn As Integer
    SelectedRow = Me.ViewState("SelectedRow")
    SelectedColumn = Me.ViewState("SelectedColumn")

    ' Output beginning of table.

    output.AddAttribute("Border", "2")
    output.RenderBeginTag("Table")

    ' Loop through each row
```

Figure 11-10   *Render* method of table control.

Figure 11-10 *(continued)*

```
Dim i, j As Integer
For i = 1 To m_Rows
    output.RenderBeginTag("TR")

    ' Loop through each column in row

    For j = 1 To m_Columns

        ' Generate table cell text containing row and column name

        Dim cellname As String
        cellname = "R" + i.ToString + "C" + j.ToString

        ' Add onClick handler that causes a postback when cell
        ' is clicked

        output.AddAttribute("onClick", _
            Page.GetPostBackEventReference(Me, cellname))

        ' If this is the selected row and column,
        ' generate HTML for a different background color

        If (i = SelectedRow And j = SelectedColumn) Then
            output.AddStyleAttribute("background-color", "green")
        End If

        ' Write table data tag and contents

        output.RenderBeginTag("TD")
        output.Write(cellname)
        output.RenderEndTag()
    Next j

    output.RenderEndTag()
Next i

output.RenderEndTag()
End Sub
```

ASP.NET accepts the postback from the browser and notifies the server-side control whose client-side HTML representation caused it.

The postback form comes to ASP.NET, which loads the target page on the server and creates the controls on it. ASP.NET needs to deliver the postback to the control to which the browser addressed it, which it knows from the hidden input control filled by the client-side script. A server-side control accepts this input notification by implementing an interface called *IPostBackEventHandler* and overriding the method *RaisePostBackEvent*. I find the method name highly misleading. It doesn't raise a postback event; it accepts a postback from the browser via ASP.NET and raises a server-side .NET event. The method exists for the sole purpose of transforming the generic form postback event sent by the browser into a named, meaningful .NET control event with useful parameters, for which other server-side controls can listen and for which a page designer can easily write code. If you think of it as "AcceptPostbackAndOptionallyRaiseServerEvent," you'll have the right mental model.

Into this poorly-named method I place the code that I want my control to execute when it receives the postback from the user's browser. You can see the code in Figure 11-11. After figuring out which control should receive the postback, ASP.NET calls this method and passes it the *eventArgument* string that the client passed to the client-side script and that got transmitted in the hidden input variable. In this case, it's the text of the table cell the user clicked. My sample code parses the row and column numbers out of the string, so my server-side handler knows which cell the user clicked.

> The control accepts the postback notification and figures out what must have happened on the browser.

```vb
Public Class TableWebControlCtrlVB
    Inherits System.Web.UI.WebControls.WebControl
    Implements IPostBackEventHandler

    ' Handler that gets called by ASP.NET when this control causes
    ' a postback

    Public Sub RaisePostBackEvent(ByVal eventArgument As String) _
    Implements System.Web.UI.IPostBackEventHandler.RaisePostBackEvent

        ' Parse row and column number of clicked cell from string

        Dim ClickedColumn, ClickedRow, Cindex As Integer

        Cindex = eventArgument.IndexOf("C")

        ClickedColumn = eventArgument.Substring(Cindex + 1)
        ClickedRow = eventArgument.Substring(1, Cindex - 1)

        ' Signal any controls on this page that might be listening that
        ' the postback was triggered by a click on this control,
        ' specifying the row and column number.

        RaiseEvent TableCellClicked(ClickedRow, ClickedColumn)

        ' Place the new row and column in the view state
        Me.ViewState("SelectedRow") = ClickedRow
        Me.ViewState("SelectedColumn") = ClickedColumn
```

Figure 11-11   Event-related code in sample table control.

Figure 11-11 *(continued)*

```
    End Sub

    ' Declare the event that our control fires when it receives a postback
    ' due to a click by the user on our table in the browser.

    Public Event TableCellClicked(ByVal Row As Integer, _
                                  ByVal Column As Integer)

End Class
```

The control will usually fire .NET events to its page or to other controls as a result of the postback.

If you know that your control is the only one that ever cares about whatever it was that caused the postback, you don't need to do anything else, just write your handler code right there in the *RaisePostBackEvent* (arrgh, that name grates every time I write it) method. But one of the main things your control might want to do after receiving a postback is to notify other controls on the page that something has happened to your control. To do this, your control needs to fire .NET events to the page and the other server controls using the same generic eventing mechanism as we saw in Windows Forms controls. In this case, I've added an event called *TableCellClicked* to my control, containing two parameters, the row and column of the click, as shown previously in Figure 11-11. Anyone who wants to can set up a handler to receive this event. In my sample, the page contains a handler that receives the event from the table control and sets the clicked cell into a label control, as shown in Figure 11-12.

```
Public Class WebForm1
    Inherits System.Web.UI.Page
    Protected WithEvents Label2 As System.Web.UI.WebControls.Label
    Protected WithEvents TableWebControlCtrlVB1 As _
        TableWebControlCtrlVB.TableWebControlCtrlVB

' Receive notification of click event from table control. Set
' name of clicked control into label control for user to see

    Private Sub TableWebControlCtrlVB1_TableCellClicked(ByVal Row _
        As Integer, ByVal Column As Integer) _
        Handles TableWebControlCtrlVB1.TableCellClicked

        Label2.Text = "You clicked row " + Row.ToString + " column " + _
                    Column.ToString

    End Sub
End Class
```

Figure 11-12 *TableCellClicked* event handler.

To summarize, eventing in Web Forms controls contains two required parts and an optional third part. First, your control must generate client-side HTML in its *Render* method that causes a postback to your control when whatever takes place in the browser that interests you occurs. Second, your control must implement the *IPostBackEventHandler* interface, so that ASP.NET can tell your control that it has received this postback and pass you additional information about it. Third, and optionally, your control can and probably will choose to fire .NET events so that other controls can receive notifications of whatever happened to it.

View State Management

Web pages are inherently stateless. By this I mean that what is shown on one page is independent of the pages that the user has previously seen, unless you write code to somehow tie them together. When users simply viewed static text pages, that wasn't too bad. But since most interaction with Web sites now involves ongoing conversations spread over many pages, that won't do. The SDK documentation says that you must "provide your user with the illusion of continuity." That author states the problem exactly backward: The user's continuity is real; it's your code's continuity that's illusory. Don't ever forget that the user's experience is the center of the universe. It is your code that must match the user's expectations, not the other way around, and if your programming model doesn't match what the user needs, it's YOUR job to write code so that it does.

> Web pages are inherently stateless.

A designer writing code on an ASPX page has access to functionality such as the *Session* and *Application* collection objects to maintain state from one page to another. But the control designer can't use these because he doesn't know when a page's session state is abandoned for a timeout or explicitly dumped by the page programmer. In fact, he doesn't even know if session state has been turned on at all, and he can't alter it if it hasn't. So if our controls want to be sure of remembering their state from one rendering of the page to another, we have to come up with some other way.

> Session state won't work well for maintaining controls' state because of the former's indeterminate lifetime.

The .NET Framework provides a mechanism that allows Web Forms controls to safely and easily maintain their state. The *System.Web.UI.Control* base class contains a member called *ViewState*. *ViewState* is a property bag collection of the same type as used by session and application object collections, except it stores its data in a hidden text field in the page. You can see the view state in the hidden input field named *__VIEWSTATE,* shown previously in Figure 11-9. When your control places data into the view state collection, ASP.NET serializes it into the view state string and transmits it to the client as part of the rendered page. When the page gets posted back to the

> Web Forms controls can easily maintain their state in a hidden property bag on the page itself.

server, ASP.NET fetches the hidden variable string and deserializes it into each control's *ViewState* member variable. This architecture is especially good for scalability in Web farm situations because it avoids any kind of server affinity. Whichever machine handles a postback can see what the state was the last time and store it, possibly updated, for the next time.

The sample control uses the view state to remember its selected cell.

I wrote my sample table control to use the view state to remember its click state, the row and column of the cell that the user had clicked. In my control's constructor, shown in Figure 11-13, you can see that I create the view state variables for remembering the clicked row and column and set them to –1, indicating no selection. When I receive a click postback from the client (Figure 11-11), I fetch the cell the user has selected and store it in the view state. When I render (Figure 11-10), I fetch the selected row and column and adjust the HTML to properly display the selected cell. That's all there is to it. I have to admire the smoothness of it.

```
' Start member variables in desired default state, indicating no
' selected cell

Public Sub New()
    Me.ViewState("SelectedRow") = -1
    Me.ViewState("SelectedColumn") = -1
    ⋮
End Sub
```

Figure 11-13   Control's constructor setting initial view state variables.

The page designer can tell the control not to use the view state, but the control might not listen.

You will note that the base class contains a member variable called *EnableViewState*, the description of which says that it tells the control whether to save its internal state in the view state control as I've just described. But if you work with the sample code, you'll find that this variable seems to have no effect on it. That's because the variable doesn't turn off the view state mechanism internally. It's simply a Boolean flag telling your control that the page designer would really like it if you would be so kind as to knock it off with the view state already. It is entirely up to you to write code that examines and responds to the state of this variable, which I've chosen not to do in this example. See how annoying it is when someone violates the Principle of Least Astonishment? So don't do it to your customers, OK?

Client-Side Scripting

Good UI design often requires client-side scripts running in the user's browser.

Most of the control functionality we have been discussing takes place on the server side, which is why the authors tried to call them "server controls." However, really good Web user interface design usually requires running at least some code on the client in the form of browser scripts. For example, the validator controls in the Web Forms toolkit ensure that a user has filled in required fields on a form with data that meets their criteria (any string, valid e-mail address, integer between 5 and 15, and so forth) before they will allow a form to be submitted. If the data doesn't meet a validator's criteria, the validator displays an error message and aborts the postback. This saves network bandwidth, server cycles, and also user frustration as the feedback is immediate; again, a lovely combination if the programming effort to obtain it isn't too high.

The ASP.NET page framework provides a built-in capability for Web Forms controls to easily emit script to be placed on a page returned to the client, and to easily access the scripts put there by themselves or other controls. I've written a sample program showing the three places where a control can place scripts on a page returned to the client. A screen shot of the running application is shown in Figure 11-14.

> Web Forms controls can and often do emit client-side script.

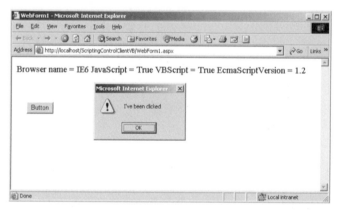

Figure 11-14   A client-side script.

The HTML page that this application emits is shown in Figure 11-15, and the code in Figure 11-16. All the methods used by a control to place script on a page reside in the *Page* member variable, representing the page on which the control resides. A control can place a startup script on a page via the method *Page.RegisterStartupScript*. This script will be automatically executed when the page is shown in the user's browser. The sample program simply pops up a message box when the page is displayed. You can also place a script block that needs to be explicitly called by other script code on the page using the method *Page.RegisterClientScriptBlock*. The sample program also pops up a message box when you click the text on the page. Both methods accept two string parameters, the name of the script block and then the script itself.

> The page on which they reside contains functions to help Web Forms controls emit scripting code.

```
<!DOCTYPE HTML PUBLIC "-//W3C//DTD HTML 4.0 Transitional//EN">
<HTML>
    <body MS_POSITIONING="GridLayout">
        <form name="Form1" method="post" action="WebForm1.aspx"
        language="javascript" onsubmit="return __ChooseToSubmit();"
        id="Form1">
    <input type="hidden" name="__VIEWSTATE"
     value="dDw0NzUyMzI2NTM7Oz4=" />
    <script language="javascript"> function __doAlert()
     {alert("I've been clicked");} </script>

    <script language="javascript"> function __ChooseToSubmit()
     {if (window.prompt ("Enter Y to allow submit") == "Y") return true;
      return false; } </script>

    <span onClick="__doAlert();" style="color:0;">Browser name = IE6
     JavaScript = True VBScript = True EcmaScriptVersion = 1.2</span>
    <input type="submit" name="Button1" value="Button" id="Button1"
     style="Z-INDEX: 102; LEFT: 32px; POSITION: absolute; TOP: 93px" />
    <script language=JavaScript> alert("startup script"); </script>

        </form>
    </body>
</HTML>
```

Figure 11-15 HTML produced by scripting sample application.

```
<DefaultProperty("Text"), ToolboxData( _
"<{0}:ScriptingControlCtrlVB runat=server></{0}:ScriptingControlCtrlVB>")>
Public Class ScriptingControlCtrlVB
    Inherits System.Web.UI.WebControls.WebControl

    Protected Overrides Sub Render(ByVal output As _
                                   System.Web.UI.HtmlTextWriter)

        ' Add attribute that calls a script when clicked

        output.AddAttribute("onClick", "__doAlert();")

        ' Create an HTML tag named "span", place the attributes from the
        ' buffer into it, and write it to the output stream.

        output.RenderBeginTag("span")

        ' Write the browser's scripting capability to the output stream.
```

Figure 11-16 Web Forms sample code that produces HTML in Figure 11-15.

```vb
            output.Write("Browser name = " + Page.Request.Browser.Type + _
                " JavaScript = " + Page.Request.Browser.JavaScript.ToString + _
                " VBScript = " + Page.Request.Browser.VBScript.ToString + _
                " EcmaScriptVersion = " + _
                Page.Request.Browser.EcmaScriptVersion.ToString)


            ' Write the close tag for the last open HTML tag, in this case
            ' span, to the output stream.

            output.RenderEndTag()

    End Sub

    Private Sub WebCustomControl1_Load(ByVal sender As Object, _
                                     ByVal e As System.EventArgs) _
                                     Handles MyBase.Load

        ' Add startup script that gets called automatically when page
        ' is shown

        Page.RegisterStartupScript("Script1", _
            "<script language=JavaScript> " & _
            "alert(""startup script""); </script>")

        ' Register script block that pops up a box announcing a click.
        ' The Render method adds a handler that calls it.

        Page.RegisterClientScriptBlock("ClientScript1", _
            "<script language=""javascript""> " & _
            "function __doAlert() {alert(""I've been clicked"");} " & _
            "</script>")

        ' Add script that gets called by OnSubmit handler to validate
        ' input and optionally abort submit process

        Page.RegisterClientScriptBlock("MyOnSubmitScript", _
            "<script language=""javascript""> " & _
            "function __ChooseToSubmit() {if (window.prompt " & _
            "(""Enter Y to allow submit"") == ""Y"") return true; " & _
            "return false; } </script>")
        ' Add OnSubmit handler that calls script added in previous line

        Page.RegisterOnSubmitStatement("SubmitScript", _
            "return __ChooseToSubmit();")

    End Sub
End Class
```

If two controls attempt to register a script with the same name, the page will ignore the second attempt. This means that, to avoid naming conflicts with other controls that you didn't write, industrial-strength controls ought to use long, distinctive names and avoid short, generic ones like "MyScript". If you want to find out if a script block is already registered before you do it yourself, you can do so via the methods *Page.IsClientScriptBlockRegistered* and *Page.IsStartupScriptBlockRegistered*. The scripts that you pass can be literal, as they are in this example. However, sometimes your scripts can get long, as can the validators. When this happens, you may want to place your scripts into a separate file to be fetched at runtime. In this case, you would write your script tag to use the *src* attribute to direct the script execution engine to the location of the script file, something like this:

```
<script language="javascript"
src="/aspnet_client/system_web/1_0_3328_4/WebUIValidation.js">
</script>
```

Your scripts can be notified of requested postback operations and block them if the scripts' demands aren't met.

Probably the main use of client-side script is to validate data before allowing a form to be submitted. In order to do this, your scripting code needs to be informed of an impending postback operation and have the ability to cancel the postback if your script's demands are not met. The ASP.NET page framework provides a convenient way for you to do this. You can register a submit handler via the method *Page.RegisterOnSubmitStatement*. When the form is submitted, the browser steps through all the registered submit statements to see if the submit should go forward. Your submit statement must contain whatever validation logic you want to have, returning true if you want to allow the submit to proceed, or false if you don't. The sample program puts out a submit handler into the generated script that pops up a message box when you click the Submit button. If you enter Y, it goes ahead; otherwise, it aborts.

Web Forms controls should check a browser's capabilities before emitting script code.

Not every browser is capable of running scripts in your preferred language, or running scripts at all. You need a way to detect whether the user's browser can do what you want it to or not, so that your control can decide to run in a degraded way, notify the user, or not run at all. The validator controls, for example, run their logic on the server side if they are unable to perform their validation on the client side. In fact, they run on the server side anyway, even if they *think* it has successfully run on the client, just to make sure that it hasn't somehow miscarried or been tampered with to inject invalid data onto the server. You can easily find out the browser's capabilities by examining the *Page.Request.Browser* object, which carries this information.

The sample code reads the properties *Type*, *VBScript*, *JavaScript*, and *Ecma-ScriptVersion* and displays them on the page for you to see. You probably also want a property on your control that will allow a page designer to turn off scripting even if the browser is capable of doing it. The validator controls contain a Boolean property called *EnableClientScript*, a design pattern you probably want to follow unless your control makes no sense whatsoever in the absence of client scripting.

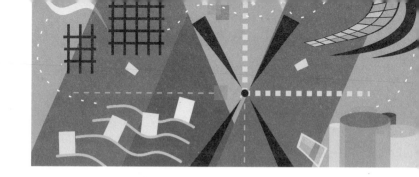

Epilogue and Benediction

Like McAndrew, I have done what I have done—written this book—and now it's up to you to judge it. Is .NET the perfect operating system? Don't be silly. Is this the perfect book about it? Don't be sillier. We won't see perfection in our lifetimes, any more than McAndrew did. But .NET will make you more money than anything else that's out there now or on the horizon, and I hope this book helps you understand how.

My daughter, born last year, belongs to the first generation that will know the Internet from the cradle, not as some recent geeky add-on, as it is for you and me. Her cousins belong to the first generation to grow up with desktop PCs, her parents to the first generation with TV, her grandparents to the first with radio. Do you have any idea how this will shape her? Do you?

Of course not, neither do I; nobody does. Or rather, lots of people have mutually contradictory ideas, and no one knows who is correct. But as I wrote these words in 2001, I remembered Arthur C. Clarke's introduction to his book *2001: A Space Odyssey*: "It is important to remember that this is a work of fiction. The truth, *as always*, will be far stranger." He's the one guy I believe.

We software developers hold much more responsibility than we ever did before. As the dean of my engineering school, a recovering metallurgist, recently wrote in our alumni journal, "Today our nation's wealth and security resides much more in bits and bytes than it does in bullets or bullion." If Freecell crashed, who cared, except the guy who lost his string of winning games? But it's different when an airline's reservation system goes down, and more different still when a hospital loses all its patients' medical histories. As Kipling wrote, speaking of McAndrew's passengers,

Maybe they steam from grace to wrath—to sin by folly led,—
It isna mine to judge their path—their lives are on my head.
Mine at the last—when all is done it all comes back to me,
The fault that leaves six thousand ton a log upon the sea.

Carry it well.

I submit to you, my fellow geeks, that we are bringing about nothing more nor less than the next step in the evolution of our species: humankind is creating its own image. Crude, limited, buggy (and what's more human than that?), but our own image nonetheless. That's why development holds a thrill that nothing we've ever experienced can match. Some people describe it as sexual, and based on the creative output, that doesn't surprise me. McAndrew felt it 100 years ago:

Uplift am I? When first in store the new-made beasties stood,
Were Ye cast down that breathed the Word declarin' all things good?

That's why we got into this crazy business, and that's why we stay. That's why you see very few geeks hanging up their mice and going to law school, even with their stock options under water.

Read what Kipling wrote about McAndrew 100 years ago. For "first-class passengers," put in your own trochaic description of an idiot—"bone-head manager" or perhaps "VB programmer." For "horse-power," substitute "megaflops" or whatever your performance metric is. Now tell me this isn't how you feel when your system goes live:

Oh for a man to weld it then, in one trip-hammer strain,
Till even first-class passengers could tell the meanin' plain!
But no one cares except mysel' that serve an' understand
My seven thousand horse-power here. Eh, Lord! They're grand, they're grand!

Index

A

Abort method, 267
AboveNormal priority, 266
ACCORD XML vocabulary, 207
Activator.CreateInstance method, 58
Active Server Pages (ASP), 82–83
ActiveX controls
  background, 270–71
  hosting in Windows Forms, 168–72
ActiveX Data Objects (ADO), 184–85
Adapter object, 199
AddAttribute method, 295
AddHandler keyword, 236
AddressOf keyword, 236
add_SomethingHappened method, 231–32, 233–34
AddStyleAttribute method, 295
ADO.NET
  architecture, 183–87
  background, 181–83
  defined, 83, 185
  examples
    disconnected operation, 191–98
    simple, 187–88
  introduced, 7
  Visual Studio .NET support and typed DataSet objects, 199–205
ADO (ActiveX Data Objects), 184–85
Application collection, 151
Application object, 105, 214, 303
ASP (Active Server Pages), 82–83
ASP.NET. *See also* Web Forms controls
  architecture, 82–85
  background, 79–82
  configuration management (web.config files), 96–99
  introduced, 6
  process management, 125–26
  security
    authentication, 106–16
    authorization, 116–22
    identity, 122–24
    introduced, 105
  Server Controls. *See* Web Forms controls
  state management (session state), 100–105
  Web page example, 85–89
ASP.NET Server Controls, 84

.ASPX pages, 92–94
assemblies
  concept of, 29–31
  configured, 38
  deployment and, 31–34
  introduced, 29
  manifests in, 29, 30–31
  multifile, 29–30
  permission sets and, 75–77
  private, 25, 31
  shared, 30–31, 32–34
  single-file, 29
  versioning and, 34–39
Assembly Cache Viewer, 32
asynchronous operation with low-level delegates, 239–44
atomic access to shared resources, 258
AttributePoint class, 216, 217, 219
AuthenticateRequest event, 118, 119
authentication, 106–16
Authenticode system, 71
authorization, 116–22
AutoPostBack property, 86

B

BackColor property, 282
base class, 41, 135
base keyword, 281
base object, 45
Begin method, 146
BeginGetTime method, 146
BeginInvoke method, 241, 242–44
BeginSomething method, 240
BelowNormal priority, 266
BlinkInterval property, 274, 275
BlinkOffColor property, 275
blocked threads, 249
BothTextBoxesBackColor property, 285
BounceThreadHolder class, 265
BounceThreadHolder object, 267
Button1_Click method, 167–68

C

callbacks. *See* events and delegates
Caption property, 20
Catch block, 69

Catch keyword, 66
CauseComponentToFireEvent method, 235
CCW (COM callable wrapper), 59–61
CheckBox control, 196
Checked property, 177
ChildNodes property, 222–23
class constructors, 46
class destructors, 46
classes. *See also specific classes*
  base, 41, 135
  defined, 40
  derived, 41, 135
Class_Initialize event, 46
Class_Terminate methods, 50
Click event, 87, 177, 239, 283
client-side scripting, 304–9
ClipRect structure, 174
ClipRectangle property, 276
Close method, 52, 190
CoCreateInstance function, 57, 61
code
  difficulty writing, 3, 13–16
  managed, 17–18, 19
code access security, 19, 70–77
code groups, 75–77
code-behind, 83
Columns property, 297
COM
  functionality, 14
    COM objects and .NET, 55–59
  interoperability
    introduced, 16, 19, 54–55
    .NET objects and COM, 59–61
  problems, 14–15
  threading and, 250
COM callable wrapper (CCW), 59–61
COM controls, 169–70
COM+, 62–64
Command object, 185, 197–98
common language runtime, 17–18, 19
CompareExchange method, 262
compatibility version, 35–36
Composite Control, 291
configured assemblies, 38
Connection object, 185, 189, 190, 192, 197, 199
Console.Write function, 24, 28
ContextBoundObject class, 259
ContextMenu property, 177–78
Control class, 282–83
Control.OnTextChanged method, 281
controls, 269. *See also* Web Forms controls; Windows Forms
  controls

cookie (forms-based) authentication, 108–12
cooperative multitasking, 246–47. *See also* threads
CopyLocal property, 33
CreateFile function, 65
CreateGraphics method, 175
CreateWindow function, 65

D

data stores, 187
DataAdapter object, 185, 187, 189–90, 192, 197–98
DataBind method, 190
DataConnection object, 187
DataReader object, 185
DataRow object, 194–96
DataSet object, 186–87, 190, 191, 192, 194, 197, 198,
  199–205
DataSet.GetChanges method, 197
DataSource property, 190
DataTable object, 194
DateTime class, 23
DateTime object, 230
Decrement method, 262
Delegate class, 242
delegate keyword, 230
delegates, 227. *See also* events and delegates
DeleteCommand property, 198
deployment, assemblies and, 31–34
derived classes, 41, 135
deserialization, 209–10
Deserialize function, 212–13
DesignMode property, 277
desktop software vs. server software, 160
deterministic finalization, 52–54
dialog boxes, 180
DialogResult property, 180
DisableCommit method, 64
Dispose method, 52–53, 68, 168, 203, 267
DLL Hell, 34–35
Document Object Model (DOM) parser, 222–24
DoSomeWork form, 251–52
drawing, 173–75
DrawString method, 276
dynamic Web pages, 80–81

E

EcmaScriptVersion property, 309
ElementPoint class, 216, 217, 219
EnableClientScript property, 309
EnableCommit method, 64
Enabled property, 177
End method, 146–47

End SyncLock keywords, 261
EndGetTime method, 146
EndInvoke method, 241, 242–44
EndSomething method, 240
Equals method, 44
ErrorProvider control, 283
Event keyword, 230
events and delegates
   architecture, 227–28
   background, 225–26
   examples
      low-level delegates (asynchronous operation),
         239–44
      more complex, 235–39
      simple, 228–35
   introduced, 7
exception handler block, 66–67
Exchange method, 262

F

FileNotFoundException exception, 69
File.Open method, 67
Finalize method, 50
finalizers, 50–52
Finally block, 69
Font property, 277
ForeColor property, 278, 292, 295
Form.Invalidate method, 175
forms, 163. *See also* Windows Forms
forms-based (cookie) authentication, 108–12
Friend keyword, 285
fully-qualified names of functions, 27

G

GAC (global assembly cache), 27–29, 32–34, 291
GACUTIL.exe utility, 32
garbage, 49
garbage collection, 18, 19–20, 49–54
generic parsing, 207–9, 222–24
GenericPrincipal object, 118
GetAuthors method, 191–92, 194, 203
GetHashCode method, 44
GetObjectContext function, 64
GetTime method, 20, 24, 133, 136, 139, 146, 241, 242
GetType method, 44
global assembly cache (GAC), 27–29, 32–34, 291
Global Assembly Cache Viewer, 32
GoTo statement, 65
Graphics object, 174, 175, 294
graphics property, 276
Grosch's law, 11

H

Handles keyword, 234, 236–37
Health Level 7 (HL7) vocabulary, 207
Highest priority, 266
HL7 (Health Level 7) vocabulary, 207
HtmlTextWriter methods, 299
HtmlTextWriter object, 294–95
HtmlTextWriter.RenderEndTag method, 295
HtmlTextWriter.Write method, 295

I

IAsyncResult object, 243–44
identity, 122–24
IDispatch interface, 58
IDisposable interface, 52
IErrorInfo interface, 65
IL (Intermediate Language), 17–18
IL Disassembler (ILDASM.exe) utility, 30
ILDASM (intermediate language disassembler), 231
impersonation-delegation model, 123–24
Implements keyword, 139
Imports keyword, 21, 28, 57, 135
Increment method, 262
informational version, in manifests, 36
infrastructure, security and, 3–5
inheritance, 41–46
Inherits keyword, 42, 135
InitializeComponent method, 166–67, 200, 234
InProcServer32 key, 60
InsertCommand property, 198
IntelliSense support, 204, 205
Intermediate Language (IL), 17–18
intermediate language disassembler (ILDASM), 231
invalid area of forms, 173
Invoke method, 145, 235, 238, 242
IPostBackEventHandler interface, 300, 303
IsCompleted property, 243
IsInRole method, 121
ISupportErrorInfo interface, 65
ItemData property, 194

J

Jablokow's corollary, 11
JavaScript property, 309
JIT (just-in-time) compilation, 18
JITter (just-in-time compiler), 18
Join method, 267
just-in-time (JIT) compilation, 18
just-in-time compiler (JITter), 18

K

keyboard handling, 179
KeyEventArgs object, 179

L

ListBox control, 194–96
Load method, 222
LoadLibrary function, 65
lock keyword, 261
Login method, 156–57
Lowest priority, 266

M

Main function, 164–65
Main method, 24
MaintainState property, 95
managed code, 17–18, 19
managed heap, 49
manifests in assemblies, 29, 30–31
Me keyword, 262, 277
membership conditions, 75–77
memory leaks, 15, 54
memory management, 18, 19–20, 48–54
menu handling, 176–78
Menu property, 176
MessageBox object, 27
metadata, 23
MethodX method, 259
MethodY method, 259
Microsoft Intermediate Language (MSIL), 17–18
Microsoft Transaction Server (MTS), 62, 64
Microsoft Web Browser ActiveX control, 171
Microsoft.VisualBasic namespace, 22
Monitor object, 261
Monitor.Enter method, 261
Monitor.Exit method, 261
Moore's law, 11
mouse handling, 175–76
MouseEventArgs object, 175
MSIL (Microsoft Intermediate Language), 17–18
MTA (multithreaded apartment), 264
MTS (Microsoft Transaction Server), 62, 64
MulticastDelegate object, 231
multifile assemblies, 29–30
multitasking, cooperative, 246–47. *See also* threads
multithreaded apartment (MTA), 264
multithreaded code support. *See* threads
MyBase object, 45, 281
MyBase.OnPaint method, 173

MyBase.OnTextChanged method, 281
MyOwnListItem class, 195

N

Namespace keyword, 22, 28
namespace URI, 154–55
namespaces, 26–28, 135. *See also specific namespaces*
Napster, 128–29, 130
Navigate method, 172
.NET
    defined, 6
    features, 6–9
.NET Framework
    callbacks. *See* events and delegates
    example, 20–26
    inheritance in, 42
    introduced, 6, 17–19
    multithreaded code support. *See* threads
    namespaces, 27–28
    prefabricated classes for Web Forms controls, 289
.NET Framework Configuration utility, 37, 72–73
.NET namespaces, 26–28
New method, 163
new operator, 25, 46, 49, 57, 63
Normal priority, 266
Nothing (object), 151
Now function, 22

O

object constructors, 46–48
object-oriented programming
    inheritance, 41–46
    introduced, 15–16, 40–41
    object constructors, 46–48
ObjectPooling attribute, 63
objects, 40. *See also specific objects*
OCX controls. *See* ActiveX controls
OLE DB, 183–86
On Error GoTo statement, 65
onClick attribute, 298
OnKeyDown method, 179
OnKeyPress method, 179
OnKeyUp method, 179
OnMouseDown method, 175–76, 178
OnPaint event, 283
OnPaint method, 173–75, 276–77, 293, 294
OnResize method, 175
OnTextChanged method, 280, 281
operating system functionality, 16
optimistic concurrency, 198

OrdinaryObject object, 241
Overridable keyword, 45–46, 281
override keyword, 45
Overrides keyword, 45
overriding methods, 44–46

P

Page.GetPostBackEventReference method, 299
Page.IsClientBlockScriptRegistered method, 308
Page.IsStartupScriptBlockRegistered method, 308
Page_Load object, 188
Page.RegisterClientScriptBlock method, 305
Page.RegisterOnSubmitStatement method, 308
Page.RegisterStartupScript method, 305
Page.Request.Browser object, 308
Page.User.Identity object, 121
PaintEventArgs type, 174
parsing, generic, 207–9, 222–24
Passport-based authentication, 112–16
permission sets, 73–77
permissions, 73–77
platform choices, 15
Platt's Second Law, 2
Point class, 47, 210, 214, 215, 219
Point object, 210–11, 212, 214, 219
Polygon class, 220, 221
polygon schema, 220
pool manager, 254–55
postback data, 94
private assemblies, 25, 31
process thread pool use, 250–55
programming language choices, 13–14, 160–61
properties in permissions, 74–75
public key cryptography, 32–33, 34
publisher policy, 37–39

Q

qualified names (q-names) of functions, 27
qualifiers, 27
QueueUserWorkitem method, 254

R

RaiseEvent keyword, 235, 278–79
RaisePostBackEvent method, 300, 302
RCW (runtime callable wrapper), 55–58
Rectangle class, 216
RegAsm.exe utility, 60
RemoveHandler keyword, 238
remove_SomethingHappened method, 231–32
Render method, 290, 293, 294, 297, 299, 303
RenderBeginTag method, 295

RequestArticle method, 156–57, 158
Response.Redirect function, 111
Return keyword, 23
Rows property, 297
Running state, 266
runtime callable wrapper (RCW), 55–58

S

schemas and serialization of XML, 218–22
security
  ASP.NET
    authentication, 106–16
    authorization, 116–22
    identity, 122–24
    introduced, 105
  code access, 19, 70–77
  difficulty of writing code, 3, 13–16
  infrastructure and, 3–5
  permissions, 73–77
  properties, 74–75
  XML Web services, 155–58
security policy, 72–77
SEH (structured exception handling), 65–69
SelectedIndexChanged event, 87
serialization of XML
  architecture, 209–10
  background, 207–9
  defined, 209
  deserialization, 209–10
  examples
    basic, 210–14
    controlling serialization, 214–18
  schemas and, 218–22
Serialize method, 211
server software vs. desktop software, 160
ServicedComponent class, 63
Session collection, 151–53
Session object, 100–101, 105, 151, 152, 303
Session property, 101
session state, 100–105
Session.Abandon method, 103
SetAbort method, 64
SetComplete method, 64
shared assemblies, 30–31, 32–34
shared (strong) names, 32–33
Shared qualifier, 165
SharedMethod method, 259
Shortcut property, 177
ShowDialog method, 180
signing components, 33
Simple Object Access Protocol (SOAP), 140–43, 153–54
SimplestHelloWorld class, 163

single-file assemblies, 29

SOAP (Simple Object Access Protocol), 140–43, 153–54

SomethingHappened event, 230, 231, 233

SomethingHappenedEvent object, 231, 235

SomethingHappenedEventHandler event, 230, 231, 237

span tag, 295

SqlConnection object, 189, 200

SqlDataAdapter object, 200

static keyword, 165

static Web pages, 79–80

strong (shared) names, 32–33

structured exception handling (SEH), 65–69

Suspended state, 266

SyncLock keyword, 261, 262

System namespace, 19, 24, 27, 28, 135

System.AsyncCallback class, 244

System.ComponentModel.Component class, 230, 232

System.Console namespace, 27

System.Console.Write function, 27, 28

System.Data.DataRow object, 194

System.Data.DataSet class, 189–90, 201

System.Data.DataTable class, 194

System.Data.OleDb.OleDbAdapter class, 189

System.Data.OleDb.OleDbCommand class, 198

System.Data.OleDb.OleDbConnection class, 189

System.Data.SqlClient.SqlCommand class, 198

System.Data.SqlClient.SqlConnection class, 189

System.Data.SqlClient.SqlDataAdapter class, 189

System.Delegate class, 227, 231, 241

System.Drawing.Graphics class, 276

System.EnterpriseServices namespace, 63

System.EnterpriseServices.AutoComplete attribute, 64

System.EnterpriseServices.ContextUtil object, 64

System.EnterpriseServices.ServicedComponent class, 62

System.EnterpriseServices.SynchronizationAttribute attribute, 259

System.EnterpriseServices.Transaction attribute, 62

System.EventHandler class, 230, 239

System.Exception class, 69

System.Exception object, 68

System.GC.Collect function, 50, 58

System.GC.SuppressFinalize function, 52

SystemMulticastDelegate class, 231

System.Object class, 42–46

System.Object.ToString method, 44

System.Runtime.InteropServices.ComVisibleAttribute attribute, 61

System.Runtime.InteropServices.Marshal.ReleaseComObject function, 28, 58

System.Runtime.InteropServices.TypeLibConverter class, 55

System.Runtime.Remoting.Contexts.SynchronizationAttribute attribute, 259

System.Security.Principal.WindowsIdentity.GetCurrent.Impersonate function, 124

System.Threading namespace, 263

System.Threading.Interlocked class, 262

System.Threading.Interlocked.Increment function, 262–63

System.Threading.Monitor class, 260, 262

System.Threading.Mutex class, 263

System.Threading.ReaderWriterLock class, 263

System.Threading.Thread class, 265

System.Threading.ThreadAbortException exception, 267

System.Threading.ThreadInterruptedException exception, 266

System.Threading.ThreadPool.QueueUserWorkitem function, 251

System.Threading.ThreadSleep method, 254

System.Web.Services namespace, 135

System.Web.Services.Protocols.SoapException exception, 154

System.Web.Services.Protocols.SoapHttpClientProtocol class, 145

System.Web.UI namespace, 290

System.Web.UI.Control class, 290, 303

System.Web.UI.HtmlTextWriter type, 294

System.Web.UI.WebControls.WebControl class, 290, 292

System.Windows.Forms namespace, 27

System.Windows.Forms.Application.Run function, 165

System.Windows.Forms.AxHost class, 169

System.Windows.Forms.Control class, 271–72, 273

System.Windows.Forms.Form class, 163, 168

System.Windows.Forms.PaintEventArgs class, 276, 294

System.Windows.Forms.TextBox class, 272, 280

System.Windows.Forms.UserControl class, 272

System.Xml.Serialization.XmlAttribute attribute, 214

System.Xml.Serialization.XmlAttributeOverrides class, 218

System.Xml.Serialization.XmlSerializer class, 209, 211

System.Xml.XmlAttribute object, 218

System.Xml.XmlDocument class, 222

System.Xml.XmlElement object, 218

System.Xml.XmlNode class, 222

System.Xml.XmlTextReader class, 224

System.Xml.XmlTextWriter class, 224

System.Xml.XmlValidatingReader class, 224

T

TableCellClicked event, 302

Tables collection, 194

target function, 227

Text property, 21, 164, 177, 277, 282, 292

TextBox.Clear method, 281–82

TextChanged event, 281

this keyword, 262, 277

Thread class, 265

Thread object, 265

Thread.Interrupt method, 266

Thread.Join method, 267

ThreadPriority property, 266
Thread.ResetAbort method, 267
Thread.Resume method, 266
threads
  architecture, 248–50
  background, 246–47
  blocked, 249
  examples
    process thread pool use, 250–55
    thread management, 264–68
    thread safety, 256–64
  introduced, 8, 245–46
  priority, 266
Thread.Sleep method, 266
Thread.Start method, 266
Thread.Suspend method, 266
Thread.ThreadState property, 266
Throw keyword, 68
TimeComponent class, 24, 25
timecomponent.dll, 23
Timeout property, 145
TimeService class, 135
timeslice, 248
ToString method, 44, 194, 221
transactions, 61–64
trusted user model, 122–23
Trustworthy Computing, 115
Try block, 66–67
Try-Finally handler, 68–69
Type property, 309
typed DataSet class, 201–2
typed DataSet objects, 199–205
Type.GetTypeFromCLSID method, 58
Type.GetTypeFromProgID method, 58
Type.InvokeMember function, 58

U

Unstarted state, 266
Update method, 198
UpdateAuthors method, 191, 197, 203
UpdateCommand property, 198
User Control, 291
UserControl class, 282–83, 285
UserControl type, 273
using keyword, 24, 28

V

VBScript property, 309
VBX controls, 270
versioning
  assemblies and, 34–39
  compatibility version, 35–36
  informational version, 36
  introduced, 15, 18
  publisher policy, 37–39
view state, 94, 303–4
virtual keyword, 45–46, 281
Visual Basic 6, Visual Studio .NET upgrade tool, 21
Visual Basic forms as Web pages, 85–86
Visual Studio .NET
  ADO.NET support for typed DataSet objects, 199–205
  Object Browser, 43
  Visual Basic 6 upgrade tool, 21
  Web Forms controls, 289
  XML Web services support, 147–48

W

WaitSleepJoin state, 266
Web Browser ActiveX control, 171
Web Forms controls. *See also* Windows Forms controls
  architecture, 288–91
  background, 287–88
  client-side scripting, 304–9
  examples
    more complex, 296–303
    simplest, 292–96
  introduced, 8, 83–84, 89–96
  server controls by function, 90–92
  view state management, 303–4
Web pages
  ASP.NET example, 85–89
  dynamic, 80–81
  static, 79–80
  Visual Basic forms as, 85–86
Web Service Description Language (WSDL) files, 138–40
Web services. *See* XML Web services
web.config files, 96–99
WebService class, 135, 151
Windows Forms
  architecture, 161–62
  background, 159–61
  defined, 161
  examples
    controls and events, 165–68
    simple, 162–65
  form enhancements
    dialog boxes, 180
    drawing, 173–75
    introduced, 172
    keyboard handling, 179
    menu handling, 176–78
    mouse handling, 175–76
  hosting ActiveX controls, 168–72
  introduced, 7, 8

Windows Forms controls. *See also* Web Forms controls
  architecture, 271–73
  background, 269–71
  examples
    containing other controls, 282–85
    extending an existing control, 280–82
    simplest, 273–79
Windows-based authentication, 108
WithEvents keyword, 233
WM_PAINT message handler, 276
WSDL (Web Service Description Language) files, 138–40

X

XML support
  generic parsing, 207–9, 222–24
  introduced, 7, 183
  serialization
    architecture, 209–10
    background, 207–9
    basic example, 210–14
    controlling serialization example, 214–18
    defined, 209
    schemas and, 218–22
XML Web services
  architecture, 130–33
  background, 127–30
  clients, 140–47
  client-side view, 132–33
  defined, 131
  design considerations
    chunkiness, 149–50
    exception handling, 153–54
    introduced, 148
    namespace URI, 154–55
    state of objects, 150–53
  example, 133–38
  introduced, 6–7
  security, 155–58
  server-side view, 131–32
  Simple Object Access Protocol (SOAP), 140–43, 153–54
  Visual Studio .NET support, 147–48
  Web Service Description Language (WSDL) files, 138–40
XmlAttribute attribute, 215
XmlAttributeAttribute attribute, 214
XmlElement attribute, 215

David S. Platt

President and founder of Rolling Thunder Computing, David S. Platt teaches programming of .NET at Harvard University and at companies all over the world. He is the author of six previous books on programming in Windows. The first edition of this book is currently outselling Tom Clancy's *Every Man a Tiger* on Amazon.com. (That shows you what kind of geeks buy their books there.) He is also a frequent contributor to *MSDN Magazine*.

Dave holds a master of engineering degree from Dartmouth College. When he stops working, he spends his free time working some more. He wonders whether he should tape down two of his daughter's fingers so that she can learn how to count in octal. He lives in Ipswich, Massachusetts, and can be contacted at *www.rollthunder.com*.

Anvil

Forging—shaping iron or other malleable metals by hammering or pressing them while they're hot—is useful because the metal can be given a desired form and the process improves the structure of the metal, particularly by refining the metal's grain size. The metal to be forged is first heated to red heat in the fire of a forge and is then beaten into shape on a metal **anvil** with sledges or hammers. Forged metal is stronger and more ductile than cast metal and exhibits greater resistance to fatigue and impact. Sometimes called black-smithing, hand forging is the simplest form of forging and is one of the methods by which metal was first worked.*

At Microsoft Press, we use tools to illustrate our books for software developers and IT professionals. Tools are an elegant symbol of human inventiveness and a powerful metaphor for how people can extend their capabilities, precision, and reach. From basic calipers and pliers to digital micrometers and lasers, our stylized illustrations of tools give each book a visual identity and each book series a personality. With tools and knowledge, there are no limits to creativity and innovation. Our tag line says it all: *The tools you need to put technology to work.*

*Microsoft® Encarta® Reference Library 2002.** © 1993-2001 Microsoft Corporation. All rights reserved.

The manuscript for this book was prepared and galleyed using Microsoft Word. Pages were composed by Microsoft Press using Adobe FrameMaker+SGML for Windows, with text in Garamond and display type in Helvetica Condensed. Composed pages were delivered to the printer as electronic prepress files. ·

Cover Graphic Designer	Methodologie, Inc.
Interior Graphic Artist	James D. Kramer
Principal Compositor	Kerri DeVault
Principal Copy Editor	Sandi Resnick
Indexer	Hugh Maddocks

Get a **Free**
e-mail newsletter, updates,
special offers, links to related books,
and more when you

register on line!

Register your Microsoft Press® title on our Web site and you'll get a FREE subscription to our e-mail newsletter, *Microsoft Press Book Connections.* You'll find out about newly released and upcoming books and learning tools, online events, software downloads, special offers and coupons for Microsoft Press customers, and information about major Microsoft® product releases. You can also read useful additional information about all the titles we publish, such as detailed book descriptions, tables of contents and indexes, sample chapters, links to related books and book series, author biographies, and reviews by other customers.

Registration is easy. Just visit this Web page and fill in your information:

http://www.microsoft.com/mspress/register

Microsoft

- -

Proof of Purchase

Use this page as proof of purchase if participating in a promotion or rebate offer on this title. Proof of purchase must be used in conjunction with other proof(s) of payment such as your dated sales receipt—see offer details.

Introducing Microsoft® .NET, Second Edition
0-7356-1571-3

CUSTOMER NAME

Microsoft Press, PO Box 97017, Redmond, WA 98073-9830